Homicide in American Fiction, 1798-1860:

A STUDY IN SOCIAL VALUES

Publication of this book has been made possible by a grant from the Hull Memorial Publication Fund of Cornell University.

Homicide in American Fiction, 1798-1860:

A STUDY IN SOCIAL VALUES

By David Brion Davis

CORNELL UNIVERSITY

Cornell University Press

ITHACA, NEW YORK

To Howard Mumford Jones

PREFACE

HUMAN aggression is a subject which haunts the minds of modern Americans. Psychological studies continue to probe at the shadowy connections among such diverse forms of violence as juvenile delinquency, racial hatred, murder, and war; social scientists urge that children be adjusted to a group because adequate recognition and a sense of "belonging" are supposed to negate aggressive impulses; yet a virtual celebration of violence pervades the cheaper novels, magazines, and television. Indeed, to be "aggressive" in one's vocation is to conform to an accepted criterion for success, although "aggression" on the part of a foreign nation or group is condemned with righteous horror. In general, Americans of the mid-twentieth century seem to think of themselves as a highly aggressive people who never commit acts of aggression, in spite of their imaginative interest in bloodshed.

On the other hand, if we could formulate a generalized image of America in the eyes of foreign peoples from the eighteenth century to the present, it would surely include, among other things, a phantasmagoria of violence, from the original Revolution and Indian wars to the sordid history of lynching; from the casual killings of the cowboy and bandit to the machine-gun murders of racketeers. If America has often been considered a country of innocence and promise in contrast to a corrupt and immoral Europe, this sparkling, smiling, domestic land of easygoing friendliness, where it is estimated that a new murder occurs every forty-five minutes, has also glorified personal whim and impulse and has ranked hardened killers with the greatest of folk heroes. Founded and preserved by acts of aggression, characterized by a continuing tradition of self-righteous violence against suspected subversion and by a vigorous sense of personal freedom, usually involving the widespread possession of firearms, the United States has evidenced a unique tolerance of homicide.

This study began with the assumption that attitudes toward intentional homicide in American literature would reveal certain beliefs and values which, in turn, would elucidate more general problems in American civilization. Since it has been an experimental study, in both objectives and methodology, it is necessary first to define its scope, purpose, and major themes. A social or legal historian might have treated the subject of homicide in America within a framework of institutional change, describing regional, social, and temporal variations in court records, newspaper accounts, and pamphlet literature. A literary historian might have confined his study to the influence of European writers on the treatment of crime in American fiction. Although this inquiry is neither institutional nor literary (in the strictest sense of the word), a lack of related investigation has made necessary occasional excursions into such associated fields.

Essentially this is a historical analysis of certain ideas associated with homicide, including beliefs concerning the origin and development of human evil, the extent of freedom and responsibility, the nature of mental and emotional abnormality, the influence of American social forces on violence, and the morality of capital punishment. It is obvious that such subjects provide material for eight or ten books. But if a wide scope precludes complete discussion of any single topic, there may be an advantage in seeing one fundamental problem in its various social and intellectual manifestations. Homicide, despite its many changing social and legal implications, is a universal problem, the culmination of all human aggression, and an ever-present means for the resolution of conflict. During the course of our inquiry, we shall examine diverse theories and distant relationships, but the unifying core will be the knowledge that man possesses, by virtue of his intelligence, an extraordinary capacity to kill. Whether judges justify lynching or reformers condemn hanging or writers of fiction uphold the "unwritten law" of a husband's revenge, there is an underlying question of how to limit man's supreme power to destroy.

We are primarily concerned, then, with analyzing American beliefs, values, and associations concerning homicide. For this purpose, the period from the late 1790's to 1860 seems to be especially promising. By the late 1790's most Americans were confident that the democratic experiment would be successful, that order could be maintained (even without the Alien and Sedition Acts), and that the new nation's future was to be one of moral progress and of individual happiness, free from the corrupting influences of European institutions. Yet territorial and economic expansion in the following decades, weak political and judicial power in frontier communities, increasing sectional conflicts, the presence of differing racial, religious, and ethnic groups, the extension of popular democracy, and the rapid growth of cities and of industrial patterns of life—all these contributed to a high incidence of violence, especially from 1830 to the Civil War. The period from the late eighteenth century to 1860 also saw the spread of new conceptions of insanity and of moral responsibility, the rise of the movement to abolish capital punishment, a persistent tolerance of dueling and lynching in the South, and changes in the legal definition of murder. Finally, the dominant issue in American life after 1850 was whether democratic institutions were capable of diminishing a profound internal conflict or whether an ultimate appeal to force was an inherent part of a society founded on the laws of nature.

Our time span may be roughly divided at 1830, and by the nature of American social and literary development, the primary emphasis must fall on the second thirty years. Chapters largely confined to the history and change of ideas are more chronological than are those which analyze themes and concepts in literature.

To appreciate the significance of homicide in American fiction, we must follow the development of related ideas in other areas, such as moral philosophy, theology, early psychiatry, and jurisprudence. Sometimes this intellectual context reaches backward or forward into time, necessitating discussions of men and ideas which are not within our period. Such material is intended to furnish a background which puts the principal themes in clearer perspective. We may assume that Americans of 1800 inherited a set of traditional values concerning homicide, largely embodied in religion and law. These dominant values, such as the biblical doctrine of "blood for blood," were challenged during the next two generations by the beliefs and theories of special groups, including reformers, defenders of lynching, Abolitionists, phrenologists, and professional alienists. Inasmuch as works of fiction often tested accepted ideas (moral freedom, for example), mediating between con-

temporary theories and traditional valuations, it is necessary to discuss examples of the dominant tradition, as well
as those of newer philosophies. In order to analyze beliefs
concerning evil and responsibility, we must first present
the views of orthodox Protestantism, John Locke, and
eighteenth-century moral philosophers.

A complex system of selection and organization is un-
avoidable in a study of this kind. The first two parts are
concerned with theories of human nature and mental
abnormality as they pertain to homicide. Since ideas from
early moral philosophy and psychiatry are applied throughout the study, the chapters introducing each of these parts
should be thought of as a framework for the entire book.
In Parts One and Two there are separate chapters containing material on human nature and insanity, followed
by chapters which analyze related subjects in American
fiction. In Parts Three and Four, however, the background
material, presented in less detail, is included within each
chapter, its extent and position being determined by the
character of the particular subject. It is necessary, for instance, to discuss the facts of an actual murder in connection with an analysis of its fictional treatment. On the
other hand, a brief survey of lynching and dueling in
America may precede a general examination of the same
subjects in fiction. Since ideas concerning evil, abnormality, and punishment were closely associated with fictional
homicide, a greater proportion of space must be devoted
to the intellectual background of these problems.

One of the central purposes of this study is to relate
and contrast theories of early psychiatry and jurisprudence
with assumptions and imaginative associations in fiction.
Certain modes of analysis may be useful in the study of
literature, yet unacceptable as standards for historical interpretation. Because modern psychological theories and
terminology often clarify imaginative expression, I have

felt justified in utilizing a general sociopsychological frame of reference in my interpretation of literature. When discussing works of fiction, I have been concerned neither with verisimilitude nor with aesthetic merit, but rather with social and psychological attitudes.

According to modern students of aggression, the murderer accomplishes through direct action what other men achieve through such symbolic gratifications as the writing and reading of literature. If we accept these contemporary theories, it is evident that imaginative fiction must express, either consciously or unconsciously, an individual's associations and emotional reactions concerning such basic factors as the acquisitive and property-getting impulses, the relation between the sexes, forces which thwart or restrict either of these impulses, and images of evil and liberation, as seen in villains and heroes. This means that such literary conventions and devices as the superman, the renegade, and the monomaniac have a psychological meaning which reflects fundamental social values.

The application of psychiatric and psychoanalytic theories to problems in history and literature is understandably suspect, yet a study of attitudes toward violence cannot ignore the significant contributions of such men as Andreas Bjerre, Franz Alexander, Frederic Wertham, Theodor Reik, and John Dollard. It must be stressed, however, that modern psychological theories are used as a technique for the interpretation of literature and are not applied as a mode of historical analysis. My objective has been to contrast the psychological assumptions of imaginative writers with certain social and intellectual currents of a contemporary period.

Fiction, of course, is never a complete index to prevailing beliefs and values, and during the first half of the nineteenth century American writers were especially sensitive to such influences as the English sentimental tale, the

Gothic romance, Byron, Wordsworth, Scott, Bulwer-
Lytton, Sue, Dickens, and Hugo. For my purpose, however, imitation is not so important as is the acceptance of
particular social values, arranged as hypothetical moral
problems.

My central theme is the imaginative reaction of writers
to a growing awareness of violence in American life, and to
the disunity implicit in material expansion accompanied
by a comparative weakness of paternal and governmental
authorities. There are four subsidiary themes which run
through most of the chapters:

1) In a reaction against eighteenth-century materialism and the extremes of sensational psychology, Americans
were inclined to accept a moral philosophy which stressed
man's nonintellectual powers. This often had the result
of increasing the relative importance of passion and impulse, which might be considered irresistible and thus justifiable; of relegating values to an inherent moral sense;
and of creating an autonomous will, free from the limitations of experience and capable of accepting or rejecting
absolute virtue, regardless of physical or social handicaps.

2) Our sixty-year span was part of a longer period of
great uncertainty over the future role and status of woman.
The liberation of many middle-class women from traditional duties, together with a disturbing suspicion that
industrialism might force the two sexes into common, undifferentiated units of labor, created a sharp tension concerning sex and the family. To compensate for this fear of
change, many writers presented a feminine ideal which
transcended all possibilities of realization. At the same
time, there was a related and widespread association of sex
with violent death. In popular fiction, the ethereal ideal of
womanhood could be physically realized only in an actual
or symbolic act of murder.

3) Although killing is an act of intimacy, the victim

often being identified with a parent or near relation, it is usually necessary that the aggressor rationalize an act of homicide by denying this close relationship. Even if the victim is a parent or friend, he must be thought of as a renegade, a betrayer of family honor who has forfeited his right to live. To hang a murderer or to avenge a woman's dishonor requires that the object of hatred be condemned as an agent of evil, instigated and moved by the devil. Throughout this study I shall use the term "alienation" to describe the psychological process which precedes or accompanies physical aggression. In this general sense "alienation" is the opposite of sympathetic identification, implying a fundamental break in the bonds of social unity. It is essential that we distinguish several specific kinds of alienation, as well as an objective and a subjective meaning of the term. Objectively, alienation is a description of an individual's movement away from sympathetic unity. In a subjective sense it implies the discovery of a dangerous enemy, of an immoral trespasser who deserves to die. Hence, for the murderer a victim is an alien, but for society the murderer himself becomes an alien. To avoid verbal confusion, we may use the terms "alienated" or "social outcast" to refer to the objective enemies of society. Groups of men psychologically isolated from the rest of society will be distinguished by the terms "out-group" or "scapegoat group," the latter being used to connote persecution.

Historically, the concept of alienation was employed to suggest three separate theories concerning the origin of human evil. Since theologians and early psychiatrists failed to provide an exact terminology, we must invent two phrases with which to refer to theories of criminal causation. We may use "physical alien" to describe a person who has been deprived of reason or judgment by external circumstances, but who retains, or is supposed to retain, his essential virtue. In other words, his subjective process of alienation (leading to hatred and murder) was the result of physical causes. "Moral alienation" implies the corruption of an inherent moral faculty through a conscious and willful choice of evil. (We shall see, however, that certain thinkers argued that moral and physical alienation could not be separated.) A man might also be alienated from God and from God's law, which meant that he was instigated by Satan and embodied a positive evil. In American literature, the theme of alienation from a central human family was often expressed as the struggle between virtuous and evil brothers for the possession of lands or women in a situation where symbols of paternal authority were either weakened or totally lacking.

4) After the Revolution, many Americans were haunted by the fear that their fathers' sacrifice had been betrayed and that some dangerous conspiracy threatened to destroy the glorious promise of democracy. A loosening of traditional ties and obligations through physical and social mobility endangered the unity of in-groups, making men aware of many out-groups in their midst. At the same time, the desire of some to expand their society to include the outcasts and the depraved ran counter to a theory of individual freedom which often implied that each man naturally possessed the powers of lawgiver, judge, and executioner. This philosophical contradiction between a belief in man's universal and uniform nature and a doctrine of individual autonomy affected interpretations of the morality of punishment, of dueling, of revenge, and of the superman.

The sources for this study have been selected with an effort to present significant or representative examples of American thought. In fiction, for example, it would be impossible to discuss all the authors who dealt with murder between 1798 and 1860. Selections have therefore been chosen with an eye to regional, cultural, and temporal representation. No attempt has been made to uncover attitudes toward *all* kinds of intentional homicide or to discuss the particular problems of every region. Since the core of the investigation is limited to American fiction, which was highly selective in interests and in subject matter before 1860, the following topics receive little or no attention: infanticide; mass murders; killings committed in the perpetration of felonies; homicides which are legally justifiable; murders committed by women for money or property; and violence in the Far West, especially in California. Analysis of homicide in American poetry and drama falls beyond my limit. I have restricted discussion of actual murder trials and legal decisions to that small number of cases which were given fictional interpretations; but the more general treatment of attitudes toward responsibility, insanity, and punishment rests on a reading of many records of murder trials which could not be discussed individually without entangling the argument in a mass of detail.

In general I have used the most available editions of novels, since the works of few American writers have been honored with a standard and authoritative edition. The dates cited in parentheses in my text refer, however, to the *first* edition in book form, not to the date of writing or to prior publication in periodicals.

DAVID BRION DAVIS

Cornell University
January 1957

CONTENTS

PART FOUR.   HOMICIDE AND SOCIETY

PART ONE

Homicide and the Nature of Man

ALL our inquiries in morals, religion, and politics must begin with human nature. The ends for which a being is made, his relations, his true course of conduct, depend upon his nature. To comprehend the former, we must understand the latter. Accordingly, certain views of man are involved in all speculation about the object of life, and the proper sphere of human action. On such views all schemes of society and legislation are built.

—W. E. CHANNING

Chapter I

BACKGROUND

A SENSE of urgency pervaded the writings of moral philosophers who were confronted in the late eighteenth and early nineteenth centuries by the dual necessity of shaping a psychology consistent with empirical method and of justifying the basic assumptions of religion and law. Such a division of allegiance between science and traditional values contributed to an obscurity and complexity of thought concerning human nature. As moral philosophers questioned the authority of dogmatic theology, legal theorists sought new sanction for guilt and punishment, while some reformers came gradually to doubt the responsibility of criminals.

Although a thorough analysis of theology and moral philosophy is beyond the province of this study, we cannot understand American attitudes toward homicide unless we recognize their historical and philosophical context. It is obvious that whatever men believe concerning the source of evil and the extent of human freedom will deeply influence the practice of law, religion, and education. In briefly

3

sketching the development of certain religious and philosophical ideas, we shall here confine the discussion to two
questions especially relevant to the subject of crime: the
source of human evil, and man's freedom to choose virtue.
In the next chapter we shall turn to the imaginative treatment of the same questions in American literature from
1798 to 1860.

II

New England theology, though it represents only a small
part of American religious history, provides a significant
record of changing attitudes toward human evil and freedom. The Westminster Confession, which defined for
American Calvinists the major theological issues from the
late seventeenth to the early nineteenth century, stated that
"man, in his state of innocency, had freedom and power
to will and to do that which is good and well-pleasing to
God." This meant that even original man was in no way
liberated from a strict chain of causality determined by
God, but possessed merely a qualitative capacity for good
if he happened to be steered in the right direction. By
Adam's fall, of course, man lost even his qualitative capacity for good actions, and, like a broken phonograph nee-
dle, his movement could produce only a grating sound in
the ears of the Lord. Even when the elect were regenerated
by divine grace and regained the capacity for harmonic
performance, it was God who determined the standards of
harmony.

Inasmuch as man was universally sinful, utterly lacking
in power to redeem himself, and incapable of measuring
his own guilt, it might be supposed that criminal acts would
be excused as the natural fruits of man's nature, especially
if the command in Romans 2:1 were taken literally:
"Therefore thou art inexcusable, O man, whosoever thou
art that judgest: for wherein thou judgest another, thou

condemnest thyself, for thou that judgest doest the same things." But if the doctrine of total depravity was intended to make man both humble before God and conscious of his own shortcomings, it did not thereby increase his tolerance for those who were manifestly alienated from God's favor. Theologians who, like John Calvin, emphasized man's depravity were also more inclined to justify rigorous civil punishment, since in no other way could the sinful will of man be thwarted.

Just as Christianity was never quite successful in eradicating Manichaean doctrines, so a primitive notion of evil persisted as long as men believed in the devil. Even when theologians argued that a criminal's guilt arose primarily from his disobedience to the will of God, he was punished not as an unruly child but as an embodiment of positive and infectious evil, as a loathsome monster whose human faculties had been made diseased by Satan. Hence, even in the early nineteenth century, indictments for murder in the United States included the ancient compromise between Christian and primitive morality: "Not having the fear of God before his eyes, but being moved and seduced by the instigations of the devil . . ."

American Calvinists in the late eighteenth century found it difficult to defend total depravity and predestination, especially after they had absorbed from pietism the belief that universal benevolence is the source of virtue. Man's sin, according to Samuel Hopkins, glorified the perfections of God, "which could not have been made to such advantage, and in so great a degree, in any other way, had not sin existed in every instance." [1] Yet Hopkins' disciple, Nathaniel Emmons, made it clear that God did not "desire" the pain or punishment of any human being, since He sincerely wished that all men might be saved. But the

[1] Samuel Hopkins, *The Works of Samuel Hopkins* . . . (Boston, 1854), III, 728.

more God desired the good of sinners, "the more he hates
their totally corrupt hearts and selfish conduct. . . . The
more he loves the happiness of sinners, the more he must
hate them for destroying it." [2] Thus it was that supreme
hatred flowed from universal benevolence. Those who
loved the goodness of God should approve and imitate his
conduct toward those "guilty and miserable objects," even
though the morally depraved were unaware of their sin
and of their inevitable punishment: "Being alienated
from the life of God, and opposed to all true benevolence,
their minds are totally involved in moral darkness." In an
effort to control man's religious aspirations and secular
desires, Calvin had justified both election and moral responsibility by the fiat of an arbitrary God, but in so
doing he had sacrificed the God of benevolence and love.
When such latter-day Calvinists as Emmons stressed the
fact that God desired the happiness and salvation of all
sinners, they reinforced the belief in man's responsibility
but at the same time undermined the doctrines of predestination and total depravity.

By 1800 it would have been impossible to have applied
Emmons' ideas with consistency in courts of law. If evil,
predestined to glorify God, was to be hated and punished
to show our approval of God's benevolence, no distinctions
could be drawn among various types of homicide, since it
would not matter whether a man had killed by premeditation, from insanity, or had merely contemplated a murder. In each instance God's command would have been
disobeyed. Each act of disobedience would emphasize the
contrast between God's virtue and man's iniquity and
thus require God-fearing men to punish the transgressor
in order to demonstrate their own respect for goodness.
Whereas the primitive savage executed or banished a

[2] Nathaniel Emmons, *The Works of Nathaniel Emmons* . . . (Boston,
1842), VI, 67.

criminal as an alien from his tribe, with the hope that such purging of evil would preserve him from similar alienation, the consistent Calvinist was required to punish the man who was alienated from God's world, trusting that an expression of such righteous hatred would secure his own position in the world to come. In both cases evil was a mysterious and infectious power, and it mattered not whether a criminal was alienated by willful choice or by physical causes.

By the time of Timothy Dwight's triumph over infidelity at Yale, provincial Calvinism had been exposed to the influence and criticism of British Unitarians, American Universalists, rationalists, and deists. The followers of Jonathan Edwards struggled against doctrines which seemed to reduce God's power or to magnify man's original goodness, but in defending this ancient moral dualism, they placed greater stress on man's natural freedom while losing sight of Adamic guilt. When an angry and vengeful God was removed from Edwards' theology, the psychology that remained seemed to suggest that a criminal was not the detestable embodiment of a mysterious and imputative guilt, whose punishment, even at the hands of sinful men, would bring an approving smile from the lips of God. On the contrary, human evil might be overcome by religious training. Hopkins and Emmons had gone considerably further than Edwards in abandoning the terror and maliciousness of the Puritan God; and, in fact, Emmons' conception of a deity who sincerely desires the good of all sinners was not so far from Hosea Ballou's Universalist God who actually saves all sinners. When the followers of Edwards denied the imputation of Adamic sin and insisted upon the supreme benevolence of God, they had, according to their Unitarian opponents, admitted that man was both free and good.

Although Timothy Dwight was a spiritual as well as an

actual descendant of Jonathan Edwards, he nevertheless succeeded in changing his grandfather's conception of sin. The final proof of man's depravity, he wrote, was the necessity of legally forbidding murder. But if murder and war were evidence of man's inherent sinfulness, the origins of evil might also be traced to social conditions which might be altered by human effort: "Murder in the proper sense, is begun in unkindness: and . . . unkindness is begun in the early and unrestrained indulgence of human passions. This indulgence, therefore, Parents, and all other Guardians of children, are bound faithfully to restrain, from the beginning." [3] The essence of sin lay not so much in a man's lacking "a disposition to love Being in general" (as Edwards had defined it) as in an individual's discontent and ambition. Dwight did not consciously revise his Calvinist heritage, but his argument against human perfection emphasized social evil and minimized supernatural sin, just as his plea for religion placed greater stress on individual effort.

Dwight was still a long way from considering criminals as accidental and pathological deviants from a basically free and benevolent human nature. He sternly warned that those who observed the law and only wished that an enemy would die would be condemned as actual criminals at the final judgment. Without the grace of God men were universally selfish, aggressive, and murderous. Yet we may classify Dwight as a transitional figure who modified the conception of metaphysical evil by stressing the social effects of sin, as well as the benefits of education and moral training.

When Horace Bushnell's theology attracted attention in the 1840's, a generation had passed since the death of Timothy Dwight. Edwards' disciples had become insignifi-

[3] Timothy Dwight, *Theology Explained and Defended, in a Series of Sermons,* 12th ed. (New York, 1846), III, 356.

cant in number compared with the millennial sects, the circuit-riding evangelists, and the urban Catholics. The impact of Kant, Herder, Jacobi, and Schleiermacher was beginning to crumble the foundations of even New England theology. For Bushnell, whose early pledges of allegiance to the principle of total depravity failed to quiet the suspicions of New England orthodoxy, salvation was not an instantaneous response to God's grace on the part of an isolated, individual man, but rather a process of a social organism whereby the natural and supernatural realms were joined in an intimate growth. Like many of his contemporaries, Bushnell loved botanical metaphors, and his descriptions of the religious experience are filled with such terms as sap, trunk, limb, matrix, and rudimental type.[4] The Christian family was likened to a kind of greenhouse, in which children were nurtured by their parents' faith, by glowing love, and by genial methods, "silent and imperceptible." Although Bushnell stopped considerably short of Wordsworth in his celebration of a child's innocence, he identified morality with the cultivation of nonintellectual faculties which contained within themselves the seeds of divine salvation. He warned parents that they should not by dull drill enforce religious lessons upon their children, since not intellectual instruction but love and a beneficent environment brought about a soul's regeneration. In 1847 Bushnell was not willing to expand the implications of Christian nurture, but it was clear to him that sin, crime, and damnation might be more the result of parental neglect and faulty emotional growth than of inherent depravity or a conscious choice of evil.

Theodore Parker, whose sympathy for the deluded and the underprivileged had once extended even to Jonathan

[4] Horace Bushnell, *Discourses on Christian Nurture* (Boston, 1847), pp. 26–28.

Edwards, was, in 1847, ready to examine the problem of those who had been denied Christian nurture. In transcendentalism, where human freedom and virtue were glorified and where traditional Christian doctrines were dismissed as "transient," there was a tendency to accept even the worst criminal as a misguided brother. For Parker there were only two kinds of criminals: the victims of society and that smaller group of men who "are born with a depraved organization, an excess of animal passions, or a deficiency of other powers to balance them." [5] Men of both groups suffered from "defective organization." Inasmuch as inheritance, poverty, or faulty education had prevented a criminal's reason, will, and emotions from developing a normal balance, "I would not kill them more than madmen." They should, in fact, be treated as patients, not punished as agencies of evil.

Parker expanded his view of crime into a theory of social progress. Each individual duplicated the history of society, climbing from animal to savage stage, and finally, progressing through a barbarous period to youth and manhood. Circumstances might stop this development in any particular man or race. A boy who matured in city slums, for instance, might live all his life on the savage level, "a Freebooter, a Privateer against society, having universal letters of Marque and Reprisal—a perpetual Arab, his rule to get what he can . . . to keep what he gets." [6] In the rapid march of civilization people were intolerant of a "Bad Boy, a black sheep in the flock, an Ishmael," and most especially intolerant of criminals, "who do not keep up with the moral advance of the mass, stragglers from the march, whom Society treats as Abraham his base-born boy . . . sending them off as Cain

[5] Theodore Parker, *A Sermon of the Dangerous Classes in Society* (Boston, 1847), p. 26.
[6] *Ibid.*, p. 6.

went—with a bad name and a mark on their foreheads!" [7]
According to Parker, human nature was the same in all
men and races except for the extent to which its capacities
had been developed. Yet criminals and backward races
were commonly treated as alien beasts, devoid of all human
rights.

It was a grave mistake to judge these "loiterers from
the march" by the standards of a more highly developed
civilization, because the rules of human behavior, like
religious doctrines, depended upon the stage of social
progress. In barbarous ages, pirates and murderers were
looked upon as leaders and heroes. Yet, Parker conceded,
a terrible question confronted parents, society, and the
civilized world. What was to be done with the alienated—
with bad boys, with murderers, and with backward races?
The transcendentalist urged society and the world to follow the example of an enlightened parent, rejecting the
use of force and punishment and removing the real causes
of evil. Thus the stragglers would be helped to rejoin "the
troop."

Theodore Parker's desire to redeem the worst criminals
and to eradicate the social causes of crime was an expression of the final movement from God to man-centered
morality. His theory held that evil resulted from uneven
development in the history of a man or of a people, especially when the divine or transcendental will had been
stifled within the soul at an early age. In so far as this will
had been permitted to develop beyond the stage of barbarism, it was free to chose the right, which was revealed
within the soul and was not dependent upon sensory experience. In a practical sense, God was therefore only the
goodness of man as revealed in man's own development of
moral, as opposed to intellectual, capacities. The hardened murderer, the self-righteous judge who condemned

[7] *Ibid.*, p. 9.

him, and the crowd which gloated at the hanging, were all examples of deformed and sickly souls, each one lacking the grace of God. It was an irony that Theodore Parker, like the Calvinist, denied any distinction between moral and physical alienation; but whereas Nathaniel Emmons condemned all but God's elect, Parker urged the reformation of "the dangerous classes in society."

III

If popular philosophy in the present age is dominated by the cult of peaceful minds and positive thinking, a theme indicating widespread fear of worry, unhappiness, and futility, American thought of the early and middle nineteenth century was obsessed in a similar way with the quest for moral certainty. American editions of Hutcheson, Paley, and Stewart multiplied through these decades; moral philosophy became the keystone of a college education; Thomas C. Upham, Laurens P. Hickok, Francis Wayland, and Joseph Haven proved that Americans could also write textbooks on the subject; innumerable "Guides," "Duties," and "Letters" addressed to girls and bachelors appealed to a popular audience; and phrenologists proclaimed triumphantly that the secret of morality had at last been discovered. Such concern over the foundation of human morality would have been inexplicable to a seventeenth-century Puritan, or, for that matter, to a devout Catholic at any age. Throughout the textbooks, the moral guides, and the popular tracts, there was a strange tenseness, a fervent appeal not so much for moral action as for an undoubting acceptance of some particular system. Since the most contradictory schools were united in their support of virtue, which, although difficult to define, was generally assumed to exclude murder, it is important to ask why moral philosophy became such a center of controversy. What did people fear and why did they seek reassurance?

Thomas Upham doubtless gave a popular explanation when he declared that "this subject is immensely important to the citizens of this country" because a representative government cannot exist "without purity in the public moral sentiment." [8] In a land where anything was capable of being changed, the only permanent law, as Jefferson had said, must be found in the virtue and intelligence of the citizens. For a Thomas Hobbes or Calvin such a view would have been absurd, since, lacking the imposition of an absolute and unchanging law, "natural man" would simply exterminate himself through mass murder. Yet even for the most optimistic exponent of man's goodness, the conditions of American society in the early nineteenth century were disturbing. A mobile and dispersed population, the presence of slaves within the country and of savages inside and beyond the frontiers, the opportunities for successful crime and fraud all contributed to the uncertainty of moral values. It was as successful rebels slightly frightened by their own freedom that Americans turned to Europe to seek positive moral laws.

The source of this interest in ethics as a positive science may be found in the eighteenth century, when such diverse Americans as Jonathan Edwards and Thomas Jefferson accepted John Locke as *the* philosopher of the human mind. As Merle Curti has pointed out, Locke's enormous popularity in America rested upon the actual conditions of colonial life, which tended to confirm an empirical philosophy, a belief that mind was shaped by experience,

[8] Thomas C. Upham, *Elements of Mental Philosophy, Embracing the Two Departments of the Intellect and the Sensibilities,* 3rd ed. (Portland, Me., 1839), II, 326.

and a conviction that natural rights were a felicitous expression of God's wisdom and justice.[9] Locke's influence extended beyond the phrasing of revolutionary documents. Early American writers of fiction assumed a Lockian psychology, as did lawyers and judges who turned to William Blackstone for the authoritative interpretation of common law. But Locke, as Jonathan Edwards discovered, was not always clear when he discussed the problems of human sin and freedom. It is significant that two of Edwards' important works were attempts to reaffirm the spiritual slavery and sinfulness of natural man without sacrificing the framework of Lockian psychology.

Locke agreed with Thomas Hobbes that man's history of murder, rape, and warfare disproved the existence of an inborn sense of the right. If moral principles were innate and did not require rational proof, why were armies praised for sacking towns, and why did duelists kill without remorse? But Locke did not use this evidence, as Calvinists did, to point toward man's hopeless depravity and dependence on God. Moral truth, Locke argued, while not inherent in the human mind or senses, could be perfectly known and deduced by reason, so that even a monkey, if he possessed reason, could foresee the consequences of his acts and thus be subject to law.[10] Despite man's history of treachery and bloodshed, it was the law of nature for rational creatures to pursue happiness by suspending desire, by comparing the consequences of proposed actions, and by choosing the greatest good.

In an attempt to give a naturalistic account of moral choice without sacrificing the concepts of guilt and responsibility, Locke divided human action into a number

[9] Merle Curti, "The Great Mr. Locke, America's Philosopher, 1783–1861," *Huntington Library Bulletin*, XI (April 1937), 111–113.

[10] John Locke, *An Essay Concerning Human Understanding* (London, 1726), II, 114.

of temporal stages. Whenever some particular action was expected to bring happiness or prevent pain, an individual experienced a "state of uneasiness" or desire. But if desire was an automatic response, the will was the power of the mind to direct or suspend desire before an actual choice was made. By use of his will, man could sublimate impatient and unruly passions and channel desire toward the most worthy ends. Yet in most cases man was not free to control *volition*, which meant that an individual must postpone choice until "he has examined, whether it be really of a Nature in its self and Consequences to make him happy or no. For when he has once chosen it, and thereby it is become a Part of his Happiness, it raises Desire . . . which determines his Will, and sets him at Work in Pursuit of his Choice on all Occasions that offer." [11]

The assumption that morality rests on a cessation of emotion and a rational examination of the nature and consequences of a possible act, was to become, as we shall see, an important element in Anglo-American criminal law. Yet Locke was not altogether clear about this power of a calm, clear judgment, which seemed to him self-evident in human experience but which was obviously *not* applied universally. Locke never doubted that a man with normal intellect should be held accountable for his crimes, which resulted from a refusal to suspend desire and examine rationally the consequences of the intended action. On the other hand, Locke thought of liberty as conformity to the dictates of reason and concluded that any liberation from "that Restraint of Examination and Judgment, which keeps us from Chusing or Doing the Worse," could be only the freedom of a madman. This was almost saying that no rational (and therefore responsible) man could choose evil. In fact, Locke very

[11] *Ibid.,* I, 220.

nearly identified evil with irresponsible error which should be eliminated by education, self-discipline, and punishment, all aiding the reason to formulate "complex ideas" of morality.

As soon as philosophers made the revolutionary shift from God-centered to man-centered morality, depriving virtue of abitrary and unchangeable sanction, there followed a disturbing ambiguity about the relativity of sin and the degree of individual responsibility. The Utilitarians, though often accused of condoning selfishness, were not attempting to subvert prevailing standards of morality, but on the contrary were seeking moral security in a world disrupted by philosophical skepticism. William Paley thought that expediency was a safer principle for moral philosophy than were reason or instinct, either of which might be used as justification for local prejudices and habits.[12] But recognizing the dangers implicit in any utilitarian theory, he stressed the supreme importance of proper training and self-discipline. Evil arose not so much from man's depravity or pride as from unregulated passions, which prevented the mind from choosing the proper and expedient course: "The criminal commerce of the sexes corrupts and depraves the mind and moral character more than any single species of vice whatsoever."

If man acted, as Jeremy Bentham said, on the principle of achieving the greatest pleasure and avoiding pain, it seemed necessary that human law should maintain the precise balance of nature by counteracting those selfish pleasures which were either inconvenient or harmful to society. Crime was essentially a social problem, not a metaphysical contest between good and evil. Circumstances, intentions, consciousness, and motives were all

[12] William Paley, *The Principles of Moral and Political Philosophy*, 7th ed. (Philadelphia, 1788), pp. 31–32.

essential in determining the degree of the crime and the nature of the punishment, for man was an intricate mechanism which could be corrected, disciplined, and trained by a scientific analysis of pleasures and pains.[13]

Paley was widely read in America before 1850, largely because he combined "expediency" in morals with a system of natural theology, but the franker forms of hedonism and materialism made little headway. It was evident to many people that, despite Bentham's confidence in his system of punishments, fundamental assumptions concerning responsibility would be undermined by pure hedonism. If man acted on no higher principle than his own pleasure, if the will was not free to choose between universal right and wrong, and if sin was not something to be punished for its own sake, who could say that a criminal was guilty or that government had a transcendent right to kill a murderer? In Europe the sensational psychology had resulted in agnosticism and skepticism, and for those Americans who looked upon the French Revolution as a kind of mass murder implicit in materialistic theory, it was essential that a different morality be defended. But though Americans generally shunned hedonism and materialism, they were to discover that, once crime was conceived as a social and psychological problem, no ethical theory was immune from the searching question: are men equally responsible for their actions?

IV

A general American acceptance of Lockian psychology, instead of, let us say, Cartesian rationalism, did not mean that American thinkers were willing to extend the influence of environment to the origins of moral knowledge.

[13] Jeremy Bentham, *An Introduction to the Principles of Morals and Legislation* (London, 1879), pp. 70–121.

If the understanding was a blank tablet where sensations traced intricate patterns of ideas and associations, there were at least bastions within the human soul which could not be stormed by scientific logic. Ideas might not be innate, yet there were innate principles and senses which provided a foundation for absolute morality. A theory which found the source of virtue in the senses, as opposed to the understanding, would also provide a new explanation for human error and evil. A man dominated by the understanding, by the mechanical laws of association, would, as the materialist claimed, be subject to the winds of circumstance. But this really meant that his well of intuition, faith, and moral certainty had gone dry, that he was living and acting in a world of surface appearances, of dusty words and fleeting sensations. A man could only truly be a man, that is, a moral being, if he could break through the mechanism of perception and emotionally "feel" an object or event. The understanding, with its ideas, associations, and word symbols, was merely a kind of convenient instrument attached to the soul, an instrument capable of being perfected by science, but not a substitute for the transcendental or instinctual capacities of the soul itself.

This point of view originated, in modern times, with Lord Shaftesbury and Francis Hutcheson, who sympathized with Locke's attempt to free ethics from rationalism and supernaturalism, but who doubted the wisdom of deducing moral truth from experience. Since all men seemed to *feel* in their hearts something recommending virtue, Hutcheson argued that moral truth depended on an instinctual love of goodness for its own sake.[14] Conscience was an expansive emotion which, if undistracted

[14] Francis Hutcheson, *A System of Moral Philosophy, in Three Books* . . . (London, 1755), I, 24.

by faulty logic or blind passion, would unfailingly arrive at virtue.[15]

There was a troubling paradox, however, in the development of the moral-sense theory. Locke had prepared the way for a rigorously naturalistic and environmental theory of ethics by rejecting the belief in intuitive knowledge of good and evil. Hutcheson and the later Scottish philosophers feared that this sensational psychology would ultimately destroy the foundations of morality and responsibility, and their theory of an immutable and universal moral sense was a defense of absolute ethical standards. All men were assumed to possess benevolent impulses (Hutcheson) or an intuitive sense of right (Thomas Reid), which was the locus of obligation and responsibility. But when philosophers made moral obligation depend on the testimony of an inner faculty and not on the synthesis of simple ideas derived from experience, it was impossible for them to furnish the kind of exact proof of responsibility desired by Locke, Blackstone, and Bentham. According to Thomas Reid:

The man who does not, by the light of his own mind, perceive some things in conduct to be right, and others to be wrong, is as incapable of reasoning about morals as a blind man is about colours. Such a man, if any such man ever was, would be no moral agent, nor capable of any moral obligation.[16]

Reid also said that a criminal act might be excused if it resulted from a diseased or disordered understanding. But he went beyond this conventional theory when he ruled that a man who lacked an innate moral sense was

[15] Francis Hutcheson, *An Essay on the Nature and Conduct of the Passions and Affections, With Illustrations on the Moral Sense* (London, 1728), p. 278.

[16] Thomas Reid, *Essays on the Powers of the Human Mind* (Edinburgh, 1803), II, 457.

not capable of moral obligation. The total absence of moral perception would thus be an example of *physical* alienation, for the subject would be removed by physical causes from sympathetic unity with his fellow men. Moral blame could be assigned only to those individuals who willfully disregarded their innate sense of right and wrong. If a man lacked such a sense, he was "morally blind" and was not responsible. Although the Scottish philosophers sought to re-establish an absolute morality and assumed that human nature was blessed with benevolent affections and an immutable sense of right, their philosophy implied that the limits of responsibility were considerably narrower than those recognized by law. But this implication would not be fully developed until the nineteenth century had modified the concept of uniformity, enabling men to question the origin and development of the moral sense.

In 1829 James Marsh, president of the University of Vermont, wrote to Coleridge that the Scottish philosophy had replaced Locke in American colleges. Two years previously, Thomas Upham had written the first serious American textbook in psychology. This work, especially in its revised editions, was a significant link between the Scottish doctrine of moral sense and the concept of transcendental reason. That there was a strong affinity between moral sense and transcendental reason (as opposed to the understanding), is a fact demonstrated by the insistence of Dugald Stewart, Pierre Laromiguière, and Maine de Biran that moral feelings were immutable and absolute. If Kant, the author of modern transcendentalism, generally mistrusted sense and feelings, it was clear in the fideism of F. H. Jacobi that pure reason could be identified with pure feeling. Those who reacted against Locke and Hume tended to seek moral certainty in the nonintellectual faculties; unintentionally, perhaps, they identified conscience with desires and emotions. Thus

American acceptance of the Scottish philosophy contributed to a growing conviction, especially after 1830, that man's uniqueness, his virtue, and his freedom, lay not in the intellect, but in "reason" or "higher feelings."

American moral philosophers, such as Thomas Upham, wanted to recognize a free will, a universal moral sense, and a clear distinction between good and bad men; but the constant dread of materialism, which they associated with sensational psychology, forced them to identify morality with emotion. It was difficult, however, to measure emotions, affections, or senses; and although the Scottish philosophers expressed faith that a knowledge of right existed within the soul of every man, this basis for responsibility was entirely subjective and incapable of proof. Locke had implied that a man was free to choose, and therefore responsible, if he had the intellectual capacity to judge the nature and consequences of his acts. But when moral choice was made to depend upon an emotional sense of rightness, it was obvious that responsibility could not be determined by so simple a test. A man might, for instance, be incapable of sensing in an emotional way that a certain act was wrong, even though his intellect knew that the act was unlawful and generally disapproved. To preserve the idea of universal responsibility, of course, it was possible to deny the disturbing belief that some men lacked sensibilities and finer emotions. The intellect might be subject to heredity and experience, to education and disease, but the moral sense was nearly inviolate, as was the autonomous will.

For simplification we may imagine two diverging lines of thought among those who accepted the supremacy of a moral sense over intellect. On the one hand, such writers as Asa Mahan and Laurens P. Hickok combined the doctrine of moral feelings with the absolutism of a Kantian will, so that within itself human nature contained law, judge, and executioner.[17] If the will was autonomous, man had the power to resist even his strongest motives and inclinations, a hypothesis which justified an assumption of uniform responsibility, despite the subordination of intellect to moral sense. It is significant that the same writers who attacked Locke as an unintentional materialist charged Jonathan Edwards with having reduced the will to a mere function of the affections. On the other hand, there were thinkers whose celebration of moral feelings, combined with an intense desire for reform and progress, resulted in an assault upon traditional assumptions of responsibility.

In the 1840's and 50's there was a growing conviction that crime was a disease of the finer sensibilities, to be prevented by improved education and social reform. Cyrus Peirce, author of the prize essay for the American Institute of Instruction in 1854, argued that cultivation of the intellect was no security against evil. In Prussia, he pointed out, where every child was required to attend school, there was fifteen times the amount of crime there was in France where the people were three-fifths illiterate.[18] If America was to reduce its increasing rate of crime, it would be necessary, Peirce felt, to encourage rigorous moral exercise, regular occupations, industrious habits, and above all, agrarian simplicity. The flood of books and pamphlets dealing with "moral culture" emphasized a single theme: it was not the intellect nor even will which served as man's shield against temptation and crime; only the proper nurture of instincts and feelings would bring eventual peace and social harmony.[19]

[17] Laurens P. Hickok, *A System of Moral Science,* 3rd ed. (New York, 1861), p. 42.

[18] Cyrus Peirce, *Crime: Its Cause and Cure, An Essay* (Boston, 1854), p. 23.

[19] Social harmony was supposed to depend primarily on the moral culture of women, since it was in the family that the feelings and affections

One the most interesting phenomena in the history of American thought was the rapid and widespread acceptance of phrenology. Phrenology solved every problem in psychology and ethics which had preoccupied Western man from the time of Plato, and it was immensely satisfying for people who worried about moral certainty. The fact that phrenology was a kind of materialism did not seem to bother its proponents, largely, one may suspect, because it retained the familiar faculty psychology, including the moral feelings. For those who associated religion with ethics and ethics with benevolent affections, it was comforting to know that morality was based on the physiology of the brain. At one stroke the disturbing gap between science and moral philosophy had been closed. God's design and purpose could be traced in the intricate brain of His highest creation.

When a phrenologist turned to the subject of human aggression, his conclusion was remarkably similar to the Freudian concept of a sado-masochistic drive. Franz Joseph Gall had identified an innate faculty of murder, which his disciple, Johann Spurzheim, changed to "destructiveness." This analogue to Freud's "death-wish" was described by M. B. Sampson:

The tendency to destroy is one of the blind propensities of man's nature, absolutely necessary to adapt him to his relation to the external world; and, when acting harmoniously with the intellect and moral sentiments, it produces only the most beneficial results; but, when roused to unbalanced action, it exhibits itself in maniacal fury, and, overpowering the reason and the feelings (which it must do before its possessor can commit murder), imparts oftentimes as strong an impulse towards the destruction of its possessor as towards the destruction of any other individual. It gives, in its morbid state, an inordinate

---

were trained. For a single example of this vast literature, see Edwin H. Chapin, *Duties of Young Women* (Boston, 1848), pp. 58–61.

tendency to violent *action,* a wild desire to overpower restraint of every kind, and to break down and destroy all that comes within its reach.[20]

E. W. Farnham, of the Female Prison at Mt. Pleasant, New York, concluded that phrenology would revolutionize criminal jurisprudence, since it abolished the belief in moral responsibility. Throughout history, society had falsely judged

all persons equally capable, and had consequently erected one standard, which none may fail to reach, however they may be incapacitated, without being judged guilty, not only of the offenses they have committed, but of the infinitely greater one of having acted in defiance of the decisions of higher powers, powers which they never possessed; of having wilfully and perversely outraged all those purer and better sentiments, and defied all that reason which saved their more fortunate brethren from the same degradation.[21]

Those who took refuge in the doctrine of free will could find little comfort in phrenology, which made clear "that the will is not a moral faculty, that it has no inherent tendency either to vice or virtue, but may be enlisted to sustain either, and that in most criminals it is unenlightened." [22] Laws, according to Sampson, had been created on the assumption that merely because most men were endowed with reason, all men enjoy an equal and perfect state of mental health. Yet the feelings and passions alone furnished motives for the intellect and will. This meant that a man whose coronal region was imperfect (depriving him of a moral sense), or whose posterior brain had been overdeveloped (giving him abnormal

[20] M. B. Sampson, *Rationale of Crime, and Its Appropriate Treatment: Being a Treatise on Criminal Jurisprudence in Relation to Cerebral Organization* (New York, 1846), p. 81.

[21] E. W. Farnham, introd. to Sampson, *Rationale,* p. xix.

[22] *Ibid.,* p. xviii.

animal propensities), would be completely incapable of conforming to the laws of average men. It was a great mistake to suppose that a criminal was normal just because he suffered from no hallucinations and could distinguish intellectually between right and wrong. The absurd injustice of criminal law was especially evident in the presumption that an inveterate offender was more guilty than a man who had committed his first crime: "Thus, that which constitutes the surest evidence of the criminal's need of remedial treatment, separates him farthest from it." [23] To say, as moralists did, that a criminal made his own career by selecting bad companions, indulging in drink, or evading responsibility, was equally fallacious, since these were only manifestations of a brain originally perverted. Those who condemned criminals were actually finding outlets for their own destructive tendencies. But they should remember that, given a similar brain at birth, they, too, would join the rank of social enemies.

Phrenology clarified the ancient problem of responsibility simply by eliminating it. According to traditional jurisprudence, a man who killed without motive might be considered insane, while a man who murdered for money had no chance of pleading insanity. Phrenology showed, however, that the destructive impulse might act either by itself or in combination with the "acquisitive tendency." Whether a man murdered for money or for no apparent purpose was relatively unimportant, since all crime resulted from impaired health or deficient development of one or more faculties.[24]

But if science "proved" that the Creator had made some men moral and others irresponsible, the safety of society obviously required that criminals and those likely to become criminals be given proper treatment. People with

[23] Sampson, *Rationale*, p. 11.   [24] *Ibid.*, p. 40.

peaked heads or with bumps behind their ears should not
be placed in positions of responsibility or temptation.
The most extreme cases should be carefully isolated in
special hospitals, where improvement under the guidance
of trained phrenologists was certain to secure the public
safety.[25]

These views, while obviously unacceptable to most
Americans, represented the final resolution of the moral-
sense theory. Locke had said that a criminal was guilty
because in refusing to be rational he violated natural
law. All men were created equal, but some, by perversity,
could morally alienate their natural rights and become
outcasts from society. According to Sampson, however,
all men were not created equal. Essentially, there were
only the elect, who possessed a moral sense and a harmonious development of passions, and the nonelect, who
were alienated from society by physical causes. Instead of
castigating their less fortunate brothers, it was the duty
of responsible men to prevent the depraved from committing the crimes they could not otherwise avoid, to sympathize with deformed affections as they might with deformed bodies, and to show patience and benevolence in
curing moral and physical diseases. In basing the moral
sense theory in man's material nature, the more consistent
phrenologists had arrived at a position approximating that
of Theodore Parker. If individual differences accounted
for crime, these differences seemed to dissolve in man's
common dependence on his mental organ or in the
brotherhood of transcendental will.

Both Theodore Parker and M. B. Sampson looked upon
crime as a social problem, and in so doing tended to obscure the question of private morality. The standards of
normal men were not to be used to judge the responsibility of defectives, but such a distinction between normal

[25] *Ibid.,* pp. 53–66.

and abnormal implied that the behavior of the majority was an expression of proper cerebral balance, or of the transcendental mind. Yet the phrenologist, after arguing that some men lack the physiological basis for conformity, found it difficult to define concepts like "normal" and "proper." Theodore Parker could not always be certain that civilization advanced in the right direction. Might not the "loiterers from the march" have a surer perception of values, especially when the marchers crossed the Rio Grande or condoned slavery? In the last analysis, morality was both subjective and relative when criminals were denied the capacity for guilt. If the moral sense was not uniform among men, if some individuals were impelled by their nature to be savages, then who could be certain of knowing universal goodness and justice? This problem, implicit in the moral-sense theory, was something that writers of fiction could not ignore.

Chapter II

FROM NATURAL MAN

TO SUPERMAN

AMERICA'S first serious writers of fiction matured in a
world strongly colored by the European Enlightenment
and at a time when educated men were assumed to be
familiar with the theories of Locke, Hutcheson, Paley,
and Reid. At one extreme, of course, there were theologians who tried to preserve the doctrines of original sin
and total depravity, while at the other end of the intellectual spectrum, a few radicals defended Thomas Paine,
William Godwin, and the French *philosophes.* By the turn
of the nineteenth century, there was a general tendency to
reject the belief that evil arose from the instigation of
Satan, from the imputation of Adam's guilt, or even from
man's disobedience to external command. The more enlightened writers of fiction assumed that evil resulted
from error, which might be defined as a delusion of
reason or as a violation of natural law. But granting
that reason depended upon the senses, and thus upon the

environment, most of these early American writers protected the concept of responsibility by emphasizing the human capacity for virtue. As we have seen, this capacity might be thought of as an inherent moral sense or as a self-correcting power to suspend desire while the reason calmly determined the greatest good. As long as man's capacity for virtue was considered to be universal, except in lunatics and idiots, moral responsibility seemed to be a self-evident truth.

Washington Irving's "The Story of the Young Italian," included in *Tales of a Traveler* (1824), was a conventional expression of this morality, but showed, at the same time, a changing attitude toward crime. To provide explanation for a brutal act of murder, Irving carefully traced the development of a moody, sensitive child, the frustrations of the criminal's youth, and the circumstances preceding his outburst of violence. First of all, the young Italian had been born with "an extreme sensibility," which, under proper guidance, might have contributed to artistic genius: "Everything affected me violently. While yet an infant in my mother's arms, and before I had learned to talk, I could be wrought upon to a wonderful degree of anguish or delight by the power of music." But as the child grew older, ignorant relatives and domestics transformed his sensitivity into a temperamental irritability: "I was moved to tears, tickled to laughter, provoked to fury, for the entertainment of company, who were amused by such a tempest of mighty passion in a pigmy frame."

When the young Italian's mother died, his "power as a spoiled child was at an end," and he was confronted by a stern, authoritarian father, whose preference for an older brother was not concealed. Thus a heart which was "naturally disposed to the extremes of tenderness and affection" was distorted by the extremes of parental attention and rejection. Sent to a convent at an early age, the boy acquired a "tinge of melancholy" from "the dismal stories of the monks, about devils and evil spirits, with which they affrighted my young imagination."

The second stage in Irving's development of a murderer came when the Italian had reached manhood and had at last found happiness. He rebelled against the injustice of his father, became a successful artist, enjoyed the patronage of a nobleman, and fell in love with the beautiful Bianca. As a climax to this change of fortune, the young Italian learned that his brother had died. He now had promise of acquiring a home, a name, and the rank of a nobleman. No longer a rejected outcast, he was able to make a formal proposal to Bianca; but first it was necessary to return to his ancestral home and win the affections of his father. He entrusted Bianca to the care of Filippo, his best friend and the only son of his benefactor.

Finding his father a helpless invalid, the Italian was forced to remain at home for eighteen months. He nursed his formerly tyrannical parent with the faithfulness of a loyal son:

I knew that his death alone would set me free; yet I never at any moment wished it. I felt too glad to be able to make any atonement for past disobedience; and, denied as I had been all endearments of relationship in my early days, my heart yearned toward a father who, in his age and helplessness, had thrown himself entirely on me for comfort.

Filippo generously served as an intermediary for the secret correspondence between Bianca and her lover.

The third state in the history of a murder began when the young Italian returned to claim Bianca after his father had died. Bianca was horrified by his appearance. Filippo, it turned out, had told Bianca that her lover had perished at sea and had then married her himself. The young

Italian could see "in her pallid and wasted features, in the prompt terror and subdued agony of her eye, a whole history of a mind broken down by tyranny." Realizing that he had been cheated out of marriage by deceit and that Bianca's life had been ruined, the Italian clenched his teeth and foamed at the mouth. At that opportune moment, Filippo appeared: "He turned pale, looked wildly to right and left, as he would have fled, and trembling drew his sword." The Italian's whole life had been a preparation for this moment. First he stabbed the villain with his poniard: "He fell with the blow, but my rage was unsated. I sprang upon him with the bloodthirsty feeling of a tiger: redoubled my blows, mangled him in my frenzy, grasped him by the throat."

Remorse, however, was the final stage in the murderer's history. In the Apennines, where he fled from justice and from the shrieks of Bianca, the young Italian could not escape from the horrible countenance of his victim, which followed him like a phantom wherever he went: "Could I but have restored my victim to life, I felt as if I could look on with transport even though Bianca were in his arms." He passed days and nights in "sleepless torment," a "never-dying worm" preyed upon his heart, an "unquenchable fire" burned within his brain, and finally, resolving that only his own blood could atone for his crime, the young Italian surrendered himself to justice.

This is a simple, unconvincing tale, doubtless intended by Irving to excite the horror and sympathy of sensitive readers, who, like himself, might look upon the young Italian's career as a sauntering American traveler might view the plight of Italian peasants. But in addition to this stereotype of Italian passion and deceit, there are several important assumptions about crime and human behavior in "The Story of the Young Italian."

It should be noted that Irving began with the theory

that a child born with "extreme sensibility" had a great chance of becoming either a genius or a criminal and therefore required special guidance and care. Presumably, a stolid, unimaginative child would not have been spoiled by relatives, would not have suffered such anguish from parental rejection (if, indeed, he had been rejected at all), and would have remained calm and rational when defeated in love. Yet Irving did not identify a passionate temperament with inherent sin, or even with a tendency toward sin. Man's fall from goodness was a result of circumstances beyond his control. These circumstances might operate in two ways: the ignorance and neglect of parents could distort a child's passions, stimulate his temper, and weaken the power of his reason to suspend impulsive desire; or external circumstances could liberate aggressive passions which, heretofore, had remained latent.

Irving also took pains to show that while reason could be temporarily overthrown in an extreme crisis, the soul of even a murderer was not totally corrupt. The young Italian, despite his abnormal temperament, seemed to possess an adequate moral sense. He sacrificed love for filial duty, he was impelled to violence only after discovering that Filippo had mistreated Bianca, and his final remorse was complete. It was this conventional treatment of remorse which kept Irving from a theory of strict environmentalism. Seemingly, the murderer's actions had been determined by a rigid chain of circumstances, yet the very fact that he felt guilty proved, according to the contemporary morality, that he had possessed the capacity to resist his criminal impulse. Responsibility, in other words, was deduced from the presence of remorse, which all criminals were supposed to have.

So far, we may conclude, Irving's assumptions were based on an adaptation of the Lockian psychology, which he vaguely associated with the theory of an inherent moral sense. The theme of this morality may be put simply: faulty training in childhood made a sensitive boy more susceptible to outbursts of passion and circumstances pushed him toward an act of violence; but while this criminal act might be understood by analyzing the subject's past, his remorse proved that his will was free to resist his desire and that he violated the natural law of his reason, or that he ignored the counsel of his moral sense.

But there is another problem in Irving's treatment of murder. If he avoided a theory of complete environmentalism, he did so only by an ending which must have seemed contrived to even the most sentimental of his readers. Every sentence of the tale relates to the central act of homicide, and every event tends to justify the protagonist. Irving lost no chance to describe the young Italian as a persecuted boy, whose attempts to achieve happiness were thwarted by a malicious plot. The Italian did not track down his victim in premeditated revenge, but he encountered Filippo by accident, immediately after his discovery of deception. Even then there was a mitigating circumstance, for Filippo's sword was drawn before the young Italian attacked. In common law this fact would have reduced the crime to manslaughter.

The question arises why Irving wrote a tale in which every incident justified an act of homicide and which was carefully constructed to arouse the reader's sympathy for a man whose haunting guilt seemed to conflict with the circumstances of his crime. To pursue the implications of this question, we must utilize certain modern concepts which, if inappropriate for historical analysis, are nevertheless useful in the interpretation of imaginative expression. If Filippo, the victim, is accepted as merely an unfaithful friend, who is otherwise unimportant to the plot, neither the Italian's guilt nor Irving's attempt to justify him can be understood. But Irving implied that Filippo represented something more than an unfaithful friend, at least in the eyes of the young Italian. It should be remembered that the Italian's original frustrations, as well as his first aggressive desires, began in a family conflict in which his brother was the favored son. After rebelling against his father's tyranny, he became a wandering outcast, whose status was regained only when his brother died. By winning his father's affection through loyal service, the Italian achieved a legitimate claim to wealth and rank which would otherwise have been his brother's. Filippo, his closest friend, was, significantly, the son of his benefactor, who had taken the place of a father in the Italian's youth. We thus arrive at the inference that Filippo represented a competing brother, whose evil deception stood for all of the injustice which the young Italian had suffered in childhood. His lonely wandering in the barren Apennines was, for the early nineteenth century, an unmistakable allusion to Cain's eternal punishment.

We have already observed that when moral philosophers discussed crime they attempted to combine a theory of environmental causation with a belief in individual guilt and responsibility. Proper education, religious discipline, or a reformed environment would protect the growing child from contamination. On the other hand, once a criminal had actually developed, he carried a personal guilt and responsibility for his acts, since he presumably retained the universal capacity for moral choice. Remorse, which appeared in even the most depraved, was evidence of every man's power to resist the force of environment and circumstance. Washington Irving tried to unify these seemingly incompatible ideas by employing a theme whose subtle overtones of feeling helped to modify the theories both of environment and of positive guilt. Fratricide, of course, was a more difficult crime to justify than was a

simple act of manslaughter. By striking at the primal
bonds of family unity, the rebelling brother proclaimed
himself an enemy of all order and authority, of all obligation and self-restraint. Irving suggested that, despite the
mitigating circumstances, an act of murder was essentially
a fratricide, an act of total anarchy, which could be
neither explained nor justified by precipitating causes.
Yet he sympathized with this persecuted Cain and emphasized the son's reconciliation with the father, so that
aggression could not be equated with a revolt against the
highest authority. By tracing the causes of violence to the
ambiguities of family conflict, and by sympathizing with
a passionate but sensitive murderer, Irving outlined a
theme which was to be repeated countless times in American magazines and popular romances before the Civil
War.

II

In briefly analyzing the history of moral philosophy
from the early eighteenth to the mid-nineteenth century,
we have seen a tendency to deny the doctrine of man's
total depravity and to restore "natural man" to the
original purity of an Adam who possessed capacities for
either good or evil. In America, especially after 1830,
"nature" was associated with the goodness of children,
with the spontaneous expression of the "real self," and
with the innocence of desires uncorrupted by civilization.
According to an increasing number of writers, morality
did not result from the discipline of passions by a stern
conscience, but rather from a liberation of the finer impulses. Yet this identification of conscience with instinct,
which was an outgrowth of the moral-sense theory, tended
to blur the ancient distinction between reason and sinful desire. Just as Jonathan Edwards, after surrendering
the intellect to Lockian psychology, had difficulty in

distinguishing religious from nonreligious affections, so nineteenth-century writers who had abandoned intellect as a source of virtue found it difficult to differentiate between pure impulse and improper desire.

If we may use for a moment the convenient terminology of Freud, this change in moral theory as reflected in literature might be described as an awakening of interest in the human libido and as a rejection of the belief that law rested upon the authority of the superego. Yet even those imaginative writers who glorified man's primal instincts as the foundation of both genius and morality were conscious of the fact that impulses, unguided by reason, might lead to violence and crime. Consequently, they went back in their search for natural virtue to man's original, undifferentiated libido, which had the capacity for either love or hatred and which, *before* it had been expressed as conscious desire, was sinless. In such a vitalistic psychology, with its confusion of various nonintellectual powers, moral purity became synonomous with unrestricted impulse, unenlightened by conscious choice, and unaware of the superego's law. Writers found obvious symbols for this sinless libido in Adam, in natural men, and in children. But since a primitive impulse is at least partly sexual and preserves its purity only in being unconscious, these same writers found it difficult to describe an uncorrupted passion without thereby corrupting it. Thus we have the misty idylls, the innocent, sylvan dance, with eunuch Satyrs and somber Pans.

Although Hawthorne's *The Marble Faun* was published in 1860, it is curiously remote from the world of Auguste Comte, Karl Marx, and Charles Darwin. It rather presents a world of pensive sculptors and fiery young painters who dare to reproduce "the exact likeness" of an old masterpiece, a world where every artist is a genius, where doves flutter, glances are bewitching, and mysterious meetings

occur in the Colosseum and catacombs. Like Irving, Hawthorne associated Italy with artistic genius, with mystery,
and with passionate violence, but Hawthorne's romance of
natural man's corruption was a significant departure from
the psychology which Irving had postulated. In *The
Marble Faun* all traces of Lockian theories have disappeared, while various human faculties have been merged
in a single flood of human passion, which contains potentialities for benevolence, artistic creation, love, and
aggression. This basic, original passion is innocent, but it
is also unstable, since it yearns for expression and self-
consciousness. Man is at first immersed in nature and
there enjoys a naïve happiness, but as he begins to tran-
scend nature, man's spontaneous and diffused impulses
coalesce into sustained desire. At this critical point, so
the theme goes, man either falls into sin or his passions
are sublimated to artistic creation. Natural man, it should
be noted, is not a rational man whose intellect calmly
selects the greatest good, nor is he even a personification
of the moral sense. Natural man is essentially a spontaneous man with a self undivided by separate senses or
faculties.

Donatello, Hawthorne's natural man, was an Italian
nobleman, not exactly a child or a man, but in "a high
and beautiful sense, an animal." He was described as a
more nearly perfect being, in his own state, than man, but
he also possessed the capacity for enlightenment and thus
for evil. This, of course, was a complete reversal of traditional morality, which regarded enlightenment as the
only source of virtue and which would have interpreted
an animal-man as a monstrosity. But if Donatello embodied the ideal of man in nature, Hilda, the mawkishly
good dove-girl, was definitely beyond nature. She was good
only because her passions had been trained and refined to
the point of elimination; but unlike Donatello, she was

not especially happy in her goodness, despite her artistic genius. After human nature had been enlightened, it would seem, no amount of cultivation could restore the freedom and happiness of the beautiful animal, who lived only for the present moment and who had never experienced guilt or shame.

But Donatello was also a man, even though he was referred to as a cousin of a satyr and took part in an expurgated sylvan dance. It was when his passions concentrated on a particular object, on a woman, that he began to rise above the sea of undifferentiated desire and into the crisp, harsh air of conscious choice. Originally, he had loved all people equally and had hated none. His corruption came, however, from directing all of his energies toward the possession of a single woman's love, whereby he excluded the rest of the human race from his affections. In a sense, then, he became alienated from humanity by his growing incapacity for universal benevolence. Hawthorne seemed to say that a man's potentiality for hatred and aggression increased in proportion to his passionate love for a single woman. When Donatello murdered Miriam's persecutor merely because her eyes consented to the act, he achieved a mystical union with his lover but he had symbolically renounced humanity.

In this allegory of man's fall, Hawthorne reinterpreted the biblical drama in terms of a vitalistic psychology. The conflict between good and evil did not arise from man's disobedience to external command, nor from an internal struggle between reason and passion. Instead of locating good and evil in different human faculties, Hawthorne saw them as possible stages in the development of a single, passionate energy. At the beginning of this process was the pristine goodness of natural man. The final, if somewhat unsatisfying, end of human development seemed to be the conventional heroine, whose tense virtue resulted from a refinement that killed her human warmth and sympathy. The question which Hawthorne posed was whether natural man could develop beyond nature without falling into sin; or, to put it another way, whether nature could become self-conscious without becoming guilty. He concluded, of course, that virtue was secure only in the bosom of a Hilda, where passionate energy had been converted into a New England conscience and a love of art; but his sympathy for the spontaneous impulse was otherwise unconcealed.

III

When we search for assumptions concerning human evil over sixty years of American literature, we find a growing tendency to reduce the importance of reason in man's moral conduct. In *Ormond* (1799), one of Charles Brockden Brown's characters expressed a theory which made man subject to the power of habit, and thus to an external moral or physical environment: "Human life is momentous or trivial in our eyes, according to the course which our habits and opinions have taken. Passion greedily accepts, and habit readily offers, the sacrifice of another's life, and reason obeys the impulse of education and desire." If native reason was subservient to habit, it also followed that a heroine like Brown's Constantia Dudley, whose habits had been properly directed to the pursuit of virtue, would be morally secure even in the face of calamitous plagues, murders, and attempted rapes.

A generation later, the elder Richard Henry Dana refused to believe that an enlightened mind would make a man invulnerable to sin: "So evil, however, is the nature of men, that almost the love of what is excellent may lead us astray, if we do not take heed to the way in which we seek it; and we may see, and understand, and wish for it, till we come to envy it in another." [1] No mistake could be greater than the rationalist's confidence in reason, for, as one Cooper character said in 1825, "The amount of human knowledge is but to know how much we are under the dominion of our passions; and he who has learned by experience how to smother the volcano, and he who never felt its fires, are surely fit associates." [2] Conscience might be an innate and divine power, as Cooper at times maintained, but it needed confirmation by habit and training.[3] The human passions were often likened to a growing plant. Capable of developing wholesome flowers, or dazzling but poisonous blossoms, as in Hawthorne's "Rappaccini's Daughter" (1846), they required careful cultivation and pruning. Seldom could conscience prevent or reason detect a gradual warping of the soul "because of that instinctive sophistry with which the mind is ever ready to defend itself from whatever is painful. . . . Indeed, evil is but another name for moral discord; its law, revulsion; and its final issue, the shutting up the soul in impenetrable solitude." [4] Thus Washington Allston described the process of rationalization in 1841, indicating a belief in the essential unity of human faculties. Four years later Cooper was even more explicit: "Seldom does man commit a wrong but he sets his ingenuity to work to frame excuses for it. When his mind thus gets to be perverted by the influence of his passions, and more especially by that of rapacity, he never fails to fancy new principles to exist to favour his schemes." [5]

[1] Richard Henry Dana, *Poems and Prose Writings* (New York, 1849), I, 271.

[2] James Fenimore Cooper, *Lionel Lincoln; or, The Leaguer of Boston* (New York, 1852), p. 66.

[3] James Fenimore Cooper, *The Heidenmauer; or, The Benedictines; A Legend of the Rhine* (New York, 1856), p. 329.

[4] Washington Allston, *Monaldi: A Tale* (Boston, 1856), p. 219.

[5] James Fenimore Cooper, *The Chainbearer; or, The Littlepage Manuscripts* (New York, 1852), II, 24.

The Christian doctrine of man's total fall received a naturalistic interpretation whenever writers stressed the interdependence of man's faculties, since either a delusion of reason or a corruption of passion would pervert an individual's total behavior. The passage just quoted from Cooper is an echo of the eighteenth-century belief in a "ruling passion," which may be seen in the antirationalism of Bernard Mandeville and David Hume.[6] This idea of a passion which dominates thoughts as well as actions was most popular in nineteenth-century literature and played, as we shall see, an important part in shaping attitudes toward insanity. In explaining the process of rationalization, it also substantiated the older doctrine that a single sin opens the way for multiple and repeated crimes. As one of Hawthorne's first villains said, in *Fanshawe* (1828), "There is a pass, when evil deeds can add nothing to guilt, nor good ones take anything from it." If a ruling passion showed that sin could infect the entire nature of a man, evil was also felt by some writers to be contagious in space and time, so that one evil act might spread outward or be transmitted to future generations (like Hawthorne's Maule's curse).

Another biblical doctrine—that evil embodies the seeds of its own destruction—was commonly given a naturalistic justification. Passions could drive a man to outward violence and maliciousness, but they could also turn inward as self-inflicted aggression. "Perhaps," as William Gilmore Simms wrote in 1835, "one of the most natural and necessary agents of man, in his progress through life, is the desire to destroy."[7] But in 1841 Simms added that this impulse could also mean self-destruction:

---

[6] Kenneth MacLean, *John Locke and English Literature of the Eighteenth Century* (New Haven, Conn., 1936), pp. 47–48.

[7] William Gilmore Simms, *The Yemassee: A Romance of Carolina* (New York, n.d.), pp. 285–286.

There is a perversity of mood which is the worst of all such penalties. There are tortures which the foolish heart equally inflicts and endures. The passions riot on their own nature; and, feeding as they do upon that blossom from which they spring . . . may [they], not inaptly, be likened to that unnatural brood which gnaws into the heart of the mother-bird, and sustains its existence at the expense of hers.[8]

Cooper, whose theories of human nature were generally less naturalistic than were Simms's, simply said that "it is a law of human nature, that the excesses of passion bring their own rebukes." [9] Such a belief in natural nemesis, as opposed to eternal punishment in an afterlife, raised disturbing questions concerning human justice. If the dominance of evil passions destroyed a criminal's happiness, and if a contorted and twisted soul was its own punishment, then sin seemed very much like a disease which no man would consciously choose. How could official punishment administered by the state cure a diseased mind which actually had an impulsive desire for suffering and self-destruction?

Moreover, as the idea of a ruling passion was adapted to a vitalistic psychology that reduced the importance of reason in even normal life, it seemed that vice might be directed by many influences which were not necessarily evil in themselves: "It carries the knife, it strikes the blow, but is not always the chooser of its own victim," according to Simms. In other words, political and religious aggression, justified by high motives and good intentions, were not essentially different from the violence of an individual criminal. Despite the fact that aggression was universal in human nature, men thought of themselves

[8] William Gilmore Simms, *Confession; or, The Blind Heart* (Chicago, 1890), pp. 11–12.
[9] Cooper, *Chainbearer,* p. 149.

as virtuous beings and justified their actions with extravagant theories:

The murderer is not unfrequently found to possess benevolence as well as veneration in a high degree; and the zealots of all countries and religions are almost invariably creatures of strong and violent passions, to which the extravagance of their zeal and devotion furnishes an outlet, which is not always innocent in its direction or effects. Thus, in their enthusiasm— which is only a minor madness—whether the Hindoo bramin [sic] or the Spanish bigot, the English roundhead . . . it is but a word and a blow—though the word be a hurried prayer to the God of their adoration, and the blow aimed with all the malevolence of hell at the bosom of a fellow-creature. There is no greater inconsistency in the one character than in the other.[10]

The more that writers abandoned reason as a firm, autonomous judge of right and wrong, the more it seemed that human personality was determined by environment. Men might not be predestined saints and sinners, but writers often referred to them as moral weathervanes or as stones "divinely kicked." When responsible moral choice was identified with refined impulse, a wholesome environment acquired a greater importance in raising moral children; it became a substitute, in some degree, for religious conversion and formal education. In the atmosphere of a tavern, according to Timothy Shay Arthur, a youth's pure, original impulses would be corrupted, his face would acquire a "sensual expression," and his natural disgust for obscenity would be transformed into a licentious smirk. An adolescent's environment required strict supervision: "Thousands and hundreds of thousands are indebted to useful work, occupying many hours through each day, and leaving them with wearied bodies at night,

[10] William Gilmore Simms, *Guy Rivers: A Tale of Georgia* (New York, 1860), p. 411.

for their safe passage from yielding youth to firm, resisting manhood." [11] The belief that moral stability may be ensured by the discipline of work was implicit in Locke as well as in the Christian doctrine of an "effectual calling," but in neither Locke nor traditional Christianity was work presented as a cultivation of pure, original impulses. For such men as Timothy Shay Arthur, it was necessary to believe that moral development depended on the environment, or there would be no need for reform; on the other hand, moral certainty and responsibility could be defended only by assuming that children possessed an original capacity for virtue, an assumption which implied an inherent moral sense within all men. Reform would bring the environment into accordance with the dictates of this original conscience and would thereby liberate the enslaved moral sense of those whom circumstances had depraved.

Between 1798 and 1860 American writers differed violently on moral questions concerning such matters as the virtue of children and Indians, but perhaps the most important contradiction pertained to the strength of human conscience and will. Most writers accepted the conviction of philosophers that good and evil were absolute terms, which could be sensed by feeling, if not understood by reason. We have seen that even a capacity for moral feeling could be interpreted as proof of responsibility by certain moral philosophers, since man was presumed to be able to will whatever he was capable of doing. Many writers assumed that if the moral sense was properly cultivated from childhood, man could resist most temptations. A heroine like Brown's Constantia Dudley, whose reason and habits had been carefully trained, was able to preserve her virtue and dignity under the pressure of a

[11] Timothy Shay Arthur, *Ten Nights in a Bar-Room, and What I Saw There* (Boston, 1855), p. 42.

most adverse environment. Cooper's Leatherstocking and the hundreds of popular heroes who followed him preserved their inner sense of justice in remote forests and on the high seas.

Yet moral feelings are intimately associated with other feelings, and a distinction between evil and moral impulses might be lost in a unity of emotion. Even those who celebrated the natural goodness of children warned that original virtue was exceedingly fragile. Writers who assumed a vital unity among the human faculties also concluded that any man could be reduced to animal madness by physical or psychic torture.

There is a striking scene in Simms's *Beauchampe* (1842), where the heroine wants to die with the imprisoned Beauchampe so that they might go together "to another country." The hero, who was perhaps familiar with Dante's Count Ugolino, was not sure about love and loyalty in other countries. He told a tale of two lovers who were imprisoned together by a tyrant. The first days only intensified their love, since they were overjoyed at finding themselves together. But as famine reached across the tiny cell, they drew apart, and the tyrant was finally able to gloat at the vision of the lover-hero with his teeth buried in the neck of the girl. That such possibilities were not totally foreign to American experience is seen in the famous Donner tragedy, which occurred four years after *Beauchampe* was published. Beauchampe himself was pessimistic concerning human strength:

In those dreadful extremes of situation, from which our feeble nature recoils, all passions and sentiments run into one. . . . It is not our love that fails us, in the hour of physical and mental torment. It is our strength. Thought and principle, truth and purity, are poor defenses, when the frame is agonized with a torture beyond what nature was intended to endure. Then the strongest man deserts his faith and disavows his principles.

Then the purest becomes profligate, and the truest dilates in falsehood. . . . Ah, of this future, dear wife! This awful, unknown future! [12]

Some writers felt that man's own evil increased as he left the limits of organized society and penetrated the heart of nature. Nature, like Dante's hell, was under the primitive law of retribution. Poe used the sea as a symbol of man's evil and violence in *The Narrative of Arthur Gordon Pym* (1838). As the "Grampus" headed away from the restraints and order of land, there were increasingly bloody scenes of mutiny and treachery. Freedom and liberty from social frustrations meant subjection to the primitive impulses of nature, especially to the impulse to eat and the necessity of being eaten. The men lost all bearings and direction, they were rootless on a sea of violence and evil, and their cannibalism on the ocean's surface was only an echo of the primeval "law" of the sea. When a character, Augustus, died from wounds after he had eaten human meat, he was thrown into the sea where he was instantly torn to pieces by sharks.

Thirteen years later another fictional voyage was to signify the collapse of reason and restraint when the psychic and physical pressure of the ocean and an even more inscrutable embodiment of power would arouse only the defiant and aggressive passions of man. In *Moby-Dick* (1851) the impotence of intellect not only appeared in Ahab's rejection of Starbuck's judgment and in Starbuck's unwillingness to mutiny, but also was symbolically expressed in the heedless destruction of nautical instruments, the instruments of reason which plotted man's course through the unknown.[13] That this black, irrational

---

[12] William Gilmore Simms, *Beauchampe; or, The Kentucky Tragedy* (New York, 1856), p. 391.

[13] Yvor Winters, *Maule's Curse, Seven Studies in the History of American Obscurantism* (Norfolk, Conn., 1938), p. 79.

aggression was latent in all men and groups was the theme of "Benito Cereno" (1856), wherein negligence and the isolation of a ship at sea once again provided the opportunity for an eruption of evil. In *Pierre* (1852) Melville pictured innocent, virtuous man as bewildered and helpless before a malicious fate. In this final statement of man's frailty, reason was illusory, the impulse to love became incestuous, and friendship resulted in murder. In no other American work of the nineteenth century was the confusion of impulses so complete.

IV

By associating the human will and conscience with instinctive impulses which at once dominated reason and were themselves shaped by circumstance, some writers were led to the pessimistic conclusion that man is incapable of knowing or choosing the greatest good. The moral impotence of Melville's Pierre Glendinning may be taken as one of the extreme developments of a psychology which reduced intellect to mechanism and searched for moral certainty in man's feeling. The moral sense, invented to preserve absolute virtue from the contingencies of experience, broke down in the ambiguities of passion. Men might glorify the pure, original impulses of nature, but as Hawthorne sensed, these impulses often lost their innocence when translated into action.

The same psychology, however, might result in an entirely different creation. Pierre Glendinning seemed morally impotent because he was driven by necessity and was therefore unable to conform to a higher law. But inner necessity might also produce the absolute outer freedom of the superman. The jutting crags, steaming volcanoes, and blasted oaks which men called sublime were considered "interesting" because they broke the natural order, the harmony and balance of a perfect system. They had been *caused*, of course, but they were not without a certain exhilarating freedom. Conformity implied diffusion and dissolution, whereas *deformity* had a stark, specific quality, a freedom in the very intensity and uniqueness of being. There was a kind of freedom in not conforming to God's law or to the inclinations of a moral sense, but in being one's true self. If there were no guiding principle, no innate ideas, and no sense which could not be transformed by environment, each man would be exceptional, a product of unique pressures and influences. He would be a law unto himself, since he differed significantly from every other man. Society might demand obedience to certain laws in the interest of order, but man would have no inner obligation to obey, except for temporary expediency.

The superman was doubtless a logical outcome of the general shift from God- to man-centered morality. Such a frightening specter was probably responsible for the tenacity with which men held to the doctrines of a divine conscience or an immanent moral sense. The concept of superman was a kind of nuclear fission in the history of ideas, from which men shrank with horror. The explosive quality of the French Revolution accentuated the dangers of this new kind of freedom and of materialistic philosophy in general; the vision of superman was too powerful to eradicate.

After the French Revolution, literature in the West was compelled to face the implications of superman, whose freedom lay in the necessity of his individual inner law and in his isolation from the transcendent laws of God or nature. If Adam's original freedom had been the power of conforming contingent actions to a necessary good, the superman's freedom was the power of conforming a contingent good to a necessary act. Inasmuch as the superman's moral standard was limited to his own actions, it followed that the actions of all other men were differ-

ent, hostile, and, in a sense, immoral. Hence the superman was self-sufficient, autonomous, and in a state of war
with the rest of humanity.

He was an ideal villain, a sublime rebel, an abrupt
fissure in the great chain of being, one who commanded
awe and wonder. Though he considered all men as essentially like himself in their true motives, the superman
was a genius because of his great sensitivity and his inherent honesty. Contemptuous of the moral hypocrisy of
others, he succeeded in worldly endeavors because he did
not allow his inner self to be stifled by slavelike submission to false values.

In American literature of the period the concept of
superman usually had four implications. The first was insanity, which will be discussed in later chapters. The second was an association with Europe, especially with the
French Revolution and its aftermath. Closely related to
this association was the idea that some organized conspiracy sought to gain control of at least part of the world.
Finally, the superman might be either a scientist, the creation of a scientist, or a man familiar with mesmerism or
Far Eastern magic.

Charles Brockden Brown was deeply troubled by the
results of the French Revolution, since he had himself
held the belief that evil was nothing more than error reduced to practice and that genuine progress was therefore
possible through social and political reforms.[14] In his
journal he had plotted a utopian commonwealth, strongly
influenced by William Godwin's *Political Justice* as well
as by the agrarian philosophy of Thomas Jefferson.[15] Yet
he had the following comment on the French Revolution:

[14] Lulu Rumsey Wiley, *The Sources and Influences of the Novels of
Charles Brockden Brown* (New York, 1950), pp. 113, 117.
[15] David Lee Clark, *Charles Brockden Brown, Pioneer Voice of America*
(Durham, N.C., 1952), pp. 17, 109, 147.

From the miscarriage of a scheme of frantic innovation, we conceive an unreasonable and undiscriminating dread of all change and reform. The failure of an attempt to make government perfect reconciles us to imperfections that might easily be removed. . . . The French revolution has thrown us back half a century in the course of political improvement and driven us to cling once more, with superstitious terror, at the feet of those idols from which we had been nearly reclaimed by the lessons of a milder philosophy.[16]

Such is the dilemma of the liberal in an age of revolution; and while Brown was repelled by the excesses of the French, he was also fascinated by the fearlessness of European radicals. Yet his gradual shift toward conservatism, as with many other liberals, implied a certain guilt, since the Revolution showed what his earlier ideas *might* have brought about. He could maintain an interest in mild reforms like women's rights or the abolition of dueling, but his impulse toward extreme radicalism found its outlet in fictional villains.

We might hypothetically suppose that Brown and many of his readers felt a curious ambivalence toward the villain supermen. Included in this complex attitude would be their original desire to see the American Revolution culminate in sweeping social changes and a man-centered morality—the realization, in other words, of the potentialities for reform implicit in the sensational psychology. But there was a disturbing awareness that such idealism might in reality be reduced to a government of unchecked and brutal power, a morality of sheer expediency, and an obliteration of man's dignity. The original desire was consequently projected as the image of the superman, and the guilt was expiated by his necessary destruction. As Bernard Shaw later put it in his analysis of the superman's

---

[16] Quoted in Clark, *Brown*, pp. 234–235.

evil and cruelty, "men felt all the charm of abounding life and abandonment to its impulses," but they did not dare "in their deep self-mistrust, conceive it otherwise than as a force making for evil—one which must lead to universal ruin." [17]

Like many of his fellow Americans, Brown was obsessed by the dangers of the Society of the Illuminati, founded by an anti-Jesuit at the University of Ingolstadt in 1776, "to reform mankind." Proclaiming itself at war with man-made religious and social institutions, the society intended to enlighten humanity by liquidating error and superstition, to which end no means were to be spared.[18] Any member who revealed the secrets of the order was supposedly doomed to certain death. Brown shared many of these beliefs about error, superstition, and the necessity of rational education, but he was also conscious of the totalitarian character of such a movement. Hence in his *Memoirs of Carwin, the Biloquist* (1815), in *Wieland* (1798), and in *Ormond* (1799), the villain supermen were all, by implication, associated with an invisible empire.

It has often been said that Brown copied his villains after William Godwin's Falkland in *Caleb Williams* (1794), but there was an important difference. Falkland represented the evil of the existing system, which Godwin wanted to change. Brown's villains were themselves radicals who preached the philosophy Brown once believed, but who proposed to put it into effect by a ruthlessly cold logic which never stopped at murder. In a young and expanding democracy, the opportunities for the superman were very great; therefore, Brown implied, these villains

[17] Bernard Shaw, *The Perfect Wagnerite: A Commentary on the Niblung's Ring* (New York, 1916), p. 66.

[18] Vernon Stauffer, *New England and the Bavarian Illuminati* (New York, 1918), pp. 157–158.

represented what we might have become and what we should avoid becoming, no matter how attractive their ultimate objectives might be.

The superman who makes his own law was a common figure in later American novels. The Byronic heroes of John Neal carried a strong imprint of Brown in their sublime passions, their unappeasable ambition, and their compulsive drive for a singe end, regardless of means.[19] When a villain in a Robert Montgomery Bird novel was accused by the heroine of being a scoundrel, he freely confessed and said that if a man cannot win one way he will win another; it was only natural that he should be a villain when she resisted him.[20]

But after 1830 a new superman began to appear in popular American literature, one whose powers included a mystical exploitation of "science." The superman scientist was related directly to the revival of mesmerism in France and England. The French Royal Academy of Medicine, which had discredited Franz Anton Mesmer's experiments in 1784, had by 1831 accepted hypotism, or "psycodunamic somnambulism," as a legitimate area for research. Joseph du Commun is alleged to have given the the first lectures in America on mesmerism in 1829, to be followed some years later by the more famous Charles Poyen de St. Sauveur.[21] As mermerism attracted popular interest in England and America, the mysterious hypnotist became a stock figure in adventure fiction.

In *The Quaker City* (1844) George Lippard combined Brown's Society of the Illuminati with a stereotype of the mystical scientist. Ravoni, a European mesmerist with a

---

[19] See especially, John Neal, *Logan: A Family History*, (Philadelphia, 1822), II, p. 124.

[20] Robert Montgomery Bird, *Nick of the Woods; or, The Jibbenainosay*, ed. by Cecil B. Williams (New York, 1939), p. 335.

[21] Theodore Leger, *Animal Magnetism; or, Psycodunamy* (New York, 1846), p. 366.

large American following, preached a new faith in the name of man and for the good of man. Since the worship of God had resulted in superstition and murder, it was time to develop the mysteries implanted in man's own bosom, so that man himself might walk the earth as a god. The leader of an ancient, secret organization with the purpose of liberating man from priestcraft and ignorance, Ravoni had a magnetic glance and an all-powerful will. He denied the existence of an afterlife, but he argued that immortality was possible through a mysterious cultivation of the senses. Unlike many of the supermen in European fiction, who were often isolated villains perverting mysterious powers for selfish purposes, Ravoni intended to transform society and to make science the instrument of ideology. Very often in popular American literature the mysterious organization for world domination was simply the Catholic church. The superman was a Jesuit priest charged with gaining control of America, while Catholic doctrine was merely a cloak to conceal his basic atheism. Whether mesmerist or Jesuit, however, the superman never hesitated at murder.

The major exception to the European superman may be seen in the literature of the South and Southwest. There the superman was definitely native, and the conspiracy involved the capture of Mexico, domination of the southern states, and ultimate control of the Western Hemisphere. Yet the motives and psychology were strikingly similar to those of Brown's Ormond. In Alfred W. Arrington's *The Rangers and Regulators of the Tanaha* (1856), a bandit leader controlled an extensive organization extending over many states and territories with the object of subverting law and order. Like Ormond, the bandit argued that sin and punishment were only idle words, since the Hand of Destiny shaped all actions. Thoughts, he maintained, follow the unalterable laws of association with the regularity of a pulse. He denied the existence of a will or conscience and said that terror and imagination made the gods. Thus could the sensational psychology of the Enlightenment be perverted to justify the ambitions of selfish and evil men, at least in American fiction.

It is important to note that the superman villain was not a representative of tradition, of authority, or of a father. Native or immigrant, he was in one sense the projected image of young America. He was a member of the peer group who was not playing according to the rules of the game, which had been handed down by tradition. In a land without the absolute authority of king or church, in a land where law ultimately rested upon the natural virtue of the people, men might confuse total amorality with rigorous individualism. It was necessary, therefore, to consider superman as a villain, as an embodiment of mysterious evil, and as an alienated competitor.

One could gaze upon the self-sufficient superman, the sublime deformity of human nature, one could follow his career with an emotional interest, achieving a certain freedom from conformity by identifying oneself with the superman's power, and at the same time it was easy to explain him as a distorted and poisonous root, a unique growth whose moral impulse had gone to rot. Despite his brief and exciting freedom from natural law, it was only proper that the superman should wither and die from his own unnatural freedom.

His very existence, however, was evidence that sensational psychology, environmentalism, and materialism, could not be ignored. Neither writers of fiction nor moral philosophers could avoid a fundamental question posed by David Hume: Do morality and immorality proceed from an amoral source? Any attempt to reform society was based on an assumption that individuals were morally influenced by their environment, a presupposition seldom questioned in American fiction. Yet such a doctrine of moral environmentalism, if allowed to stand as a final explanation, would endanger the concept of human guilt. Imaginative writers were united with theologians and philosophers in their effort to find some autonomous faculty within man's nature, some divine prism which would automatically break the light of experience into its moral components, revealing eternal laws to the human will and reason, regardless of individual misfortune or handicaps. After Locke had refuted the theory of innate ideas, it was obvious that the understanding, dependent on sensory impressions, would not satisfy the need for an independent moral faculty. But as men abandoned the intellect and turned to the senses and emotions for moral certainty, they were made even more aware of individual differences and of the subjectivity of ethical judgment. Imaginative writers tended to identify the moral sense with natural man, implying that improper environment might blunt such a delicate sensitivity. The relations between brothers or between father and son were of supreme importance, since only in the love and unity of a family could mortality be nurtured. Yet the literature of our period was haunted by a basic problem which has never been answered: if the moral sense is innate and universal, why are some men evil? and if the moral sense is corrupted by external forces, are evil men truly guilty? This question was central to the interpretation of insanity.

PART TWO

The Abnormal Heart and Mind

THE will might be deranged even in many instances of persons of sound understandings and some of uncommon talents, the will becoming the involuntary vehicle of vicious actions through the instrumentality of the passions. Persons thus diseased cannot speak the truth upon any subject nor tell the same story twice in the same way.

—BENJAMIN RUSH

Chapter III

BACKGROUND

THE subject of mental and moral abnormality is in one sense a continuation of our discussion concerning human evil and freedom. Like Chapter I, the present chapter provides a historical framework for the entire study, but is immediately followed by an analysis of mental and moral insanity in American fiction (Chapters IV and V). After briefly describing legal views of insanity and responsibility from the early eighteenth century to 1860, we shall trace the development of psychiatric theory as it pertained to causes and types of abnormality and then discuss the debate over "moral insanity" and "irresistible impulse." The inherent conservatism of legal thought necessitates an occasional reference to men or concepts which precede our period. On the other hand, the full meaning of such psychiatric theories as moral insanity can be apprehended only by an allusion to discoveries which occurred after 1860. Our principal emphasis, however, will fall upon the discrepancy between legal principles and psychiatric theories from 1800 to 1860. In Chapters IV and V we may then contrast these changing medicolegal attitudes toward insanity with assumptions and imaginative associations in fiction.

II

Thinking that a recognition of absolute guilt and innocence was essential to maintain social order, legal theorists from Sir Matthew Hale to Sir James Fitzjames Stephen, and from the M'Naghten judges to those of the present day, have defined insanity in the narrowest terms, and have presumed that most criminals are psychologically normal, essentially guilty, and deserving of punishment. The fear that a widened conception of mental disorder might endanger society by a diffusion of guilt undoubtedly arises from what Edmond Cahn has called man's natural "sense of injustice." According to Cahn, law is based on the obvious principle that human beings are shocked and outraged by crime, that they sympathetically regard the violation of another man's dignity as a personal aggression, and that the conviction and punishment of the offender satisfies a biological need for retaliation, affording a release from the original shock and emotional tension.[1]

The sense of injustice is a useful principle with which to explain society's resistance to penological reform and to liberal definitions of insanity, but to understand this natural desire for revenge, we must analyze the assumptions it involves. If men are outraged by a crime, it is because the criminal has done what people are supposedly taught not to do. In most societies children learn that violent expressions of temper, willful vengeance, and outward aggression are modes of behavior to be suppressed. Whenever the normal man suffers a real or imagined wrong, his conscience transforms his aggression into harmless anger,

---

[1] Edmond N. Cahn, *The Sense of Injustice: An Anthropocentric View of Law* (New York, 1949), pp. 18–24, 111.

loud complaints, or socially approved methods of revenge. Certain types of homicide, such as that in war or self-defense, do not arouse his sense of injustice. But when some other man actually commits a murder, giving evidence of a disorganized conscience, the normal man is revolted and outraged. This means that the revulsion and horror he associates with his own aggressive impulses are directed outward, to another ego. Because he is capable of suppressing criminal desires and is therefore a righteous man, he thinks that justice requires that the criminal be made to feel guilty through punishment. The sense of injustice makes crime proportionate to guilt, but it is important to observe that the guilt is that which a "good" man would feel, or would imagine he might feel, if he had committed the crime. Thus a murder with extraordinarily sordid details arouses the greatest shock and desire for retaliation, precisely because the abnormal killer expresses impulses which are most deeply repressed in the normal mind. But the righteous citizen, assuming that all men are the same, measures the criminal's guilt by the standards of men who are able to resist crime.

In tracing ideas concerning insanity and criminal responsibility, we must keep in mind the juridical assumption that all men, despite their difference in personality, intellect, and training, are endowed with a conscience and with an equal capacity for guilt. As a specific example we may consider the distinction between premeditated murder and negligent homicide. It is doubtful that relatives of a murdered man feel greater shock or grief than if he had been killed through criminal negligence. Surely criminal negligence is at least as great a threat to society, and the negligent killer is just as likely to repeat his offence as is the average murderer, since he may have an incurably reckless temperament. Yet society is seldom deeply shocked or horrified by negligent homicide, and jurists have seldom questioned the belief that murder deserves the harsher penalty. Such a distinction in penalties may be justified only by assuming it is less difficult to suppress murderous intentions than it is to avoid criminal negligence; and this assumption presupposes that all men are normal.

Since a man with delusions of persecution sometimes planned a murder in minute detail, eighteenth-century jurists concluded that he possessed both reason and will and was therefore legally sane. In 1724 an Englishman named Edward Arnold was positive that Lord Onslow was sending armies of devils to invade his bedroom each night. When this became intolerable, he tried to kill Onslow. Mr. Justice Tracey, in a ruling which English and American courts followed, dismissed Arnold's plea of insanity on the ground that he was not totally deprived of understanding and memory. Unless a man completely and permanently lacked reason, unless it could be proved that he was like a "wild beast," there was no hope of exemption.

According to Blackstone, crime resulted from a vicious will, from a "disposition to do an evil thing," and could be excused only by "a want or defect of will," or by a *"defect of understanding,"* which prevented the will from joining in the act.[2] Courts were to assume that any unprovoked homicide implied malice, unless the contrary was sufficiently proved, "for no person but one of a wicked heart, would be guilty of such an act." Despite the ambiguity implicit in such a phrase as "a want or defect of will," which might logically include a malicious disposition, most of the symptoms of mental disorder were regarded as the essence of criminal guilt. Hence Blackstone

[2] Sir William Blackstone, *Commentaries on the Laws of England* (4 vols.; Oxford, 1765–1769), IV, 20–26, quoted by Nathan Dane as a basis for American jurisprudence in *A General Abridgement and Digest of American Law, with Occasional Notes and Comments* (Boston, 1824), VI, 638–644.

ruled that a man who resolves to kill the next person he meets is guilty of a general or "universal malice" which would be evidence of a depraved and criminal heart.

Such a view of insanity and legal responsibility clearly drew from the old faculty psychology which was well suited for the deductive reasoning and certainty of objectives demanded by the law. Man was a rational animal, and his reason ruled from an elevated and exclusive quarter-deck. As long as reason had any strength to command, as long as reason lived, there was legal and moral responsibility. Mutinies could justify a ship's erratic course only when the captain had been killed or imprisoned. Lawyers were not interested in such fantasies as Melville later described in "Benito Cereno" (1856), where the captain seemed to control the ship, the slaves seemed to be suppressed, and slight appearances of disorder were logically explained, even though a mutiny had taken place. Reason and sea captains were not supposed to behave that way.

In 1800 the issue of legal insanity exploded in a sensational conflict. For the English people, it was not a year to confirm convictions about the inherent rationality of man, with Moreau and Napoleon spreading the madness of the Revolution across Austria and Italy, and a king of doubtful sanity on the English throne. A man named Hadfield, who suffered from delusions of persecution, attempted to execute in the Drury Lane Theatre the Lord's command that he sacrifice George III. Although Hadfield did not conform to the "wild beast" test and had an abstract knowledge of right and wrong, Lord Erskine argued that "without the disease there would have been no murderous attack." By shifting the question from whether Hadfield possessed reason to whether insanity had caused the crime, Erskine challenged the juridical assumption that only raving madness and loss of intellect prove a man to be *non compos mentis*. Hadfield's aquittal destroyed the sharp distinction between partial and total insanity, but jurists were extremely reluctant to admit that delusions constituted an adequate defense. When John Bellingham was tried, convicted, and executed within a week for the murder of the Right Hon. Spencer Perceval, Sir Vicary Gibbs adopted the interpretations of Hale and Hawkins on partial insanity, cited for precedent the Arnold case of 1724, and argued "that if even insanity in all his other acts had been manifest, yet the systematic correctness with which the prisoner contrived the murder of Mr. Perceval, shewed a mind *at the time* capable of distinguishing right and wrong." [3]

Such cases show that the jurisprudence of insanity in England and America was characterized by an extraordinary confusion in the first half of the nineteenth century. In the famous Selfridge case of 1805, Chief Justice Parker of Massachusetts adopted the curious English rule that delusions might be accepted as an excuse for murder only if the insane defendant imagined that his life depended on "self-defense." [4] This compromise with Erskine's rule in the Hadfield case was more clearly expressed by Chief Justice Lemuel Shaw in Commonwealth *v.* Rogers (1844). When monomania was to be accepted as an excuse for homicide, "the delusion is such that the person under its influence has a real and firm belief of some fact, not true in itself, but which, if it were true, would excuse his act. . . . *A common instance is where he fully believes that the act he is doing is done by the immediate command of God, and he acts under the delusive but sincere belief that what he is doing is by the command of a superior power, which supersedes all human laws and the laws of*

[3] *Trial and Execution of Bellingham, for the Murder of Mr. Perceval. Sessions-House, Old Bailey, Friday, May 15, 1812* (n.p., 1812), p. 5.

[4] Francis Wharton, *A Treatise on Mental Unsoundness, Embracing a General View of Psychological Law,* 4th ed. (Philadelphia, 1882), p. 123.

nature." [5] Evidently Justice Shaw believed that a religious delusion was purer than a secular delusion and that motives maintained their rigid hierarchy in even an abnormal mind. Francis Wharton, a leading authority on criminal law in the nineteenth century, approved of Justice Shaw's interpretation, but sternly warned that Mormons could not use religious delusions to justify polygamy and crime, since "they are shrewd, sane men, and must be held responsible for their delusions."

Francis S. Key, as counsel on behalf of the United States, accepted a more liberal view in the trial of one Lawrence, who was charged in 1835 with attempting to assassinate President Jackson. Lawrence believed that Jackson had prevented him from obtaining money which would have enabled him rightfully to claim the English crown. Such a delusion did not meet Justice Shaw's test, for surely no American would admit the right of an English king to murder the president of the United States, even if the president had deprived the king of money and crown. But Key chose to follow Erskine's principle that insanity could be proved by establishing a connection between the delusion and the criminal act. Under this rule Lawrence was declared insane.[6]

Examples of conflicting judicial decisions might be multiplied indefinitely, but a common source of difficulty runs through the contradictory definitions and changes in phrase. Judges measured the guilt of criminals by the values and motives of normal men; yet as knowledge of mental disease increased, it appeared that conscience as well as intellect was affected by insanity. When jurists held that delusions excused an offender only when involving a command from God, an imagined self-defense, or, in the most liberal construction, when the crime was

[5] Quoted in Wharton, *Mental Unsoundness*, p. 130.
[6] *Niles' Weekly Register* . . . , XLVIII (April 18, 1835), 119–124.

closely associated with the delusion, they assumed with Locke that madmen reason correctly from an erroneous impression or principle. If a man was not an idiot or a "wild beast," his faculties were supposed to maintain a harmonious balance and his abnormality was limited to a defect in the original perception of ideas. Benjamin Rush apologized in 1786 for disagreeing with "that justly-celebrated oracle, who first unfolded to us a map of the intellectual world," but he confessed that Locke had been wrong in thinking of partial insanity as a problem in epistemology.[7] In 1838 Isaac Ray, who, next to Rush, was the most important American psychiatrist before the 1880's, bluntly said that Locke was ignorant of mental disorder. Nothing could be more absurd, according to Ray, than the supposition that certain faculties and powers are healthy, simply because a man is capable of specious planning and thinking.[8]

As psychiatry moved toward the conception of a unified personality, however, the law searched for some area in the mind of the paranoid, the schizophrenic, and the psychopath which remained inviolate and capable of bearing the burden of normal guilt. The ambiguous and fluctuating status of legal insanity by the 1840's necessitated some clear and definite statement of authority, when French and English psychiatry threatened to undermine the basic principles of criminal jurisprudence. No longer satisfied with the uncertain and antiquated definitions of Hale and Blackstone, judges were beginning to show interest in the theories of Jean Esquirol and James C. Prichard. Those who feared that the most heinous crimes might eventually be equated with insanity were alarmed by the use in court

[7] Benjamin Rush, *An Oration Delivered before the American Philosophical Society . . . Containing an Enquiry into the Influence of Physical Causes upon the Moral Faculty* (Philadelphia, 1786), pp. 21–22.

[8] Isaac Ray, *A Treatise on the Medical Jurisprudence of Insanity* (Boston, 1838), p. 158.

of such terms as "homicidal mania," "moral insanity," and "irresistible impulse."

On January 20, 1843, Daniel M'Naghten set out to shoot Sir Robert Peel, but killed his secretary, Mr. Drummond, by mistake. There followed a momentous trial, destined to influence Anglo-American criminal law for the next century. Alexander Cockburn of the defense quoted from Erskine's famous speech, from the writings of Isaac Ray, and from the works of Esquirol and Philippe Pinel. M'Naghten was acquitted on the ground that partial insanity or monomania was a state without legal responsibility. During early March, the House of Lords, reflecting a widespread fear that the decision would subvert the criminal law, submitted a series of questions to a judicial committee. The answers, known as the M'Naghten Rules, were soon incorporated in the penal laws of most American states, where they have remained as the authoritative definition of legal insanity for more than one hundred years.[9] This was the test of criminal responsibility:

The jurors ought to be told in all cases that every man is to be presumed to be sane, and to possess a sufficient degree of reason to be responsible for his crimes, until the contrary be proved to their satisfaction; and that, to establish a defense on the ground of insanity, it must be clearly proved that, at the time of the committing of the act, the party accused was labouring under such a defect of reason, from disease of the mind, as not to know the nature and quality of the act he was doing, or, if he did know it, that he did not know he was doing what was wrong.[10]

[9] Despite a continuing attack by criminologists and psychiatrists, the M'Naghten Rules have persisted with only slight modifications. The present case of Durham v. United States, 214 Federal Reporter 2nd ser. (Oct. 4, 1954), 871, represents the first serious challenge of the M'Naghten Rules in court. The long history of the right-wrong test, while falling beyond the province of this study, reflects, nevertheless, the depth of the crisis in legal psychiatry in the 1840's.

[10] 8 Eng. Rep. 718, 722 (1843), quoted in Durham v. United States, 214 Fed. Rep. 2nd ser. 869–870.

The learned judges also accepted the rule that a man with delusions that he was in serious danger of being killed might be exonerated for a murder in "self-defense," but that delusions of simple persecution would no more justify revenge than if the persecution were real. By sharply dividing mental from moral error, the judges maintained belief in an unimpaired faculty which, though dependent on the diseased intellect for knowledge of external objects, was nevertheless capable of preserving moral standards. If the intellect was so disordered that a man could not perceive the nature and quality of his acts, then this "inner sense" was imprisoned and not responsible. But if a partially diseased intellect gave a man the false perception that his wife was secretly ruining his character, his will was free to resist a murderous impulse, as much as if the perception were true. Partial insanity was merely a kind of distorted vision which made a man mistake objects and relations but in no way affected reason's natural power to suspend desire and to choose the greatest good.[11]

The M'Naghten Rules were clearly based on Lockian psychology, which reduced moral responsibility to an epistemological test, presuming that man's mind was divided between a mechanism of sensation, on the one hand, and an impartial capacity for judgment, on the other. For knowledge of the nature and quality of acts, judgment depended on the mechanism of sensation and association, but when this knowledge was impaired by mechanical failure, the faculty of judgment, though liable to error, was not altered in its essential composition. Actually, the judges were saying that a man's guilt or innocence depended on the nature and quality of *his own* capacity for

[11] Francis Wharton, *A Treatise on the Law of Homicide in the United States; to Which Is Appended a Series of Leading Cases,* 2nd ed. (Philadelphia, 1875), pp. 474–476.

judgment or natural disposition; that this inner state of guilt or innocence could usually be inferred from his actions; but that in certain cases of insanity, actions gave no indication of the heart's disposition. Therefore, legal insanity might be defined as a state in which a man's guilty or innocent disposition could not be deduced from his acts, and was consequently unknowable. Symptoms of insanity were no longer explained by theories of Satan's *incubi,* but the devil lived on as a hypostatized guilt, as a malicious heart, which, unlike the intellect, was responsible for its own abnormality.

Disease might alienate a man's reason, but the law implied that human nature included a faculty which was inalienable except through a conscious choice of evil. John F. Dillon, who had a long career as judge and chief justice of the Iowa Supreme Court before becoming Storrs Professor at Yale, expressed confidence in 1894 that man's moral nature was indivisible and inalienable: "Conscience having its imperial and divine seat in every breast, susceptible of having its vision made more comprehensive . . . by enlightened education, yet incapable of being torn from the breast of man . . . is a universal judge, holding its assize at every man's door." [12] Legal theorists of the nineteenth century, despite their differing interpretations, considered demented man as if he were a warrior who had been captured by another tribe; a criminal, on the other hand, was a man who had willingly surrendered to the devil. The physical alien could not be punished, but the moral alien was a renegade and traitor to society.

[12] John F. Dillon, *The Laws and Jurisprudence of England and America: Being a Series of Lectures Delivered before Yale University* (Boston, 1894), p. 4.

III

Between 1790 and 1850, when legal theorists were revising Hale's conceptions of insanity to conform with Lockian psychology, a few pioneer psychiatrists were exploring the mysterious and uncharted realm of the abnormal mind. In 1792 an obscure French physician named Philippe Pinel initiated a revolution which shocked even radical leaders in the new government. He unchained the lunatics at the Salpêtrière and Bicêtre and established a tradition in French psychiatry which extended to Jean Charcot, Pierre Janet, and, through his French training, to Sigmund Freud. Seventeen hundred ninety-two was also the year when English Quakers, led by William Tuke, rebelled against time-honored methods of beating and torturing for "gathering the remembrance of a lunatic" and started a movement which resulted in the York Retreat. Nearly a half-century later, Dorothea Lynde Dix was to combine the theories of the English Quakers with the humanitarianism of her idol, William Ellery Channing, who was himself strongly influenced by Francis Hutcheson and the Scottish philosophers. Previously some of these seemingly diverse influences had converged in the thought of Benjamin Rush, father of American psychiatry. Born in a Quaker settlement in Pennsylvania, he caught the lingering spirit of the Great Awakening from George Whitefield and from Samuel Davies at Princeton, he was exposed to the theories of Hutcheson and Reid at Edinburgh, and he completed his formative education in the atmosphere of the French Enlightenment. Modern psychiatry began with the belief that scientific observation would further humanitarian reform and with the conviction that man naturally possesses an inner light or moral sense, which, if properly nourished and treated, would restore happiness and reason to the diseased mind.

Most American alienists in the early nineteenth century followed Rush and Esquirol in dividing cases of mental disease into mania, monomania, dementia, and idiotism.[13] The symptoms of mania included hallucinations, intense excitement, and wandering, glassy eyes. Feigned maniacs could be detected because they lacked a characteristic "peculiar animal odour." Monomania or "partial insanity" evinced symptoms which today would fall under the categories of paranoid schizophrenia, catatonia, and depressive psychosis. Theodric Romeyn Beck described the disease as involving systematized delusions, irrational depression, and inanimate stupor. Although monomania might lead to dementia, or a total and permanent loss of understanding and memory, only victims of this latter disease were consistently judged *non compos mentis*.[14]

Religion was thought to be a major cause of insanity, especially in the 1840's. "Mistaken ideas on religious subjects" commonly resulted in "demonomania," a form of partial insanity which sometimes led to acts of violence. In 1843 the New Hampshire superintendent of the Asylum for the Insane listed the causes of insanity, as attributed by friends of the inmates, as follows: excitement over religion, particularly Millerism—21; ill health—10; pecuniary embarrassment—6; intemperance—3; head injury—3; taking cold—2; hard study—2; disappointed affection (female)—2.[15] This classification corresponds with the beliefs expressed in professional treatises, although Benjamin Rush put greater emphasis on the dangers of hard study:

---

[13] Theodric Romeyn Beck, *Elements of Medical Jurisprudence* (Albany, 1823), I, 335–336.

[14] Beck, *Elements*, I, 346–347. The distinction between forms of mania and dementia resembled the ancient division in Roman law between *mente capti*, whose understandings were weak or null, and *furiosi*, who were restless and violent (Ray, *Medical Jurisprudence*, p. 5).

[15] *Journals of the Senate and House*, 1843, app. (Concord, N.H., 1843), pp. 280–282.

"The frequent and rapid transition of the mind from one subject to another. It is said booksellers have sometimes been deranged from this cause. The debilitating effects of these sudden transitions upon the mind, are sensibly felt after reading a volume of reviews or magazines." [16]

Rush described the mental faculties as innate and internal senses, including understanding, memory, imagination, passions, the will, a principle of faith, conscience, a moral faculty, and a sense of deity. These faculties were likened to external senses, because they depended on bodily sensations to produce specific operations. Since these mental functions were intimately connected with man's organic and nervous systems, they were all subject to physical disease, which might affect two or more faculties in succession, in rotation, or all at once.

It was not a theory of diseased intellect that brought alarm to legal circles and seemed to threaten the basic principles of jurisprudence. Early psychiatrists were groping for a concept of insanity which would include the whole personality, and in so doing they invented two phrases which struck terror in the hearts of conservative judges—moral insanity and irresistible impulse.

On February 27, 1786, Benjamin Rush made an address to the American Philosophical Society in which he combined the moral-sense theory with a modified materialism. He expressed his debt to Francis Hutcheson and Jean Jacques Rousseau for the concept of a moral sense or instinct, and said that by "moral faculty I mean a power in the human mind of distinguishing and chusing good and evil; or, in other words, virtue and vice. It is a native principle, and though it is capable of improvement by experience and reflection, it is not derived from either of them." [17] Man's conscience, he observed, was seated in the

[16] Benjamin Rush, *Medical Inquiries and Observations, upon the Diseases of the Mind* (Philadelphia, 1812), p. 37.
[17] Rush, *Oration,* p. 2.

understanding and was dependent on the laws which the moral faculty provided. But if man had a moral sense, as Hutcheson and the Scottish philosophers had said, then it was only logical to assume that this separate faculty, like memory, imagination, and judgment, was subject to hereditary defects and to physical disease.

Rush illustrated his point by recalling the celebrated Servin in the Duke of Sully's *Memoirs*. Servin had been a virtual superman, with a prodigious memory, a knowledge of languages, philosophy, and religion, a genius for poetry, dazzling musical skill, ability as an actor and comedian, and physical prowess which was unequaled. Yet he was also a treacherous liar, a cheat, a drunkard, and an addict of every vice, who died in a brothel "with the glass in his hand, cursing and denying God." The moral faculty, Rush concluded, was not immune from disease, but was subject to the effects of diet, climate, idleness, and environment. Hunger, pain, exposure to cruel punishments, filth, or an atmosphere of crime could all distort and corrupt man's sense of right and wrong. It is important to notice that Rush identified disease with undesirable influences, and the moral faculty with emotions, sensibility, and will. Essentially he was arguing that man's total emotional development determines his values and conduct in life. He confessed that such a theory made it difficult to draw a line between responsible and irresponsible action, but he later added that the morally deranged are "in a pre-eminent degree, objects of compassion . . . ; it is the business of medicine to aid both religion and law, in curing their moral alienation of mind.[18] The only trouble was, as Rush himself knew, that religion and law were principally interested in punishing "moral alienation of mind."

When Pinel examined symptoms of mental disease at the Bicêtre, he found to his surprise that some maniacs

[18] Rush, *Medical Inquiries*, p. 360.

were "under the dominion of instinctive and abstract fury," although they lacked delusions or impairment of the intellect.[19] The first case reported by Pinel of such *"manie sans délire"* was an only son of a weak and indulgent mother, "encouraged in the gratification of every caprice and passion of which an untutored and violent temper was susceptible!" He was especially dangerous because "every instance of opposition or resistance roused him to acts of fury. He assaulted his adversaries with the audacity of a savage. . . . If a dog, a horse, or any other animal offended him, he instantly put it to death." [20]

Moral insanity, or what would today be known as psychopathic personality, was first described by Pinel and Rush but was soon accepted by Heinroth and Hoffbauer in Germany, by Andrew Combe and Prichard in England, and by Esquirol, Georget, and Gall in France. George Combe wrote an introduction to the 1839 edition of Rush's Philosophical Society *Oration,* wherein he referred to Rush's conception of a moral faculty shaped by physical causes as "the nearest approach to Dr. Gall's discovery, which has come under my notice." Prichard and Ray both welcomed the support given by phrenology to psychiatric theory; and according to Wharton, who strenuously opposed the concept of moral insanity, it was phrenology, combined with the "sentimental humanitarianism" of Rousseau's disciples, that first threatened the courts with the absurd doctrine that all criminals are insane.[21]

Until the 1830's the theory of moral insanity was obscured by the fact that Pinel's cases of *manie sans délire* evidenced a violent and impulsive aggression which might be explained either by a diseased or atrophied moral faculty or by a morbid passion that could not be resisted. When moral insanity was defined in the latter sense, it im-

---

[19] Ray, *Medical Jurisprudence,* pp. 168–169.　　　[20] *Ibid.,* p. 175.
[21] Wharton, *Mental Unsoundness,* pp. ix–xii.

plied that the moral faculty was itself unimpaired, but
that reason and will were overwhelmed by an "irresistible
impulse." Closely resembling the eighteenth-century belief in a "ruling passion," the impulse theory accepted the
fact of nonintellectual insanity, but tended to preserve the
Lockian assumption that all men possess a *capacity* for
moral action. An insane man might find a certain impulse
irresistible, but there was a strong implication in such
a phrase that he knew, at least, that he *should* resist it.

The difference between irresistible impulse and moral
insanity, not sufficiently clarified until the 1830's, lay
primarily in the distinction between will and moral faculty. Benjamin Rush thought of the moral faculty as
seated in the will, whose derangement would tend to pervert the emotional response to good and evil. If, however,
the will was considered as entirely separate from the
moral faculty, it was conceivable that a sudden impulse
might overpower the will but leave the *capacity* for moral
choice unaffected. Thus a man with an innocent heart
might be irresistibly impelled to commit a murder; and
since his act resulted from a "want or defect of will" and
not from a malicious disposition, he would be innocent
of crime even by the rule of Blackstone.[22]

What seems to be a slight semantic difficulty was actually the most significant point of conflict between psychiatry and the law. The basic issue was whether moral actions
are determined by nonmoral causes, or, in other words,
whether *any* human capacity or faculty could be alienated
by external causes, or whether some area remained in
man's mind which could be annulled only by conscious
choice. From the time of Locke, philosophers and psychologists had slowly circumscribed the reason, the conscience,
and the will by physical causes; the theory of moral insan-

[22] Robert B. Warden, *A Familiar Forensic View of Man and Law*
(Columbus, O., 1860), p. 510.

ity now threatened to subject that last refuge, the moral sense, to materialism. The irresistible impulse was a frantic, last-minute concession from law to the forces of radicalism. If Thomas Upham and Laurens P. Hickok were correct in separating will from moral feeling, the ultimate guilt or innocence of an individual was still unaffected by physical defects, since either the mind or will could be diseased or overpowered without implying moral alienation. By recognizing an impulse which, like delusions or hallucinations, might lead a "good" man into evil, philosophers and judges avoided the frightening thought that even a "bad" man's disposition is not without causes.

IV

In 1838 Isaac Ray described a series of American murders in which the principle feature was an *"irresistible, motiveless impulse to destroy life."* Such homicidal insanity was usually characterized by a

morbid activity of the *propensity to destroy;* where the individual without provocation or any other rational motive, apparently in the full possession of his reason, and oftentimes, in spite of his most strenuous efforts to resist, imbrues his hands in the blood of others; oftener than otherwise, of the partner of his bosom, or the children of his affections.[23]

Because of the frequent brutality and mutilation accompanying these crimes, people were shocked and sought an explanation in "that time-honored solution, of all the mysteries of human delinquency, the instigation of the devil." Yet certain American courts abandoned English

[23] Ray, *Medical Jurisprudence*, pp. 197–198. Esquirol and Prichard held that homicidal madness could result either from mental hallucinations without "malignant or destructive . . . dispositions" or from an emotional disorder which did not affect the intellect (James C. Prichard, *A Treatise on Insanity and Other Disorders Affecting the Mind* [Philadelphia, 1837], p. 16).

precedent and recognized the theory of Esquirol. In State
(of Ohio) *v.* Thompson in 1834 the jury was instructed
that the defendant must be acquitted if he could not dis-
criminate between right and wrong or if he had no power
to forbear even though he knew that the act was wrong.

In a historic decision in Commonwealth *v.* Rogers
(1844), Chief Justice Lemuel Shaw ruled that to constitute
a crime, a person

must have intelligence and capacity enough to have a criminal
intent and purpose; and if his reason and mental powers are
either so deficient that he has no will, no conscience, or con-
trolling mental power, *or* if, through the overwhelming violence of mental disease, his intellectual power is for the time
obliterated, he is not a responsible moral agent, and is not punishable for criminal acts.[24]

Although some judges suspected that an irresistible impulse was nothing more than a depraved heart, it was
accepted as a legitimate test for insanity in several states
before the Civil War. The more conservative M'Naghten
Rules were adopted with less hesitation, however, so that
it was not until 1872 that a case of irresistible impulse was
recognized by the United States Supreme Court.[25]

But if psychiatrists had partially succeeded in convinc-
ing judges that a homicidal impulse might be irresistible,
they found less sympathy for a theory of total moral derangement. Prichard, the first to use the phrase "moral
insanity," defined it as "a morbid perversion of the natural feelings, affections, inclinations, temper, habits, moral
dispositions, and natural impulses without any remark-

[24] Quoted in Wharton, *Treatise*, p. 479.

[25] Wharton, *Treatise*, p. 482. North Carolina emphatically repudiated
the test in State *v.* Brandon, 8 Jones, 463 (1861), and the District of
Columbia refused to accept it until 1929. It was a rare state that, like
New Hampshire, defined legal irresponsibility as simply the product of a
mental disease or defect: State *v.* Pike, 1870, 49 N.H. 399, quoted in
Durham *v.* United States, 214 *Fed. Rep.*, 2nd ser., 874–875.

able disorder or defect of the intellect." [26] This is a good definition of what we know today as psychopathic personality, but the terms Prichard used were those of eighteenth-century philosophy and literature. For Jonathan Edwards and his followers, the depraved were precisely those whose natural inclinations and affections were unable to respond to the new "simple idea" of God. When philosophers had partially substituted the concepts of immanence and process for God, it was the human inclinations, affections, and impulses that were to be nurtured and refined by social institutions. It was one thing, however, to believe that social progress could be achieved through a cultivation of human drives and emotions, and quite another to recognize the social responsibility involved when men's emotions and impulses had become perverted. As Isaac Ray acidly observed,

When the public feeling has become too refined to tolerate the infliction of blows and stripes on the imbecile and the mad in the institution, . . . it can still be gratified by gazing on the dying agonies of a being unable to comprehend the connexion between his crime and the penalty attached to it, and utterly insensible of the nature of his awful situation.[27]

Yet lawyers and judges were faced with the difficult task of determining the exact degree of guilt in a particular criminal case; and if equal justice was to be achieved it was necessary to fix upon some standard of reference which would not fluctuate with every new psychological theory. Ray said that a man's abnormality could be measured only by comparing his actions with his previous habits, since "madness is not indicated so much by any particular extravagance of thought or feeling, as by a well-marked change of character, or departure from the ordinary habits of thinking, feeling and acting, without any

---

[26] Prichard, *Treatise*, p. 16.   [27] Ray, *Medical Jurisprudence*, p. 126.

adequate external cause." [28] If the question were merely whether an individual was capable of managing his property, Ray's criterion of comparing actions with former habits would not seem radical.[29] But criminal guilt demanded an absolute test, for if standards of insanity changed with each individual, there was no certainty that the evil would be separated from the virtuous. Even such a liberal judge as Robert B. Warden, who was deeply concerned with the problem of abnormality and whose knowledge of medical psychology led him to repudiate the M'Naghten Rules, searched for an "Ideal Standard Man," for some point of reference by which the law could measure guilt.

The effort to find "standard men" sometimes resulted in strange conceptions of justice, as in the trial of William Freeman in 1846. Two years previously, Judge John Worth Edmonds of New York had ruled that a man with deficient moral or intellectual powers was not responsible. But then Judge Edmonds had been presiding in the case of Kleim, a white man who had killed a poor and obscure woman. William Freeman, on the other hand, was part Indian and part Negro and he had wiped out the rich and powerful family of John G. Van Nest. In his first trial it had been demonstrated that Freeman could count to twenty, that he knew his parents, and that he was not a "brute beast," which, by the authority of Coke and Hale, established his sanity and convicted him of murder.[30]

[28] *Ibid.*, pp. 142–143.

[29] English and American law traditionally made a sharp distinction between responsibility for crime and insanity which rendered a person incapable of managing property. Jurists gave many logical reasons for defining civil incapacity in broader terms than criminal irresponsibility, but the psychiatrist, Georget, who was not familiar with such discriminations in French law, could only conclude that the English valued property more than life (Prichard, *Treatise*, p. 267).

[30] Quoted in *Argument of William H. Seward, in Defense of William Freeman, on His Trial for Murder, at Auburn . . . Reported by S. Blatchford* (Auburn, N.Y., 1846), pp. 15–17.

William H. Seward, who defended Freeman in his second trial, was outraged by the curious rule used to justify such a primitive test for insanity. Because of his inferior racial blood, it had been held that Freeman could not be judged by the standards of a white man:

Hence it is held that the prisoner's intellect is to be compared with the depreciating standard of the African, and his passions with the violent and ferocious character erroneously imputed to the Aborigines. Indications of manifest derangement, or at least of imbecility, approaching to Idiocy, are therefore set aside, on the ground that they harmonize with the legitimate but degraded characteristics of the races from which he is descended.[31]

Seward, who quoted liberally from Isaac Ray, was not alone in his attempts to expand the meaning of legal insanity. Two years after the Freeman case, an article in *The American Review* pointed out that most of the inmates of asylums were capable of telling right from wrong. The author also hinted that guilt might be a projection of the normal mind:

We assume to punish guilt, because we understand what constitutes crime in the case of a sane man; possessing, as we do, his thoughts and feelings, with enough of his motives to enable us to pronounce upon his conduct. But in respect to the insane, who knows the operations of his mind, or what dark power reigns over him? [32]

Isaac Ray proclaimed, perhaps with undue confidence, that the existence of moral insanity was "too well established, to be questioned by those who have any scientific reputation to lose." In a series of reports to *The Boston Medical and Surgical Journal*, Dr. S. B. Woodward advo-

[31] Seward, *Argument*, p. 10.
[32] "Insanity—How Far a Legal Defence," *The American Review: A Whig Journal, Devoted to Politics and Literature*, XLV (Sept. 1848), 274.

cated legal recognition of moral insanity and of "moral idiocy" as "an imbecile state of the moral faculties, from birth, as to make the individual irresponsible for his moral conduct." [33] But by 1850, the legal profession had rallied for a concerted attack against any theory which, like a Trojan horse, would permit the infiltration of humanitarian reformers behind the rigid lines of criminal law.[34]

In 1851 Dr. Benedict's report from the New York State Lunatic Asylum hinted that childhood discipline might prevent moral insanity and that, in any event, the "disease" might be controlled by such "nauseating remedies, as ipecacuanha and antimony, and purgatives," or by applying "blisters and setons to the back of his neck." [35] An article in *The American Journal of Insanity* in 1857 complained that the new category would shield the worst criminals from punishment and urged that stricter legal tests be adopted. Looking back on the conflict, Francis Wharton reported in 1882 that moral insanity had become "an exploded psychological fiction," that since 1860 there had been a complete "denunciation of a scheme of psychological romanticism," and that science and law had advanced together to protect society from "the romanticism of the French psychological followers of Rousseau, afterwards aided by phrenology, which refined crime into insanity." [36]

Yet the concept of moral insanity had not been abolished, it had merely started a devious line of development. Benjamin Rush and Isaac Ray had assumed that the de-

[33] S. B. Woodward, "Moral Insanity," *Boston Medical and Surgical Journal*, ed. by J. V. C. Smith, XXX (April 17, 1844), 228; XVIII (March 28, 1838), 126.

[34] Sydney Maughs, "A Concept of Psychopathy and Psychopathic Personality: Its Evolution and Historical Development," *Journal of Criminal Psychopathology*, II (Jan. 1941), 335, 337.

[35] "Moral Insanity," *Boston Medical and Surgical Journal*, XLIV (May 7, 1851), 285.

[36] Wharton, *Mental Unsoundness*, pp. 487, xiv.

rangement was largely caused by environment, that it was curable, and that the victims were "objects of compassion." But in 1857 John Kitching, drawing on the writings of George Combe, argued that men differ in inherent moral, as well as intellectual, capacities. Some fifteen years before, a Spanish physician named Soler had written on the theory of the "born criminal" or "criminal type," which was to receive definitive treatment a generation later in the works of the Italian criminologist, Cesare Lombroso. It would seem that, once society recognized the psychopathic personality, there was a rapid denial of all social responsibility. Certain types of insanity might be explained by head injuries, alcohol, or faulty education, but the morally insane were *born* criminals. Later, with the triumph of the science of race and physiognomy, the criminal type would result from irresponsible crossbreeding, miscegenation, or inferior racial stock. As the unwholesome spawn of a Jukes or a Kallikak, the morally insane could be recognized by his faulty cephalic index, his body hair, his prognathous jaw, or his simian nose. Though J. A. L. Koch used the phrase "phychopathic personality," as early as 1891, its relation to other psychic abnormalities was not seen before the investigations of Freud.

V

The theory of moral insanity should have been meaningful for Americans in the second quarter of the nineteenth century, since it implied a dynamic, rather than a static view of human behavior; it emphasized innate motions and impulses rather than a passive reception of knowledge and automatic response. A more recent list of the symptoms of the morally insane or psychopath has a striking resemblance to the fictional villain of 1840: superficial charm and good intelligence; no delusions; no nervousness or psychoneurotic symptoms; unreliability, untruthfulness, and insincerity; lack of remorse or shame; inadequate motives for antisocial behavior; pathologic selfishness and incapacity for love; general poverty of the major affective reactions, such as sympathy; failure to follow any important plan, poor judgment; suicide rarely carried out; inability to withstand tedium or pressure, and evidence of a quick temper.[37]

Such an individual would, of course, be a challenge to the prevailing social values. He would be a living instance of the failure of those values or of the social mechanism for transmitting them. If the psychopath had any ideals, they would conform to a group code of violence and daring which filled the vacuum left by an undeveloped conscience, providing an outlet for an insatiable desire to destroy.

In the early nineteenth century America was not without its gangs and violence, its city riots and frontier outlawry. In a land where limitless opportunities stimulated imagination and desire, where the restraining force of tradition and order was often ineffective, a psychopath might become a successful burglar, land pirate, or slave stealer. It was in fiction, however, and not in the courts that the diseased heart would be described, analyzed, and judged. But before examining the fictional treatment of moral insanity, we must first discuss some literary implications of intellectual disorder.

[37] Manfred S. Guttmacher and Henry Weihofen, *Psychiatry and the Law* (New York, 1952), p. 90.

Chapter IV

THE DISORDERED MIND

BEFORE analyzing the treatment of the disordered mind in American fiction, let us summarize the central concepts and theories discussed in the preceding chapter.

Legal theorists of the eighteenth and early nineteenth centuries preserved the ancient division between the totally insane and the lunatics or monomaniacs whose reason was only partially diseased. The law assumed that all men, regardless of mental defects, possess an autonomous moral faculty or disposition. The state of a man's soul could usually be deduced by examining his actions, but among the totally insane whose hearts were unenlightened by reason, this fundamental goodness or evil was beyond the scrutiny of law. Moral alienation, as opposed to mental disease, was always synonymous with guilt, since it represented a conscious and willful disobedience to divine and human law. Legally, the lunatic or victim of partial insanity was an eccentric who might not be capable of managing property but who was nevertheless responsible for criminal acts committed during lucid intervals. Such distinctions cannot be fully understood unless we keep in mind the underlying assumption that the moral faculty, while dependent on reason and sensation for information, was at the same time immune from outside contamination.

The debate over insanity and responsibility was therefore largely confined to lunacy or monomania. After such a victim of partial insanity had committed a crime, the fundamental question was whether his unlawful act was a result of a disease which rendered impotent his innate moral sense, or whether the crime stemmed from malicious motives arising from a corrupt heart. Liberals stressed the interdependence of human faculties, but they seldom challenged the basic premise concerning the nature of guilt. For conservatives, physical alienation was never an excuse for moral alienation, though the two might become indistinguishable when the reason was badly disordered, in which case a maniac was beyond the reach of justice.

From the Shakespearean drama to the nineteenth-century opera and from the Gothic romance to the early psychological novel, two images of insanity expressed the ancient distinction between physical and moral alienation. Sometimes a sympathetic character, preferably a young woman, was pictured as suffering from mania or dementia after a traumatic experience. Ophelia was perhaps the inspiration for the succession of white-robed heroines, pathetically innocent, childlike, and unresisting, that appealed to refined sensibilities in the 1840's and 50's. But horror rather than pity was associated with the cunning lunatic, whose lucid intervals were mistaken for sanity but whose fiendish plots and eventual deliriums gave proof of a wicked soul, controlled by the devil.

If a woman lost her reason because of a lover's betrayal, or if, like Cooper's Hetty Hutter, she lacked reason from the beginning, it was often imagined that her moral sense developed a unique purity and that, like the Pythia at Delphi, her pronouncements revealed a higher truth. Though strange and perhaps even eccentric, the demented heroine was more like an oracle or a traveler from an unknown land than like a witch. Cooper used a familiar American legend in *The Wept of Wish-ton-Wish* (1829), where a girl named Ruth Heathcote, after being captured and reared by Indians, returned to her family as one alienated in mind and habits. Now, there was a striking resemblance between Ruth Heathcote and the conventional demented heroine. They shared an *involuntary* alienation from society, a partial loss of memory, especially for family ties and affections, and a heightened devotion to certain ideas and people, which seemed unrealistic or incongruous to parents and relatives. Their moral sense, in other words, had developed without being directed by civilization or by practical reason. The wicked lunatic, on the other hand, resembled the white renegade, who adopted the customs of savages for his own evil purposes and who used barbarous allies in carrying out schemes of private revenge. In stories, a distinction between physical and moral alienation was often symbolized by the virtuous oracle and the witch, by the captured heroine and the renegade, and by the demented lover and malicious lunatic.

Although writers of fiction generally accepted the division between partial and total insanity, we shall confine our discussion to the former, since fictional victims of dementia and total mania were seldom involved in murder. The types of insanity which attracted the attention of novelists were precisely those cases involving obsessions and delusions that, obscuring moral responsibility, occasioned the greatest debate among judges and psychologists. It is important to note that legal writers discussed insanity in terms of abstract faculties, as if the individual could be isolated from the social forces of his environment. Imaginative writers, on the other hand, were free to explore emotional associations and social relationships; and if the fictional maniac was often a stereotype, his malady was at least presented within a wider context. When a court was faced with the problem of a man who had killed as the result of a delusion, the judge tried to determine whether the motive would be justifiable, had the delusion been real. But the novelist, by tracing the origins and by examining the implications and overtones of the delusion, had a different device for finding the degree of moral guilt.

Thus far we have used physical and moral alienation as terms to distinguish between a mind disordered by disease and a moral faculty perverted through a conscious choice of evil. Writers of fiction accepted this traditional distinction, but they tended to merge the various faculties so that intellectual and moral responses were closely related. Moral alienation became identified with rebellion against familial or social authority, an expanded meaning which had implications concerning both the causes of private revolt and the nature of guilt.

II

Conforming to the classical American belief in progress, science, and reform, Charles Brockden Brown referred to seduction and dueling as "remnants of the ancient manners of Europe," and in 1807 he attacked the popularity of murder in fiction, which, "like all departures from nature and common sense, will have but a short reign." [1] Yet Brown himself, more than any other early American writer, had contributed to the fictional study of murder and abnormal psychology. Although he believed in politi-

[1] Quoted in David Lee Clark, *Charles Brockden Brown, Pioneer Voice of America* (Durham, N.C., 1952), pp. 142–146, 241.

cal and social democracy, he sensed that freedom might also imply a psychic liberation from the forces of tradition and authority. Men might, he wrote,

imagine themselves laboring for the happiness of mankind, loosening the bonds of superstition, breaking the fetters of commerce, outrooting the prejudice of birth; they may, in reality, be merely pulling down the props which uphold human society, and annihilate not merely the chains of false religion but the foundations of morality—not merely the fetters of commerce and feudal usurpations upon property, but commerce and property themselves.[2]

In *Wieland* (1798) Brown examined one of the results of American freedom: a European conscience, cut loose from tradition and authoritative standards, confused by the uncertainty of knowledge, might mistake dark passion for divine law. In Germany the Wielands' grandfather had enjoyed the opportunity for an orderly expression of his talents as a musician and writer, but sudden misfortune subjected his uneducated son both to economic servitude and to emotional freedom. He had been prepared for neither. Consequently, the younger Wieland found an outlet for his stifled passions in religious fanaticism, stimulated by an accidental reading of a book on the Albigenses. Emigrating to America, the son attempted to convert the Indians, made an unexpected fortune in trade, and settled with his own family in Pennsylvania, where he had freedom to practice mysterious rites in a temple he had built on a hilltop. Wieland was obsessed with a strange sense of guilt, and his moral agonies finally culminated in a case of "spontaneous combustion," which left him a mass of "crawling putrefaction." After the father's death, Clara Wieland and her brother grew up in an atmosphere of "natural religion" and were left to the guidance of their own intellects.

[2] *Ibid.*, p. 190.

The story thus far is almost an allegory of American colonial history. It includes disrupting economic changes in Europe, religious fervor which was not unrelated to these changes, frequent references to predestination and to stern self-analysis, the vision and failure of spreading truth among the savages, unexpected economic success, and even the well-known figure of a temple (or city) on the hill. The parallel continues with the disorganization and self-consumption of the original religious fanaticism and with the appropriation of the temple by rationalistic descendants. Finally, the continental Enlightenment appeared in the character of Henry Pleyel, "the champion of intellectual liberty . . . who rejected all guidance but that of his reason."

For the new generation of Wielands who sang, talked, and read in the temple scorched by their father's combustion, "time was supposed to have only new delights in store." But if Pleyel's cheerful and confident rationalism signified one meaning of eighteenth-century Europe, there was a note of ambiguity in the mysterious and anarchic figure of Carwin. Young Wieland himself was unable to escape from his father's shadow, or from an obsession with guilt and moral justification. New delights were not inevitable, therefore, in a land where the ultimate source of morality lay in the individual conscience, and where European science and revolution (Carwin) collided with a tradition of religious enthusiasm (Wieland).

Such a drama of historical allegory cannot be pushed too far, but it is important to note that *Wieland* is not simply an imitation of Godwin and Schiller, and that Brown was concerned with the problems of a society which imposed few limitations on self-expansion. Like Melville's *Pierre*, *Wieland* might well have been subtitled "The Ambiguities," since the characters constantly mistake one another's intentions and see neither the truth nor the consequences of their acts: Wieland and Pleyel both thought that Clara was having a secret affair with Carwin; Clara thought that Carwin was pursuing her, when he was actually making love to her maid and using his gift of ventriloquism to avoid detection; Carwin was innocent of malicious intentions, but brought ruin to the Wieland family; and Wieland finally killed his wife and children, thinking that such a sacrifice proved his fidelity to God's commands. These ambiguities, according to Brown, resulted from the imperfections of reason and from the devious nature of human passions.

To understand Brown's association of conscience, insanity, and murder, it is necessary to examine certain psychological overtones of which he doubtless was unaware. Since we wish to illuminate Brown's imaginative expression, we cannot accept ambiguity as a final conclusion concerning human motives. To analyze the symbolic language of fiction we may therefore utilize techniques unsuitable for the interpretation of historical fact.

Although the Wielands had rejected their pathetic father and had converted his consecrated temple into a kind of picnic ground, Clara and her brother showed symptoms of great anxiety and guilt. Part of this vague dread involved the memory of the elder Wieland's death, but there was also tension in the closeness of the married brother and the unmarried sister. After a period of deep depression, Clara had a striking dream. She was walking in the evening toward her brother's house. Suddenly she saw him in the distance, motioning that she make haste, though she did not notice that Wieland was actually standing on the opposite side of a deep pit. She would have plunged to her death, had a mysterious man (Carwin) not caught her from behind. This dream suggested that Carwin had saved Clara from an incestuous relation with her brother.

At another time, after Clara had been brooding over the memory of her father, an ominous voice called for her to stop walking toward her bedroom closet. Actually, Carwin was hiding inside, after making love to the maid, but the significant fact was that Clara had the frantic thought that her *brother* was in the closet, though she had no basis for such fear or suspicion. Again, the symbolism hinted at a dread of incest. That this dread was not entirely disassociated from desire was suggested when Clara confessed, after Wieland had gone insane and had killed his wife and children: "I acknowledge that my guilt surpasses that of all mankind. . . . Is there a thing in the world worthy of infinite abhorrence? It is I."

There are other indications that insanity and murder were in some way associated with a mysterious guilt, that this guilt involved Wieland's relationship with his sister, and that violence as a substitute for suppressed desires was sanctioned by a perverted conscience. When Wieland was disturbed by the thought that Clara was unsafe in the presence of Carwin, he wandered aimlessly to her house. On the way his contemplations "soared above earth and its inhabitants," and he longed to make some testimonial of his faith to God. Disappointed in finding the house empty, his ambiguous fears and desires intensified by Clara's absence, Wieland was suddenly confronted by a "luminous glowing" and was then ordered to render his wife to the Lord. After executing the command, "I lifted the corpse in my arms and laid it on the bed. I gazed upon it with delight. Such was the elation of my thoughts, that I even broke into laughter. I clapped my hands and exclaimed, 'It is done! My sacred duty is fulfilled!' "

Brown's description of the circumstances accompanying Wieland's hallucinations and murders hinted at concealed motives beyond the derangement of an intellect. The contrast between his feelings for his wife and those for his sister appeared after the first murders, when Clara found him happy and exultant, as if some "joyous occurrence had betided." But when Wieland heard the command to kill Clara, he lifted his eyes to heaven and said, "This is too much! Any victim but this." He could murder his wife and children without remorse, for the divine will transcended human obligations, but his sister was endowed with a "sanctity and excellence surpassing human." It was as if Wieland's obsession with supernatural religion provided his suppressed desires with an outlet in a murder that removed one of the obstacles between Clara and himself. Yet an act of violence could be justified only by religious sanction, which might obscure but could never eradicate the underlying guilt of an incestuous wish. Although Wieland at first rebelled against the act, he knew that he could possess his sister only by killing her. As soon as murder and death are translated into libidinal desire, Wieland's horror and reluctance become even more understandable.

An attempt to explain *Wieland* wholly in terms of an incestuous relation would, of course, be misleading. For our purposes, the important fact is that Brown associated delusions with guilt and with unconscious motives, though the precise nature of Wieland's motives was never made explicit. In the freedom of the American environment, the Wielands had been left to the guidance of their own understandings; yet, as Wieland himself concluded, guilt was meaningless when determined by "halting reason." Guilt and virtue were beyond the province of simple rationalism and depended ultimately upon the complex relationships between parents and children, brother and sister, and husband and wife. Without the authority of tradition or of a respected father, Wieland searched for God's will and for moral certainty. In so doing, however, he found the justification for his own desires only. When

Wieland finally realized the true nature of his wishes and desires, he was forced, in a blinding moment of sanity, to commit suicide.

We have already noted that cases similar to Wieland's attracted the attention of British and American judges who were faced in the early nineteenth century with the problem of separating delusions from guilty or justifiable motives. In 1844 Chief Justice Lemuel Shaw of Massachusetts ruled that a murder was excusable if the killer acted under the delusive but sincere belief that he was obeying a command of God, which would supersede all human and natural laws. Such a decision rested on the assumption that supposedly valid motives never conceal a malicious heart. Judges interpreted delusions as simple mistakes in perception, which in no way obscured the purity or corruption of the moral faculty as evidenced by worthy or evil motives. Had Wieland gone before an American court in the 1840's, it is probable that his crime would have been excused as an accident, in the sense that neither his delusion nor his choice of victims was related to purposeful desire.[3]

Unlike judges and legal theorists, Charles Brockden Brown did not describe delusions as an isolated psychological fact. Wieland had been conditioned by his background of religious fanaticism to seek a release from his morbid guilt in violence justified by the voice of God. Carwin's mysterious ventriloquism, added to Wieland's inner tension and growing suspicion of his sister's virtue, precipitated hallucinations which allowed a momentary escape from guilt. Both the content of Wieland's delusions

[3] To qualify this hypothesis, however, it is necessary to add that much would depend on the state of public opinion, the status and popularity of the victims, and the character of the judge. Yet the important point is that the assumption underlying Justice Shaw's decision also served as the foundation for the M'Naghten Rules and can be found in American decisions at least as early as 1805.

and the choice of his victims were related to illicit and unconscious desires. His moral alienation was symbolized by his final self-destruction.

A generation after the publication of *Wieland,* John Neal's Harold argued that a man like Wieland, who acted with good intentions, was innocent in the eyes of God: "And if he *meant* rightly, God will hold him guiltless, as he would the maniack who should dip his hands in the blood of his own mother!" [4] But Brown was not sure about the guiltlessness of maniacs, especially those who desired the blood of their mothers. In *Edgar Huntley* (1799) he continued his exploration of criminal insanity and arrived at several pessimistic conclusions. This novel was an attack upon simple rationalism, upon the belief in moral progress, and upon naïve theories of reform. A quiet, steady worker, normal to all appearances, was really an insane killer. Education, wealth, and a benevolent guardian failed to prevent the development of a criminal; Christian forgiveness, sympathy, and understanding proved to be useless when they were confronted by man's unsuspected evil. Even the rational and seemingly able Edgar Huntley was a somnabulist, and innocent individuals were murdered by savages as the result of social injustice and of a primitive desire for revenge. "How little cognizance," Brown wrote, "have men over the actions and motives of each other! How total is our blindness with regard to our own performances!" Hence, somnambulism was more than a sensational element to create dramatic suspense; it was also a symbol of the vast unconscious life of man.

For Clithero, an intelligent and aspiring peasant boy in Ireland, Mrs. Lorimer was an ideal mother image. He loved his patroness, waited on her, sought only to please her, and resisted all temptations leading to dissipation and

[4] John Neal, *Logan: A Family History* (Philadelphia, 1822), II, 228.

to sensuality. It was a pure and intimate love between an idolized mother and a boy who was not quite a son. Such a utopian affection was clouded by the fact that Mrs. Lorimer, who was the lady of an Irish manor, had an evil twin brother who repaid her sisterly love with scorn and hatred. Through his influence with their parents, he had even violated his sister's sexual freedom by forcing her to marry a man against her choice. Significantly, Mr. Lorimer was dead before the arrival of Clithero, so that Arthur Wiatte, the brother, had become a conveniently detached father figure. Mrs. Lorimer cautioned Clithero: "Of whatever outrage he be guilty, suffer him to pass in safety. Despise me; abandon me; kill me . . . but spare, I implore you, my unhappy brother." Thus the mother sympathized with the son's dislike for the evil father, but pleaded for understanding and tolerance.

A sign of the son's increasing maturity appeared in his love for Arthur Wiatte's illegitimate daughter, Clarice. Writers have frequently used the device of love among cousins, stepchildren, or near relations to intensify the conflict between generations, especially one between a son and various figures of authority. In this case, Clithero felt guilty in loving Clarice because of his attachment and responsibility to Mrs. Lorimer. When the kind patroness discovered the love affair and approved of it, the problem seemed to be resolved. Then Clithero had an accidental fight with Arthur Wiatte. By killing the father in self-defense, Clithero removed the only obstacle both to Mrs. Lorimer and to Clarice.

After describing this disguised parricide, Brown was primarily interested in the delusions resulting from Clithero's unconscious guilt. At first Clithero felt great anxiety over the injury he had unintentionally done to Mrs. Lorimer and Clarice. He became obsessed with the idea that his patroness might die after hearing of her brother's fate.

Using this fear as an excuse to enter her bedroom, Clithero stood beside the sleeping woman, was suddenly seized by an irresistible impulse to murder her, and picked up a dagger from the table. In the darkness he could not see that Clarice was sleeping in Mrs. Lorimer's bed. At the crucial moment Mrs. Lorimer entered the room and shrieked, whereupon Clithero discovered that he was about to kill Clarice. When he tried to explain the death of Wiatte, Mrs. Lorimer sank to the floor in a swoon, and Clithero fled to America.

As a servant in Pennsylvania, Clithero was a sober, gentle, and sometimes melancholy workman, but his guilt drove him to sleepwalking and to compulsive actions. Edgar Huntley, the young American hero, suspected him of murdering a friend named Waldegrave, but Huntley was reasonable and benevolent:

I am no stranger to your gnawing cares; to the deep and incurable despair that haunts you, to which your waking thoughts are a prey, and from which sleep cannot secure you. I know the enormity of your crime, but I know not your inducements. . . . I see proofs of that remorse which must ever be attendant on guilt. . . . I once imagined that he who killed Waldegrave inflicted the greatest possible injury on me. That was an error, which reflection has cured. Were futurity laid open to my view, and events, with their consequences, unfolded, I might see reason to embrace the assassin as my best friend.

This was the expression of an optimistic, Quakerlike morality, one which considers signs of guilt genuine repentance, and symptoms of suffering, expiation. Huntley, after hearing Clithero's story, could not understand why he should feel guilt over the killing of Wiatte: "Shall a man extract food for self-reproach from an action to which . . . he was actuated by no culpable intention?" The rational explanation for the whole affair seemed to lie in Mrs. Lorimer's "absurd opinions of the sacredness of consanguinity," and in Clithero's excessive gratitude, "dread of unjust upbraiding," and "imputation of imaginary guilt."

When it appeared that both Mrs. Lorimer and Clarice were alive and in America, that Clithero had only imagined his patroness' death, and that Huntley's friend had been killed by Indians, the story of Clithero seemed to dwindle into a superficial tale of temporary madness. But a darker note was introduced in the character of Sarsefield, once the materialistic, worldly-wise lover of Mrs. Lorimer and a former teacher of Edgar Huntley. Sarsefield called Clithero a maniac, "an agent from Hell," and "the engine of infernal malice." After Clithero had been wounded by Indians, Sarsefield refused to help him, saying that "to prolong his life would be merely to protract his misery."

Huntley, however, could not accept such a brutal and unenlightened view of human error. But when he saved Clithero and tried to ease the wounded man's sense of guilt by reporting that Mrs. Lorimer was alive and in America, Huntley discovered that Sarsefield's seeming inhumanity was justified. Roused to an unexpected fury, Clithero suddenly announced his determination to kill Mrs. Lorimer at any cost and was saved only by suicide from "lingering for years in the noisome dungeon of a hospital." The confused Huntley had to confess to Sarsefield: "I have erred, not through sinister or malignant intentions, but from the impulse of misguided . . . but powerful benevolence. . . . I imagined that Clithero was merely the victim of erroneous education and the prejudices of his rank; that his understanding was deluded by phantoms in the mask of virtue and duty, and not, as you have strenuously maintained, utterly subverted."

Brown concluded, in other words, that Clithero's will and moral faculty had been alienated, though his reason was but partially deranged. If the Irishman's understanding had been "utterly subverted," the subversion was certainly not in the sense of the "wild beast" defined by law, nor were his delusions the product of his reasoning from false assumptions. In so far as Wieland was a split personality, a man who believed that he murdered from the highest possible motive, he could not distinguish between right and wrong. But Clithero suffered from no hallucinations, his sense of guilt was more persistent and conscious than Wieland's, and his madness took the form of an irresistible impulse to kill. Brown seemed to agree with Sarsefield that Clithero was a moral alien, an "engine of infernal malice" who deserved neither sympathy nor help, since his impulse to kill arose not from a deranged understanding, but rather from a perverted heart.

Yet Brown was primarily interested in developing the causes of homicidal insanity, for which purpose the devices of a novelist were at times more suggestive than were the contemporary theories of psychiatrists. Instead of explaining Clithero's insanity by means of a head injury, erroneous education or religious beliefs, intense study, or economic misfortune, Brown emphasized the ambiguous emotions of a foster son. Without embarking upon an extravagant Freudian analysis, we may assume that Brown sensed the vague sexual tensions between parents and children. Arthur Mervyn was revolted by his father's marriage to a young servant girl, whom he had previously seen in intercourse with a neighbor boy.[5] His fear of a possible incestuous relationship with this servant-girl-mother contributed to his moral outrage and to his flight from home. Ormond's efficiency and seeming benevolence was a contrast to the disability and drunkenness of Constantia Dudley's father; after murdering Dudley in

[5] Charles Brockden Brown, *Arthur Mervyn; or, Memoirs of the Year 1793* (Philadelphia, 1887), I, 21.

order to possess Constantia, Ormond himself became a threatening father image. Whenever Brown described deep personal conflicts, he suggested an ambivalent sexual attraction and aggression between the generations of a single family.

Clithero's extreme guilt after killing Arthur Wiatte was precisely that of a son who had murdered his father. The central fact was that his relationship with Mrs. Lorimer had suddenly changed with her brother's accidental death. Clithero was in love with Clarice, a girl of his own generation, but he could marry her only if he escaped the guilt implied by the new mother relationship. Hence the murder of Mrs. Lorimer would prove that the killing of Wiatte had been truly an accident and that it had not been a primitive, Oedipal murder. In another sense, the killing of Mrs. Lorimer would be the only possible way for Clithero to preserve the former relationship, which had been untainted by elements of blood and sex. Clithero rationalized his impulse as an attempt to *protect* Mrs. Lorimer from anguish and grief; Huntley interpreted the madness as a desire to escape from a patroness' disapproval; but both explanations became meaningless when Clithero persisted in his efforts to murder. In Brown's completed picture, the essential elements contributing to homicidal insanity were an abnormal devotion to a mother, an excessive desire for approval, and an overpowering sense of guilt. The horror and shock which Clithero felt upon discovery by Mrs. Lorimer did not result from remorse, but from the hideous mistake he was about to make. Had he killed Clarice, the path to the future would have been cut off, he would have been condemned in his own eyes as an Oedipal murderer, and even matricide could not have saved him from the multiplying guilt. In both *Wieland* and *Edgar Huntley* an original murder is linked with a concealed and unlawful desire, which, for the diseased mind, necessitates a second murder as the only means of removing an unbearable guilt.

III

The plot of Cooper's *Lionel Lincoln* (1825) is tortuous and illogical, but like the more abbreviated symbols of other writers, Cooper's plots convey important attitudes and relationships. *Lionel Lincoln* traces the development of a specific case of monomania from the human sins of lust, jealousy, and avarice, which, in Cooper's philosophy, were responsible for most of the evil and unhappiness in the world.

Making the conventional male error, the elder Lionel Lincoln had sired a bastard named Job Pray, whose feeble-mindedness was a natural mark of his origin. The mother, Abigail Pray, was jealous when Sir Lionel later married a girl named Priscilla, who gave birth to a legitimate son, Lionel the younger (we shall refer to the son as "Lionel" and to the father as "Sir Lionel" or "Ralph"). It so happened that Abigail's guardian was also Sir Lionel's aunt, Mrs. Lechmere, a cold-blooded, avaricious woman with eyes firmly set on the Lincoln estate in England. She had hoped to entangle Sir Lionel with her own daughter, and was outraged when he married Priscilla, who had also been her ward. When Sir Lionel went to England to claim his rightful estate, he foolishly left his wife under the care of Mrs. Lechmere and Abigail Pray, both of whom desired her destruction. Driven by jealousy and greed, Abigail and Mrs. Lechmere plotted murder, but were saved the trouble when Priscilla contracted smallpox. Cooper could imagine a terrifying feminine death-wish: "Vain, weak and foolish as I had been," said Abigail, "never did I regard my own fresh beauty with half the inward pleasure that I looked upon the foulness of my rival."

When Sir Lionel returned from England, he was told
that his wife had died in giving birth to the offspring of
an adulterous romance. Mrs. Lechmere had planned this
deception to drive the disillusioned husband toward her
own daughter or toward Abigail. But despite his original
sexual transgression, Sir Lionel was stunned by the information and driven insane. In this instance, insanity
resulted from the trauma of thinking that his wife was
unfaithful, even though the victim had himself put the
complex forces of evil into motion.

The actual story occurred some fifteen years later, after
Sir Lionel, who had escaped from an English insane asylum, had returned to America under the name of "Ralph."
Feeling that he had suffered intolerable slavery, Ralph
identified England and the king with the demons at the
asylum, his monomania including both a desire for political rebellion and a thirst for revenge against Mrs.
Lechmere. Cooper thus gave family conflicts a wider social
significance, as young Lionel, a Loyalist, is ranged against
his insane father and half-wit brother, both of whom supported the radical cause. Neither side in the Revolution
was described as especially virtuous or evil, though violence
and even sadism resulted from the struggle. The novel is,
in fact, filled with murderous intentions. When Lionel
learned that his mother had supposedly been seduced and
had died in childbirth, he swore to kill the adulteror.
Finally discovering that he had been deceived, Ralph tried
to kill Abigail, his former mistress, whereupon Lionel was
saved only at the last moment from slaying his father in
Abigail's defense. To keep Lionel from parricide, Cooper
allowed a keeper from the asylum to deliver the fatal
blow, adding enigmatically that the keeper never returned to England: "Perhaps he was conscious of a motive,
that none but an inward monitor might detect."

With the exception of a few background scenes of

Revolutionary violence, the tale was strictly limited to a tight family situation wherein characters were related either by blood or by sex. The division of the generations was not so important, however, as the division between the two sexes. Every female character was in some way related to or controlled by Mrs. Lechmere, whose subtle evil transcended the forthright criminality of Cooper's worst villains. In an age of increasing deference to the gentle and noble sex, nothing was so striking in this novel as the corrosive feminine dishonesty and the vicious but hidden female aggressiveness. Lionel's mother and bride, though pure in heart, were, respectively, the ward and granddaughter of Mrs. Lechmere; in the plot, they were only facets of the central, female nature. It is important that Lionel, like his father, believed that his mother had committed adultery; and his marriage to Cecil was planned and blessed by Mrs. Lechmere.

The essential plot, then, may be interpreted as a struggle between the masculine and feminine sides of a family, the former being decidedly the weaker of the two. Young Lionel's quest was, in effect, an attempt to join forces with his father against the power of feminine evil. But Sir Lionel had already been reduced to a state of impotent mania, since woman's nature is at once so pure and deceptive that Mrs. Lechmere could effectively mobilize the dead Priscilla as a fifth-column agent. Just as unwittingly, her granddaughter, Cecil, helped to steer the son away from his father.

Sir Lionel had committed an original sin, but his subsequent sufferings were out of proportion to his evil, for, despite his monomania, he never killed or injured his opponents, his desire for revenge being deflected by political obsession. Insanity was clearly a consequence of evil and not a source of it.

The relations between young Lionel and his father grew

increasingly ambiguous as Ralph's mental alienation became more complete. When Lionel first beheld the mysterious Ralph, walking like a phantom through the fog,
he was tempted "to kneel, and ask a benediction." The
son said that colonists should be as loyal to the king as
children to a common parent, though Ralph ironically
accused the king of being an unnatural father. After
Lexington and Concord, Ralph saved his son's life, and
Lionel temporarily abandoned his bride to go with Ralph
in order to learn the secret of his past. Yet the son was
constantly confused, unable to discover his true position.
He was torn between the bad mother-image of Mrs.
Lechmere and the good mother-image of Cecil, who together represented the possibilities of feminine nature. In
a sense, the character, Job Pray, was a projection of
Lionel's loyalty to his father. When Job died of smallpox,
Lionel was finally committed to the feminine side, which
Cooper purified by Mrs. Lechmere's death and by Abigail's remorse. The parricide was put into execution by
a stranger, but the actual intention was Lionel's.

Such a lengthy analysis is necessary to show the important assumptions in this novel concerning insanity
and aggression. The impulse to kill and destroy emerges
from innate passions, especially from greed. Man's weakness in abusing the sexual relation opens him to attack
and aligns the sexes against each other. The father, who
suffered most, was a helpless ineffectual, not basically evil
but unable to resist sexual desire, suspicion, and jealousy.
The son's attempt to identify himself with the father was
frustrated by the latter's inherent weakness and by the
dual potentiality of woman. Woman here has the terrible
and supreme power over sexual fidelity which may enable
even a loyal and loving wife to contribute to her husband's destruction. Yet, in the final picture, the husband
was by no means blameless. The son who knelt at his

father's feet and gave him unswerving support was the
half-wit Job.

There was nothing new in Cooper's theory of the passions or in his explanation of Ralph's insanity. But the
outlets for passion and obsession were determined by a
specific social situation, which had a peculiar slackness
and ambiguity about it. American society in *Lionel Lincoln* was a society where men had to travel great distances
to claim inherited fortunes, where the status of women
was vague, where an emphasis on sexual morality opened
new sources of feminine power, where paternal authority
and tradition dissipated or became perverted, where, instead of conserving the past and protecting the weaker
females, the fathers destroyed the past and eventually
succumbed to woman's strength. Loyal to his king, yet the
son of a radical, Lionel searched for the firm, reassuring
voice of a patriarch. He found a wild-eyed fool and discovered that he must choose between half-witted obeisance
to a pathetic lunatic and submission to an enigmatic ideal
of woman.

IV

In the novels discussed so far, insanity was precipitated
by traumatic experiences which upset the balance between
an individual's self-ideal and his actual status as reflected
in his social relations. Thus Wieland's intimate relations
with Clara seemed securely innocent until Carwin's presence made the brother suddenly aware of his sister's
sexuality. As long as Arthur Wiatte lived, Clithero could
love his patroness without guilt, and Sir Lionel Lincoln
could excuse his early transgression until he thought his
wife unfaithful. In the deranged mind there was a curious
perversion of the self-ideal, which, instead of compelling
conformity to accepted standards of virtue, permitted the
liberation of darker passions, a massing of latent hatreds

which might surge upward in a blinding monomania. If the ideal heroine reacted to trauma by stringing flowers through her hair and wasting away to innocent and ethereal death, a stroke of lightning might also sear a character's finer affections, igniting his frozen and half-forgotten depths of evil.

"A diseased self-esteem," said William Gilmore Simms, "is apt to be an active condition in the mind of most lunatics, and has contributed not a little to their mental overthrow." Many of the symptoms of insanity, Simms thought, were efforts to startle other people in order to win recognition by any means. But a monomaniac, whose aggression took a specific direction, could be understood only by discovering the relation between some trauma and his previous state of insecurity.

In *The Partisan* (1835) Simms explored the causes of insanity in a character named Frampton. Frampton was a Carolinian whose pregnant wife had been tortured and brutally killed by a gang of Tories. The backwoods partisan warfare in 1780 was in truth characterized by sadism and atrocities of this kind. But Simms was not content with a simple plot of revenge. Since Frampton had never been especially close to his wife, the shock of her ruthless murder was accentuated by self-accusing memories of his own cruelty. He prayed to her, asking forgiveness for his neglect and unkindness. He became very sentimental when he thought of her, perhaps unconsciously recalling that he had himself once wished her death. Such extreme guilt was, of course, a blow to Frampton's self-esteem. Feeling that he must prove that he had not been unkind to his wife and that he had not desired her death, Frampton lived only for revenge and for self-justification.

Hiding in a swamp and hunted by Loyalist war parties, the maniac killed and mutilated stray soldiers. When he found an injured Tory named Clough, he pulled the man's bandages open and drove his weapon into the wounds. After another Tory cried for mercy, "the speech was silenced, as, crushing through bone and brain, the thick sword dug its way down into the very eyes of the pleader. The avenger knelt on the senseless body . . . and poured forth above it a strain of impious Thanksgiving to Heaven for so much granted and gained of the desired vengeance."

Simms was ahead of his time in attempting to provide a psychological explanation for the extreme depths of human cruelty; but in 1837, two years after *The Partisan*, Robert Montgomery Bird described a similar case of monomania in *Nick of the Woods*. Nathan Slaughter was a Quaker farmer living on the Pennsylvania frontier in the late eighteenth century. When a party of Shawnees came to his farm, Nathan gave them his knife and gun to show that he was a friend. The Shawnee chief answered by killing Nathan's wife, mother, and five children. As Slaughter later said:

When thee has children that Injuns murder, as thee stands by, —a wife that clasps thee legs in the writhings of death,—her blood, spouting up to thee bosom, where she has slept—an old mother calling thee to help her in the death struggle!—then, friend, then thee may see—then thee may know—then thee may feel—then thee may call theeself wretched.

Nathan's resulting monomania was complicated by a racial and religious implication. On the one hand, Indians were presented as only half-human and consequently easier to hate and kill, but on the other hand, Nathan Slaughter was a Quaker, who did not believe in physical resistance to bloodshed although he tried to prevent the massacre. Where Simms utilized a husband's guilt to explain a pathological sadism, Bird rather mechanically relied on a head injury. Nathan survived a brutal scalping which presumably shattered his Quaker convictions and which provided him with the distinguishing marks of a monomaniac, including epileptic fits.

Moving to the Kentucky frontier, Slaughter became a split personality, at once a meek Quaker hunter, tormented by the settlers for his refusal to fight Indians, and also the mysterious Jibbenainosay, or Nick of the Woods, who murdered Indians indiscriminately, leaving them scalped and with a bloody cross on their chests. This double life and hidden identity, intended by Bird to add to the narrative suspense, also dramatized the morality of killing. It was the accepted attitude in the Kentucky settlement that Indians were vicious animals that had to be exterminated. But Nathan was not part of the community justifying racial murder, and thus he had to make a compromise with his own conscience.

Creating his own morality, Nathan Slaughter was a kind of superman as well as maniac. His physical skills were easily equal to those of Leatherstocking, while his undeviating and unquenchable urge to murder gave him an added supernatural aura. In his maddened state, revenge was holy, plunging a knife into the breast of an Indian was a divine ecstasy, and the spirit of Jibbenainosay could not rest until he held the bloody scalp of Wenonga, the chief, beside the dried locks and ringlets of his own murdered family. Yet Nathan, the timid hunter, the gentle Quaker, guilt-ridden and apologetic when he killed an Indian to save the hero's life, argued against revenge and against the killing of killers. Thus it was that Nathan maintained his social position as a moralizing dissenter, a Christian outcast, though his secret, savage deeds evoked a horror even in the hearts of blood-stained frontiersmen.

Such a division was more than mere hypocrisy or literary convention. It was a portrayal of the intricate relation between aggression and conscience, and between group

violence and the moral alien. By his Quaker protest against
the rationalized values of the frontier community Nathan
could justify a more extreme aggression on the personal
level. He could achieve an intimate satisfaction from his
own private and bloody rites, at a time when social values
were so ambiguous that no clear distinction could be
made between pathologic and normal violence. Even
though Nathan Slaughter killed Indians, he was essentially
a moral outcast, seeking personal revenge in a land disrupted by group warfare.

In his literary portrait, the monomaniac usually possessed acute senses, as did Nathan Slaughter, or a powerful
intellect, as did John Neal's Harold. The murderer in
Poe's "The Tell-Tale Heart" described his sensitive hearing as proof of his sanity. But if the monomaniac appeared
supernormal in certain of his senses and faculties, the
relationship between his conscience and passions had been
distorted. Simms and Bird, who were principally interested
in the mechanisms of guilt and justification, described
maniacs who consciously killed for vengeance. Frampton
might be compelled to pray to his dead wife and Nathan
might condemn the frontier's hatred of Indians, but theirs
was no devious route in choosing Tories and Shawnees for
private revenge. But Poe, who brought a new dimension
to the concept of monomania, emphasized a total perversion of the will. His killers were frustrated, impulsive
men, seething with an undetermined hatred, blindly groping for an object to destroy. In Poe's deceptive, moon-lit
world, the nerves and senses were tautly drawn to a point
where their very rigidity had snapped the fragile web of
logic, even though the intellect retained its capacity for
planned action. It was not simply a question of killing
Indians or Tories *because* they had brought death and
grief, since the mind was incapable of such conscious deduction. Instead, unrelated objects advanced in the con-

sciousness and stood glaring and unnaturally bright in the reflected light of anger. They provoked and irritated a deranged mind—like a bull-fighter's cape.

The images which precipitated violence were the haunting eyes of an old man, the bright, clean teeth of a girl named Berenice, or a sinister cat named Pluto. There was a concentration on the flickering and shifting light on the surface of consciousness, as seen from the slightly distorted perspective of a man submerged in the fluid of passion. Poe did not enlighten the reader concerning the original frustration or desire. We are presented with a character suffering from a serious but obscure mental disorganization, his essential symptom being a rupture in the relation between logical thought and emotional feeling. As the tension increased, escape seemed to lie only in an act of violent aggression. A plan crystallized, and a chain of ideas led irresistibly to an action which was both illogical and beyond the understanding. Sometimes, this violence was so horrifying to the normal consciousness that, like Egaeus in "Berenice" (1835), the man could not remember it. And yet the act brought a relaxation, a temporary calmness and rationality, perhaps even satisfaction and pride.

The central characteristics of most of Poe's insane killers were a feeling of guilt *before* the murder, a conviction that violence was the only solution for some deep emotional problem, and a relief from tension and anxiety in the act itself. Thus Egaeus did not openly desire to kill Berenice, nor are we told why he feared her.[6] Yet he felt that the possession of her teeth could restore him to reason and peace of mind. It is fairly obvious that the protagonist in "The Black Cat" (1843) in some way associated the cat with his wife, though he did not himself recognize this

---

[6] There is an ingenious and perhaps far-fetched explanation in Marie Bonaparte, *The Life and Works of Edgar Allan Poe: A Psycho-Analytic Interpretation* (London, 1949), p. 229.

identification. When his obsession and anxiety only increased after he blinded the cat, he hanged the creature as if it were a criminal to be justly executed. That the animal was not the real object of his fear and hatred was evidenced by the arrival of a second cat. It seemed to be only the accidental interference of his wife which diverted his passions, yet in that moment the identification was suddenly complete. He could justify the murder of his wife by her annoying interruption as he was righteously pursuing the cat, but the emotional relief and satisfaction lay in the realization of his original desire.

It is important that most of Poe's unhappy maniacs were temporarily liberated by an act of violence. Like Nathan Slaughter and Frampton, they were freed from anxiety and guilt, from a frowning conscience or from moral insecurity. Freedom does, after all, lie in action. But action may be restricted or guided by parents, society, and natural forces. An escape from these restrictions might mean slavery to individual passions, but this, in turn, might be the essence of a particular kind of freedom. A man who felt a crushing weight of guilt or fear might seek his liberty in a supreme act of will, focusing his passionate energy on one frustrating image, and, with a concentrated effort, break through the net of confining powers.

V

America proclaimed itself a land of liberty. It was a land where men had once dissolved political bands and had accused a single man of absolute tyranny, intolerable abuse, and usurpation of power, though the king was scarcely responsible for the charges. The king, however, was being tried before the Supreme Judge, and there was no appeal. Yet this quest for liberty could lead to an increasing denial of limits. "Who's to doom," Captain

Ahab asked, "when the judge himself is dragged to the bar?"

Opposed to the fathers, the laws, the kings, and the gods, there was always the wounded, intimate self, the animal being that yearned for unrestricted expression, for an expansive gushing forth, an acting, grasping, possession of the world. In America there were many selves expanding, receiving fuel from claims in land, clothes, banks, or, vicariously, in the gratifying national extension and enrichment. But then expanding selves can rub against one another, and even without such friction, a few remaining limits irritate and challenge ascending spirits. If man at last seemed free, free to plot his course or free to throw the instruments overboard, could a man, an American in the nineteenth century, strike out and kill all opposing forces? Could one supreme act of will shatter the complex and shifting images of restriction? When a baby attempts to claim the world, his desires are blunted and driven underground by a ruling father. For Americans, at least, one father was dead.

A monomaniac may be driven by an irresistible impulse, but he imagines at times that this impulse is an expression of his true self and that each act of murder is an act of freedom. Only in the wildest insanity, however, could a man strike out to obliterate every opposing will. From the time of the first tantrum rebuked, the mind incorporates certain restricting and guiding forces. Hence the monomaniac has an obsession to kill Tories, Indians, or black cats. "Human madness," said Melville, "is oftentimes a cunning and most feline thing. When you think it fled, it may have become transfigured into some still subtler form."

In America the literary study of monomania reached its highest point, of course, when the "Pequod" sailed out from Nantucket across the watery part of the world. In his "masoned, walled-town of a Captain's exclusiveness," Ahab was beyond the secure, yet restrictive, shore of civilization, and lived for the supreme act. Unlike Frampton and Nathan Slaughter, Ahab's initial trauma had not involved injury to an extended self, in the form of a murdered wife or children. The injury had penetrated directly into the heart of Ahab's soul, insulting his masculine power, ruining the source of his assurance and pride. Ahab's imagination enhanced the whale with supernatural significance. As long as Moby-Dick lived, there was a force to humble Ahab's manhood and to mock his pretensions of freedom.

It is simple enough to say that Moby-Dick represents a father, or God, or Nature, or the Unknowable, but Ahab's voyage was not an intellectual quest. The whale was not a man nor an idea, but a feeling. Killing the whale was not a matter of subduing Nature or of revenge against a castrating father. It was the attempted assertion of a wounded self at bay. Moby-Dick embodied the feeling of restriction and limitation, external power, the essence of every thwarting, baffling, hurting thing, supreme and concentrated, malign and maddeningly confident. For a lesser injury or a lesser hatred, a black cat or an Indian might suffice. But for Ahab, who had a majesty above all ordinary supermen and maniacs, no simple murder could avenge such a profound grievance or pacify such a towering aggression. It was Melville's genius to avoid an allegory of parricide and to choose a whale, whose size and power could signify the inclusiveness of Ahab's feeling and the enormity of his challenge.

In the fictional treatment of monomania it was generally assumed that innate passions had the capacity for causing violent aggression, especially when directed and stimulated by reason and imagination. Normally, these

aggressive passions were subdued and controlled either by
divine conscience or by inculcated social values. Nevertheless, some trauma or injury might provide a justification for violence and an immediate object for aggression.
The victim would feel that his ego had been outrageously
violated, that the ordinary codes had been broken, and
that his was a special case. In addition, he might have received a physical injury like scalping or the loss of a leg,
or he might have had a previous guilt or anxiety which
would contribute to his madness.

In so far as the monomaniac had lucid intervals, he
might technically be able to distinguish right from wrong,
although he created his own morality with respect to the
hated object. Freedom and self-esteem could only come
from yielding to the desire to act, or to kill. Conformity
to traditional or social prohibitions would only be slavery
to external force and a denial of inner certainty. Even
though the monomaniac might appear normal, as Ahab
did on shore, he was in this sense driven by an irresistible
impulse. Thus knowledge could coexist with deep emotional abnormality.

Writers often expressed sympathy for these driven and
obsessed souls, who were seldom described as responsible
criminals. And yet they had lost their instruments of
navigation, they blindly sailed away from the light and
warmth of society and attacked white monsters in a black
and icy sea.

VI

At the cost of repetition, it seems appropriate at this
point to summarize certain fictional ideas and associations
concerning insanity and murder, including their similarity
to and difference from contemporary legal conceptions.
Although we have analyzed only a small sampling of
American fiction from 1798 to 1860, similar themes and

ideas may be found in the works of many other writers. In a discussion of the fictional treatment of insanity it would be possible to stress minor differences in interpretation, to show, for example, the early influence of Pinel and Rush or the gradual acceptance of Esquirol's classification of symptoms. For the limited purposes of this study, however, it seems more important to note the divergence between the basic assumptions in jurisprudence and fiction.

An American judge in the first half of the nineteenth century might have defined legal guilt as a causal connection between an unlawful act and the malicious disposition of an inner, nonintellectual faculty, which might variously be called the heart, will, or moral sense. Whether the will and moral sense were thought to be united or independent was relatively unimportant in this sense, since the final seat of moral action was autonomous, regardless of terminology. It was, essentially, the "heart," as described in scholastic philosophy, a philosophy still uncontaminated by sensational psychology. For the theologian, of course, a malicious heart was guilty even if it failed to produce illicit acts, but the law assumed that guilt could not be punished unless made manifest in crime.

In the legal view, insanity was an impairment of the understanding in varying degrees and could be classed with other accidental diseases. It presented a problem in criminal law because a diseased intellect tended to obscure the causal connection between an evil heart and an unlawful act. Such a connection was impossible to establish in cases of total insanity, but monomania, or "reasoning madness," which often involved systematized delusions, seemed to imply that the understanding was only partially damaged, and that certain actions, at least, reflected the true nature and quality of the heart. From the Hadfield case in 1800 to the general acceptance of the M'Naghten Rules, partial insanity was a subject of dispute in criminal law. There was general agreement, however, that moral guilt could be theoretically distinguished from a physical alienation of mind. An evil will was only accidentally associated with mental disorder.

If writers of fiction stressed the innocence of the demented heroine, they also tended to identify murder with monomania. We have already seen that four ideas concerning insanity and aggression were at least implicit in most of the works discussed. First, the immediate cause of monomania was a traumatic experience which destroyed an individual's ideal conception of his own moral status. Whenever judges equated insanity with physical disease, the selection of victims was viewed as fortuitous, at least in the same sense that plagues and fevers disregard human standards of morality. In fiction, however, monomania was not amoral, since only certain individuals having specific ideals and temperaments could respond to shock with pathologic aggression. Had Nathan Slaughter not been a Quaker, for instance, he could have joined the Kentuckians in their war against Indians without experiencing inner conflict. If Wieland had been a deist, he would not have been tempted to hear the voice of God. From its very inception, then, partial insanity was related to the nature and content of an individual's moral faculty.

The second idea follows logically from the first. An insane murderer's delusions and choice of victims were not matters of chance, but were rather determined by the inner disposition of his heart. This meant that no sharp line could be drawn between physical and moral alienation, since physical symptoms, such as impairment of reason, were a reflection of moral conflict. We should note again, however, that total insanity, which was seldom related to murder or crime in fiction, was described as physical alienation. Writers did not extend the moral connotation from monomania to dementia.

Third, moral alienation was given a wider meaning by its association with social isolation. Monomania often implied a revolt against primary obligations and restrictions, a revolt bringing about a disintegration of parental authority, tradition, and social order, as we have seen in the analysis of *Lionel Lincoln*. Finally, monomania resulted automatically in its own punishment, usually by suffering and death. Although *Nick of the Woods* is a significant exception, guilt was often synonymous with self-deception and final destruction.

Whereas judges and moral philosophers had tried to clarify and separate the human faculties, these four ideas reflect a belief in a unified personality, whose reason was merely an instrument of will and desire. A malicious heart might conceal itself from consciousness by generating delusions or specious motives for evil acts. The depraved soul mistook the workings of Satan for divine grace. Yet this theory, while resembling the ancient doctrine of total depravity, was opposed to a fundamental assumption of jurisprudence. If the faculties were so intimately and subtly joined, good intentions and worthy motives were not necessarily proof of innocence. In other words, the guilt of an insane murderer could not be deduced from external circumstances or measured by the standards of normal men. But judges, of course, were denied the privileges of novelists. They could neither scrutinize the inner soul of criminals nor assume that moral guilt would inevitably bring its own punishment.

Chapter V

THE MORALLY PERVERSE

SINCE one of the purposes of this study is to clarify the relationship between fiction and social values, we should make careful distinctions among several theories of alienation before analyzing the literary treatment of moral insanity. We have seen that one of the principal assumptions of theology, moral philosophy, and law in the early nineteenth century was a belief that man inherently possesses the capacity to distinguish good from evil. Because this capacity was universal in human nature, even the worst criminal might be judged by the standards of normal men. Moreover, the democratic principle of legal equality was based on the premise that men cannot choose evil without experiencing inner conflict. But if justice was thus related to natural law and was not synonomous with the arbitrary command of a sovereign, it is important to note that equality of responsibility was inseparably united to equality of moral capacity.

We have already traced several implications of the belief in an equal moral capacity. In the eyes of the law a murderer had willfully chosen evil. This meant that he had morally alienated himself and deserved to be killed as an enemy of man. The only exception was the killer whose mind had been alienated by physical disease, thereby separating his actions from inherent moral capacity. Our analysis of the fictional monomaniac brought us to a third variety of alienation, in which a divided mind chooses evil by self-deception. In both the conscious and unconscious forms of moral alienation the murderer experienced an inner conflict between selfish desire and natural law; and in fiction this struggle usually led to delusions or to remorse. As sinful passion gradually triumphed over an inherent respect for law, it was imagined that the murderer moved away from the warmth of social unity until, like Cain, he wandered alone and despised. As he was generally conceived, then, the moral alien was a man who, by disregarding his inner moral standards, had renounced his equal membership in the human family. Either by conscious or by unconscious rebellion, the moral alien became a social outcast, cut off from bonds of sympathetic identification.

In our brief surveys of theology, moral philosophy, and psychology, we have noted the evolution of a theory which flatly contradicted the traditional premise of equal moral capacity. For Theodore Parker the criminal had not alienated himself from society, nor had he rebelled against his inherent moral sense. Even the murderer was but an unfortunate straggler from the march of civilization, a man who had never shared full membership in society. If morality was the product of enlightened Christian nurture, the alienated were victims of social deprivation only. Similarly, the phrenologists argued that criminals lacked moral capacity and should therefore be treated as victims of improper training or heredity. The same idea found clearer expression in the theory of moral insanity, which presented a definite challenge to American jurisprudence in the 1840's. This theoretical denial of equal responsibility was, as we have seen, a logical development from the moral-sense philosophy. For Benjamin Rush a "sense" was a *physical* capacity subject to conditioning by culture. As Pinel suggested, there might be a causal relation between indulgent mothers and children who lacked a moral sense. The totally depraved were, in other words, physical and not moral aliens, since they experienced no inner conflict, nor had they consciously renounced a social membership they had never possessed. Confronted with such doctrines, the legal profession could either deny the importance of social conditioning and argue that moral capacity transcended experience, or it could fall back on a Hobbesian conception of law as command. We shall return to this question in our discussion of punishment, but we must now analyze the treatment of moral insanity in fiction, keeping in mind the conflict between traditional Lockian assumptions and the newer theories of varying moral capacity.

II

Presumably, there have always been psychopathic personalities, men possessing neither an internalized moral code nor a respect for external authority, but the fact that medical recognition of such delinquents occurred at the time of accelerating growth of urban areas and of urban problems was more than coincidence. In the 1830's and 40's there was a flood of American and European novels dealing with city crime and with urban villains nurtured in degrading slums or trained by the brutal contest for economic survival. In the anti-Godwinian fiction, characters appeared who lacked the finer impulses, the moral sense, and the benevolent regard for their fellow men which some moral philosophers had thought to be instinctive human attributes. Though some of these villains acquired the social graces and qualities of leadership necessary for success, they justified their amorality by a fatalistic philosophy or by sheer materialism.

Our objective in this chapter is to consider beliefs and values concerning those fictional villains who evinced a kind of moral insanity. To understand these attitudes expressed in literature, however, we must briefly discuss the psychological significance of the fictional villain. A thorough analysis of this subject would fall beyond the intended limits of our study, but we may make two general observations. First, we shall consider the role of the villain as a scapegoat, and second, we shall discuss certain changing values which led to an ambivalent attitude toward moral aliens.

If society forbids certain forms of outward aggression, it also provides substitute targets in unpopular groups, criminals, and fictional villains, who may be condemned and attacked with justification.[1] Sometimes the scapegoat merely replaces an original frustrating person or object, but the mechanism of socially approved aggression may also involve a projection of guilty desires from one individual or group to another.[2] There can be little quarrel with the conclusion of modern social psychologists that a fictional villain is either a symbol of frustrating forces or a projection of guilt and thus a device for vicarious punishment.

Of course, it would be impossible to prove that the popularity of villains in early nineteenth-century literature reflected a specified amount of social frustration. Yet we may suspect that the particular character of fictional

[1] John Dollard, Neal E. Miller, et al., Frustration and Aggression (New Haven, 1939), pp. 87–121.
[2] J. C. Flugel, Man, Morals and Society (New York, 1947), pp. 164–174.

villains was not unrelated to general social conditions. Throughout the early nineteenth century the American environment was marked by an unpredictable future and by a variety of opportunities for individual men. The realization of many of these opportunities, however, required that social order be rigorously maintained. Unlike that in Europe, expansion in America was not associated with a revolt against tradition and authority but rather with an attainment of greater unity. As long as social continuity could be preserved, as long as high moral standards could be transmitted from generation to generation so that brothers would not conspire against brothers, the Americans would be secure in their freedom and abundance. An appeal for unity in the name of Revolutionary "tradition" was a theme echoed in political speeches, public orations, and editorials from the time of Jefferson to the election of Lincoln. Many Americans accepted the values and decisions of the past, praising the supreme wisdom of the Founding Fathers, looking with optimism to future national expansion and prosperity, yet they feared that some evil conspiracy threatened to destroy both the heritage and promise of American life. There is a parallel between such attitudes and the specific nature of the villain in American fiction.

In American literature the traditional conflict between father and son, which was nearly as old as the written word, was at least partially replaced by the struggle between peers. In the early American novels there are surprisingly few tyrants or titans, the counterparts of Falkland, Brian de Bois-Guilbert, Murdstone, Sikes, and William Brandon, who clearly symbolize oppressive fathers. American fathers are often Revolutionary veterans or at least idealistic old gentlemen, slightly confused by the quickening pace of life, perhaps temporarily associated with or dominated by a villain, but ultimately on the side of virtue. If we may generalize further, villains often appear to be men or women in the hero's age group, representing unlawful competitors or projections of aggressive forces within the writer (or reader) himself. Such a pattern of villainy implies that the democratic ideals (the glorious traditions of the forefathers) are threatened by various sinister forces. Hence a man who felt that his generation might fail to realize the promise of the Revolution, and who blamed Jesuits, slavery, or alcohol for social evil, might also receive a symbolic justification in literature by sympathizing with a kindly old father, and by exulting in the defeat of a crafty villain.

If American writers expressed an ambivalence toward the morally depraved villain, who stood for an unscrupulous competitor instead of a tyrannical father, it was partly the result of American social conditions and partly a reflection of more pervasive intellectual currents which were transfroming Western thought. In American society there was often a tendency toward excessive individualism, in the sense of disregarding rules and restrictions, and we may interpret the fictional villain as a device whereby good men pledged loyalty to natural law and order, after first achieving symbolic liberation from all restraint. But this alternate identification with and rejection of an anarchic villain was also associated with a changing Western *Weltanschauung*. If the dominant idea in the eighteenth century was a belief in the uniformity of man's nature, in the universality of reason, and in the balance and order of natural law, then a villain was evil precisely because he was radically different, and thus contrary to the harmony of nature. From the late eighteenth to the mid-nineteenth century, however, there was a development and persistence of certain philosophical concepts which partly changed the character and role of fictional villains. Whenever the idea of progress and perfectibility was accepted, it was obvious that the criminal villain represented an earlier stage in man's development and that he had been merely retarded in his normal growth. In so far as the idea of progress was combined with the earlier belief in man's unity, the morally depraved was considered mainly as an unfortunate brother who deserved sympathy and help. But when men identified progress with a given race or group, the criminal became a degenerate half-animal who was not fit to live. On the other hand, as writers began to glorify individual uniqueness, emotion, and temperament, the total moral alien, who represented a dramatic break in the uniformity of nature, acquired a fascinating dignity and power. From Schiller's Karl Moor to Byron's Cain and onward to Bulwer-Lytton's Paul Clifford, writers sympathized with sublime insurgents, satanic heroes, and supermen murderers. We have already examined some of the implications of the superman, but it is important to note that he was essentially related to any murderer who lacked an inner conflict and remorse.

The ambivalent attitude toward the morally insane is clearly seen in Edgar Allan Poe, who accused previous philosophers of disregarding man's innate impulse to be "perverse." [3] Man, according to Poe, had an instinct to submit to the compulsions of society, but he also had a counterimpulse to do wrong for wrong's sake. Poe's murderer in "The Imp of the Perverse" (1845) had not acted from a sudden or blind passion, but only after months of deliberation, and he had received more delight from the act and its success than from the money gained. Yet, when he compulsively surrendered himself, perverseness turned against even his own well-being.

Poe had a vague theory that the "sublime" geological disorders and natural disturbances which fascinated paint-

[3] Edgar Allan Poe, *The Works of Edgar Allan Poe,* ed. by Edmund Clarence Stedman and George Edward Woodberry (Chicago, 1894), II, 33.

ers and writers of his time were prognostic of death. He also believed that man's mind was "unparticled matter" in motion.[4] He seemed to imply that the perverse impulse was the "unparticled" form of geological disorders, that it too was "sublime," and that both were God's way of announcing death to the universe. It is certain that Poe identified the sublime, and thus the most meaningful human emotions, with aggression, murder, and death. The agents and victims of this violence were probably either substitutes for competitive figures in Poe's life or projections of suppressed desires, personified and punished through the medium of literature. The importance of Poe's theory lies in the fact that he carried a romantic philosophy to its pathologic extreme, raising the non-intellectual life to a point where even perverseness and sadism were glorified. Happiness for Poe could only accompany pain, while death itself was only a painful metamorphosis.[5] Intellect was so impotent that actually its dictates aroused the reverse action, since "reflection but urges us to forbear, and *therefore* it is, I say, that we *cannot.*" Poe, of course, was not in every way typical of American thought in the 1830's and 40's, but his fascination with villains and murderers, his rejection of rationalism, and his denial of uniformitarianism, all represent the direction in which thought was moving.

We may thus distinguish two factors which influenced attitudes toward moral insanity in American fiction. Economic abundance, intense competition, and the absence of traditional restrictions tended to make the individual both insecure and ambitious. The fictional villain, as a ruthless and immoral competitor, was a convenient scapegoat for deflected aggression and a means for the vicarious expression and punishment of illicit desires. From the late eighteenth to the mid-nineteenth

[4] *Ibid.*, pp. 100, 316.   [5] *Ibid.*, pp. 320, 317.

century there were also certain intellectual currents which glorified the uniqueness of individual passions and emotions, stressed the weakness of intellect and the diversity of moral standards, and deified the independent self, which was associated with "natural" inclinations. These two factors doubtless contributed to the increasing interest in crime and criminal trials in America, evidenced by the many editions of *The Newgate Calendar,* collections of famous trials, pamphlet accounts of criminals' lives, and newspaper coverage of local and foreign crime.

III

Before we consider the origins and significance of moral insanity as interpreted by American writers, we must first describe several typical examples of the murderous villain. The hardened criminal, whose essential attribute was a total absence of remorse, was well defined in popular American literature by the 1850's. Such was Captain Robert Dashington, a young man of twenty-five who had escaped from a New York prison and had walked all the way to Boston. It was a rainy, autumn evening, bleak and cold, when Captain Dashington sat on a bench in Boston Common, reflecting upon his position in the world. His long beard, uncombed hair, dirty clothing, and old, glazed cap were all marks against him. Feeling in his pockets, he found only one chew of tobacco, a dull jack-knife, a broken pocket comb, and two York shillings. Sitting on the cold bench in a New England drizzle, Dashington was about as low and hopeless a man as one could imagine.[6]

Yet the brave Dashington's strength lay in the very fact that he was a moral alien, a competitor who lacked inhibitions. He went to a respectable public house, ate a

---

[6] [George Thompson], *Dashington; or, The Mysteries of a Private Mad-House,* by Greenhorn [pseud.] (New York, n.d.), p. 3.

good dinner, paying his last shillings for the meal, and then asked the landlord for lodging, after explaining that he was really a gentleman in disguise, tracing his adulterous wife who eloped with the footman. Because the villain had a good education, spoke well, and signed his name in faultless penmanship, the landlord apologized for his original hesitation. Late at night, Dashington rose and crept into the next room, where a young man was fast asleep. He found some fashionable clothes of the right size on a chair, with money in the pockets. When the sleeper stirred, the resourceful captain strangled him "with as much deliberation as he would have displayed in the killing of an insect." Calmly setting the room on fire, he walked from the building. A shave and haircut the next morning transformed him into a respectable-looking gentleman. Despite a conventional deference to morality, the author presented Dashington as an admirable character, whose shrewd plans, amazing self-reliance, and uninhibited desires typified an ideal of freedom and independence. That Dashington had to suffer for his sins did not detract from his original fascination; the most exhilarating freedom is the most ephemeral.

A Gothic version of the totally perverse criminal may be seen in George Lippard's famous "Devil-Bug." Lippard attacked "effeminate" and "shallow" critics who were not concerned with "reality," yet he observed that the character of Devil-Bug was full of interest not because he seemed real, but because he represented the "grotesque-sublime." [7] Perhaps a description of Devil-Bug will clarify the meaning of the "grotesque-sublime." Born in a brothel, raised in the sight of vice and squalor, Devil-Bug was the doorkeeper and general handy man at notorious Monk-Hall, which seemed to be the source of all evil and cor-

[7] George Lippard, *The Quaker City; or, The Monks of Monk-Hall* (Philadelphia, 1845), p. 258.

ruption in Philadelphia. Devil-Bug was thickly set, with immense shoulders and long arms, thin, distorted legs, a ludicrously large head, and a shriveled, orbless eye. He had a protruding forehead, a flat nose, and flaring nostrils. His principal hobby was human torture.

Devil-Bug talked continually of mangled corpses and delighted in dashing out the brains of an old woman against the brass knob of an andiron. Nevertheless, even Devil-Bug had the vestige of a moral sense. He was plagued by ghosts of murdered people, he rescued a girl named Mabel from being raped by a parson, and he even resisted the strong temptation to rape Mabel himself. A trace of animal generosity was often associated with human deformity, which implied greater physical than moral alienation. In this respect, Devil-Bug resembled Robert Swale in John Pendleton Kennedy's *Rob of the Bowl* (1838), who was also led to repentance and to the betrayal of a criminal band after being outraged by an abduction.

Devil-Bug is interesting primarily as an early ancestor of the countless modern creatures of horror that infest contemporary comic strips and cheap literature generally. Even the crude dialogue of this popular image of the morally depraved has changed surprisingly little. Essentially, three elements constitute the stereotype: unquenchable sadism, physical distortion, and extremely low mentality. Closely related to ape men, werewolves, and Frankenstein monsters, the character symbolized the criminal impulse for the most illiterate and unimaginative readers, who could feel superior at least to such a figure of depravity.

Yet the villain who lacked a conscience was not necessarily an animal-man with twisted features and primitive desires. It was in the very nature of the superman to lack or to deny a moral sense. Brown's Ormond had received his training in the Russian army at an early age. At eighteen he captured a Tartar girl, murdered a friend who claimed her, raped and killed the girl, and expiated any lingering guilt by taking the heads of five Turks the next day, for which act he was commissioned for valor. Since all actions, regardless of motives, seemed to produce evil, Ormond concluded that virtue and duty had meaning only in so far as they promoted individual happiness. Moral codes and lofty principles could never influence the machinelike course of existence. For Ormond, true morality was simply the science of egoism.

Just as the cosmopolitan superman differed from Devil-Bug, so in the novels of the South and West there was often a distinction between the criminal aristocrat and the lower-class, cracker-type of gang leader. Alfred W. Arrington portrayed this hierarchy in *The Rangers and Regulators of the Tanaha* (1856). A Byronic character named Curran, least culpable of the criminals in the Texas Republic, was a poet of the twinkling spur and billowy cape variety who had been converted to robbery by the "infernal logic" of his cousin, Captain Carlyle. Curran admitted that he loved the hourly perils, the "fetterless freedom," and the romantic vigils of the criminal. He even confessed that he had killed men, but this had only been in the burning heat of battle, where the odds were against him. He believed in the southern code of honor, in free will and full responsibility, and he firmly refused to commit a cool, premeditated murder.

His cousin Carlyle was an aristocratic leader of a gang, a once-promising lawyer who, after meeting the wrong woman, had been drawn from love to murder, and from specific revenge to general crime. Carlyle had all of the qualities of a southern hero, except for his sinister sweetness of voice. Like Ormond, he justified his life by a fatalistic philosophy, arguing that repentance for crime and murder was ridiculous, since life was determined by destiny.

But Jack Morrow lacked even Carlyle's pretense of being a gentleman. The son of a poor Missouri farmer, Morrow was a simple, straightforward boy, who distinguished himself as a great hunter. Like Poe's Politian and Simm's Beauchampe, he fell in love with a dishonored girl, who urged him to kill her seducer. But in this version of the formula, the villain lawyer, Ellsman, was a crack-shot Southerner who refused to fight only because Jack Morrow was a ruffian. Southern gentlemen may not have wanted to fight ruffians, but the code of honor and class distinctions were difficult to enforce on the western border. To solve the problem, Jack Morrow simply grabbed Ellsman's nose with one hand and his chin with the other, jerked the lawyer's mouth wide open and discharged a full volley of tobacco juice into his throat. After that indignity, even a southern gentleman was willing to fight a western hunter.

Morrow shot and killed the haughty lawyer and then went to fetch the girl, since she had promised to marry him if he avenged her dishonor. When her father objected to the sudden turn of events, Jack Morrow calmly broke his neck. Inured to violence by these killings, Morrow became a chief of the Missouri lynchers, who were struggling for power with another group known as moderators. Morrow's band captured one suspected moderator, accusing him of a murder he had not committed. Jack forced him into a grave to examine the dead body, then shot his legs, and buried him alive.

During the 1830's Jack Morrow became a prominent lyncher and outlaw in Texas, his ruthlessness growing with his power. When he suffered defeat, he had a sudden emotional reaction to his past murders and cruelty, although this convulsive remorse was temporary and associated only with a wounded ego. The criminal finally lashed back in revenge, defying the law to his death.

It might be supposed that such characters as Dashington, Devil-Bug, Ormond, Carlyle, and Morrow are merely examples of evil men, in no way distinguishable from the general category of literary villains. It is certainly true that Ormond and Devil-Bug, at least, are not distinctively American. Yet when we summarize the important characteristics of these murderers, their resemblance to the morally insane becomes apparent. In each case evil was not the product of a particular faculty or passion, but was rather identified with the total personality. Dashington, Ormond, and Carlyle, who benefited from native intelligence and intellectual training, were just as ruthless and sadistic as were the slum-bred monster and frontier thug. Benjamin Rush used the example of Servin to make the same point. Intellect and training led only to rationalization. The second characteristic, which is related to the first, was the absence of inner conflict and genuine remorse. It took little provocation for such men to commit a murder, and they neither hesitated nor disguised their motives with delusions. Since they totally lacked the capacity for virtue, we may conclude that they were not morally responsible. Such characters might, of course, have an intellectual knowledge of the nature and quality of their acts, but this becomes meaningless without a sense of emotional identification with their fellow men. Unlike most of the fictional murderers described in this study, the morally insane villain was a general criminal, a man whose good actions were only accidental, since his motives were governed neither by a concern for virtue nor by evil. An individual who thus lacked what Adam Smith called "sympathy" was totally alienated, in the sense that he was morally unaffected by his relations with society.

We have already seen that this concept of total moral depravity presented a fundamental problem in values. Traditional ethics as well as criminal law rested ultimately upon the theory distinguishing moral from physical alienation, a theory which seemed contradicted by the very existence of the psychopath. In one sense, he was the final product of moral alienation, the end point on a scale of guilt graduated according to the degree of inherent evil. But in another sense, he was a physical alien, since his capacity for moral choice had been destroyed by physical or social causes. American courts found it absurd to accept total depravity as an excuse for crime, but then judges were concerned with a specific act of injustice and not with original causes. If novelists intended to recognize the existence of moral insanity, they could not fail to give an explanation.

IV

One of the causes assigned to moral depravity was the ancient one of excessive luxury and sensual indulgence, which at first implied guilt on the part of the sinner. There was a strong tendency in the Christian tradition to glorify work and a legitimate calling. There was also a suspicion that unearned wealth would lead to indolence, to sensual sins, and ultimately, to crime. Morality was associated with self-discipline, especially in adolescence, which was to be enforced by hard work, and, to a certain extent, by economic necessity.

Charles Brockden Brown gave a conventional explanation of moral depravity in his portrait of Welbeck in *Arthur Mervyn* (1799–1800). A close affinity may be seen between Welbeck's history and the morality of Richardson's novels, to say nothing of Franklin's philosophy of work and discipline.

According to his own confession, Welbeck's primary

sin was his lack of economic virtue. He had the "cureless disease" of indolence, depending on his kinsmen for support, and making no attempt to help himself. Such economic sin was followed logically by sexual sin, a succession which conformed to the prevailing eighteenth-century theory of moral discipline. The intellect could dominate the passions only by imposing a rigid schedule upon the daily life; inherently lawless impulses could then be drilled and marched to the rhythm of regular hours and continuous work.

Welbeck's moral insensitivity was a natural consequence of his early slothfulness. He violated the trust of friendship, seduced impressionable women, disregarded legitimate opportunities for success, and achieved a specious position of opulence and rank by deception and villainy. He was too cowardly to commit suicide, but he murdered the brother of a girl he had wronged. Although he resembled the stereotyped villains in many English eighteenth-century novels, Welbeck was also a portrait of moral insanity as it had been described by Benjamin Rush.

Welbeck was a product of England, where he had reached a crucial point of development at an early age, his villainy having been successfully detected and exposed. About to begin a life of crime as a necessity for survival, he chose the easier course of emigrating to America. Hence America provided the morally depraved with a chance for escape and regeneration. In America there were more possibilities both for improvement and for unrestrained crime. But a man of Welbeck's temperament, arriving in a land where pretty young wives missed their traveling husbands, and where wealthy but naïve immigrants were easy prey for seemingly benevolent strangers, was not to profit from legitimate opportunities.

By 1850 the concept of indolence as a cause of crim-

inality had different connotations, at least in popular
literature. Cheap novels of the 1840's and 50's showed
an increasing awareness of city slums, poverty-stricken
workers, and a decadent money-aristocracy. In 1850 Newton Mallory Curtis defined the problem:

The fatal policy, so prevalent amongst the wealthy citizens of
large towns, of educating their children to believe that the
wealth their parents possess refines their blood, refines their intellect, refines their tastes, and even refines the very flesh upon
their bones, is the bane and curse of society, when the great
masses, the toiling masses . . . are firm in the belief that all
are "created free and equal"—that worth makes the man." [8]

Such novelist-reformers were not interested in attacking
the economic pioneers, men who had founded the textile
mills and banks, the ironworks and steamship companies.
A half-century before Curtis wrote, Brown's Welbeck and
Thomas Craig had sinned by *not* choosing to work for
lawful fortunes and by lacking proper economic in-
itiative. Yet the very success of the acceptable enterprises,
like the success of the Revolution, created disturbing
problems for the fortunate heirs of the next generation.
How were they to avoid the indolence and sensuality
which would accompany inherited wealth? How were they
to prevent independence from becoming license or individual freedom from resulting in anarchy?

Curtis chose a member of New York's aristocracy for
his portrait of moral insanity. At forty-five, Seymour
Sydenham was a tall, handsome man, a fashionable
dresser, well educated, and highly esteemed as a philanthropist. But he also lived in luxury, drank too much,

[8] Newton Mallory Curtis, *The Matricide's Daughter: A Tale of Life in
the Great Metropolis* (n.p., n.d.), p. 68. This first volume of Curtis' trilogy
seems to have been published in 1850, but the date is not certain. Editions
of the three novels appeared in the 1870's, but internal evidence suggests
that all three were written in the 1850's.

and anxiously awaited the full inheritance of his mother's fortune. Taught to look down with scorn on the miserable men who worked for a living, he found that his own extravagance led only to mounting indebtedness. Since his mortgaged property and his reputation as one of the loudest professors of Christianity were at stake, Seymour finally entered an alliance with organized crime. Curtis made it clear that such moral desolation resulted from faulty training, and not from a want of natural abilities. Moral depravity was a product of social evil, of maternal indulgence, and of a betrayal of the forefathers' ideals.

Seymour's new associates included a once-celebrated Methodist preacher who had stolen church funds to support a reckless wife also the mistress of a Wall Street cashier. The preacher had subsequently become a burglar and murderer. Another acquaintance was the reigning beau of New York's fashionable circles, the son of a millionaire, who had married at twenty, seduced two of his wife's sisters, eloped to the South with a circus woman, forged notes, received a sentence and pardon, and then thanked the governor by seducing his daughter's mulatto servant before selling her for a high price in Virginia.

When Sydenham discovered that even counterfeiting did not alleviate his embarrassed financial position, he concluded that it would take one-half of his mother's fortune to satisfy his demanding creditors. Without a twinge of conscience he decided to kill his mother, and for that purpose he enlisted the aid of a famous Philadelphia criminal, one "Quaker Fletcher." Fletcher did not like bloodshed but agreed to do the job for fifty thousand dollars. Trying to answer the burglar's increasing doubts, Sydenham said, "It is not like murdering a young person in the bloom of life and the height of enjoyment. My mother is very old, and at the best, could have but a short time to live." Quaker Fletcher thought that life still might be sweet for the old lady, whereupon Sydenham fell back upon elemental philosophy: "I am compelled to the course I am pursuing to preserve myself and my own; and self-preservation is an instinct that we cannot resist." [9]

Because Quaker Fletcher wavered, Sydenham himself was forced to execute the crime. The professional burglar was sick with guilt over the affair, though he had never had qualms about a simple crime of robbery. Sydenham, on the other hand, felt no remorse from the murder, his upbringing having deprived him of both conscience and moral feeling. Guilt, for Sydenham, was synonymous with being caught; after he had been tried and convicted of murder, he went into a childish tantrum and committed suicide.[10]

Increasing wealth might also bring a new leisure and independence for women, especially after state laws in the 1840's gave more liberal property rights to the gentle sex. Before the new laws, it was difficult for a woman to run away from her husband without starving, or at least without finding another man. But for certain critics like James Fenimore Cooper in *The Ways of the Hour* (1850), this "cup and saucer" law in New York had subverted the social order: "There is no mode by which an errant wife can be made to perform her duties."

Mary Monson, a young, aristocratic woman who had left her vicomte husband and had been unjustly accused of murder, was perhaps the strangest of Cooper's heroines. Her eccentricities only intensified the public's suspicion of her guilt. Cooper seemed to be torn between a sympathy for her, since she was persecuted by the vulgar major-

[9] Newton Mallory Curtis, *The Star of the Fallen: A Tale* (New York, n.d.), p. 73.

[10] Newton Mallory Curtis, *The Victim's Revenge: A Sequel* . . . (New York, n.d.), pp. 88–89.

ity, and in intense dislike of her feminine independence.

Mary Monson was first of all a lady (described as one who can give grounds for scandal but cannot talk scandal herself); and Cooper admired her for such superiority to public opinion. The novel is confusing, however, because Cooper mixed several unrelated ideas in trying to resolve Mary's unattractive qualities into a vague notion of insanity. The fact relevant to this discussion was that Mary's alleged insanity was something like moral insanity, and this was explained in terms of her social position. The heroine herself confessed that wilfulness had been her great enemy, that independence and too much money had only stimulated her stubborn disregard for male authority: "I doubt if it is good for a woman to be thus tried. We were created for dependence—" she told her stern lawyer, Thomas Dunscomb "—dependence on our fathers, on our brothers, and perhaps on our husbands?" Dunscomb, who had the most traditional and respectable ideals of feminine propriety, quickly deleted the "perhaps," and replied that women should lean on their husbands "for support, guidance, authority, and advice."

It was Cooper's thesis that Mary Monson's insanity was aggravated by the pernicious "ways of the hour" which gave women an unwholesome and unnatural independence. Yet he was enigmatic about the precise nature of her malady. She had an impulsiveness and a cunning which practically ruined the case for her defense. She had, Cooper tells us, "erred in many things that are duties as grave as that of being chaste." But though temporarily convicted of murder, she was innocent of any specific crime.

Mary's lawyers rejected the possibility of an insanity plea because "insanity had been worn out by too much use of late." Cooper added that her insanity might have been impossible to establish legally, even though the judge noted her haughty gaze and air of "stealthy cunning" with a certain suspicion. But since there was no evidence of delusion or of a split personality, and since Mary Monson's chief traits were an assertiveness, a love of temporary pleasure, and a disregard for consequences, it would seem that she represented the kind of moral insanity that aroused debate in the 1840's and 50's. Cooper's own remedy, at least for the female victims, was simply obedience to a husband's authority.

V

For William Gilmore Simms it was improper education and not wealth, indolence, or faulty laws that contributed primarily to moral perverseness. But education was not to be intellectual alone: "It is not at the university," Simms wrote, "that the affections and the moral faculties are to be tutored." The old conception of an enlightened mind disciplining unruly passions was useless if morality could be achieved only by a careful cultivation of the passions themselves.

Simms's first novel, *Martin Faber* (1833), was a study in criminology and psychopathy. Like the Wielands, the Fabers had emigrated from Germany, but Nicholas Faber had become a leading citizen of a town. Because he was weak and ineffectual and spent most of his time away from his family, Nicholas was in large part responsible for his son's delinquency. Petted and spoiled by his mother, young Martin became a rude and insolent boy who delighted in defying the local schoolmaster. At thirteen, after ruining the master's globes, he provoked him to physical combat, after which he lied to his father about the master's brutality. Thereupon a group of outraged villagers, led by Nicholas Faber, drove the bewildered

teacher from the town, much to Martin's gloating satisfaction.

As he matured, Martin Faber exhibited more of the
conventional symptoms of the morally insane. His manners improved as he suppressed the crude and brutal traits
of his childhood, but he continued to be completely selfish
and stubborn. Totally lacking in moral standards, he lived
only to assert and elevate his ego. Yet in Simms's interpretation Martin was not happy: "The moral darkness is
the most solid—and what cold is there like that, where,
walled in a dungeon of hates and fears and sleepless hostility, the heart broods in bitterness and solitude, over its
own cankering and malignant purposes."

The real trouble began when Martin seduced fifteen-
year-old Emily and then married a prominent heiress. But
before the marriage Martin was forced to strangle Emily,
who was well advanced in pregnancy, because she had
threatened to reveal her secret to the heiress. After
wedging the body in a cavity between some rocks, Faber
felt loftier and manlier than ever before: "There is something elevating—something attractive to the human brute,
in being a destroyer." He delighted in associating the
word "murder" with his own name, and received great
satisfaction in horrifying his best friend, William Harding, by an account of the event. Even in a supposed confession, however, Martin could not tell the whole truth.
When Harding was finally driven by his conscience to
report to the authorities, the body could not be found.

Inasmuch as public opinion was naturally hostile to a
man who bore false witness, William Harding was placed
in a most embarrassing position. His efforts to find Emily's
body and thus to clear his own reputation and conscience
constitute a primitive American detective story. But
Simms was primarily concerned with the total depravity
of Martin Faber, who, discovering that his wife and Hard-

ing were attracted to each other, expended much effort in stimulating the romance in a perverse attempt to dishonor his bride and friend.

After finally bringing Martin to justice, Harding sympathetically gave the prisoner a dagger to prevent the shame of his dying upon the scaffold. Faber's last act of violence, however, was to stab his wife when she refused to curse Harding as the destroyer of her husband. In the end, lacking courage to commit suicide, Martin Faber died on the gallows.

Richard Henry Dana's "Tom Thornton" (1833) was also a tale about an excitable, impetuous youth who was spoiled by an indulgent mother. Tom echoed the sentiment of many boys in many ages when he thought, "They must have been but simple lads in my father's day." Unfortunately, Tom was not a simple lad, but a self-reliant one, a New England Martin Faber, who led his schoolmates in an assault upon the master. "Yes," he told his mother, "we had the old pedagogue flat on his back; and he could no more turn over than a turtle. And such a sprawling as he made of it!" Whether or not American schoolmasters actually endured such revolts in the early nineteenth century, it is certain that American writers were concerned with the disintegration of adult authority.

Being a New Englander, Tom ran away to sea and received his first baptism of blood on board ship. At home, he was pushed by his best friend into an unwise marriage with a licentious widow. His extravagance and selfishness led to enormous debts, which his wife paid off by sleeping with the friend. Thus was Tom moved toward the inevitable murder.

Simms elaborated upon the identical theme in *Guy Rivers* (1834). This time he was determined to trace the causes of criminality without any deference to the idol of motherhood or to popular prejudice:

Our philosophers are content with declaiming upon effects—
they will not permit themselves or others to trace them up to
their causes. . . . The popular cant would have us forbear
even to look at the history of the criminal. Hang the wretch,
say they, but say nothing about him. Why trace his progress?—
what good can come out of the knowledge of those influences
and tendencies, which have made him a criminal? Let them
answer the question themselves!

Not a born criminal, Guy Rivers actually possessed a
fine intellect which had been adequately trained by formal
education. The mistake, Simms wrote, "a mistake quite
too common to society—consisted in an education limited
entirely to the mind, and entirely neglectful of the *morale*
of the boy. He was taught, like thousands of others; and
the standards set up for his moral government, for his
passions, for his emotions, were all false from the first." [11]
It should be noted that Simms equated moral government
with a cultivation of the passions and emotions, and not
with religious training or with achieving a supremacy of
reason.

Again a doting mother was responsible for the creation
of a murderer. It is not likely that a morally insane criminal would be able to analyze the causes of his own malady,
but for us it is the philosophy of crime and not the realism
that is important. Guy Rivers voiced one of the harshest
indictments of American motherhood to be found in all
of our literature; and because this pertains directly to an
entire theory of moral alienation, it is worth quoting at
some length:

She taught me the love of evil with her milk—she sang it in
lullabies over my cradle—she gave it me in the playthings of
my boyhood. . . . It is not strange; we see it every day—in
almost every family. She did not *tell* me to lie, or to swindle,

[11] William Gilmore Simms, *Guy Rivers: A Tale of Georgia* (New York,
1860), pp. 496–497.

or to stab—no! oh, no! she would have told me that all these
things were bad; but she *taught* me to perform them all. She
roused my *passions,* and not my *principles,* into activity. She
provoked the one, and suppressed the other.

Since the first ten years of a man's life determined his
moral character, it was primarily the effectiveness and uniformity of parental authority that prevented delinquency.
Like Cooper, Simms was worried about wives who acted
independently of husbands:

Did my father reprove my improprieties, she petted me, and
denounced him. She crossed his better purposes, and defeated
all his designs, until, at last, she made my passions too strong
for my government, not less than hers, and left me, knowing
the true, yet the victim of the false. Thus it was that, while my
intellect, in its calmer hours, taught me that virtue is the only
source of true felicity, my ungovernable passions set the otherwise sovereign reason at defiance, and trampled it under foot.
Yes, in that last hour of eternal retribution, if called upon to
denounce or to accuse, I can point but to one as the author
of all—the weakly-fond, misjudging, misguiding woman who
gave me birth! [12]

Although he accepted the traditional dualism between
subversive passions and a sovereign reason which beholds
the truth in calm interludes, Guy Rivers believed that
a man might be capable of knowing right and wrong and
yet lack the power to resist evil. He could recall the specific ways in which his mother had corrupted him:

I have been thinking how I had been cursed in childhood by
one who surely loved me beyond all other things besides, . . .
how sedulously she encouraged and prompted my infant passions, uncontrolled by her authority and reason. . . . How she
stimulated me to artifices, and set me the example of herself, by
frequently deceiving my father, and teaching me to disobey and
deceive him! She told me not to lie; and she lied all day to

[12] *Ibid.,* pp. 453–454.

him, on my account. . . . She taught me the catechism, to say on Sunday, while during the week she schooled me in almost every possible form of ingenuity to violate all its precepts. She bribed me to do my duty, and hence my duty could only be done under the stimulating promise of a reward; and, without the reward, I went counter to duty. She taught me that God was superior to all; . . . yet, as she hourly violated those laws in my behalf, I was taught to regard myself as far superior to him! . . . It is all her work. The greatest enemy my life has ever known has been my mother! [13]

This is quite a different view of motherhood from what one finds in Washington Irving or in Mrs. Lydia Howard Huntley Sigourney.

Guy Rivers had a clear mind, he knew that virtue was the only source of happiness, he had no definite motivation for his villainy, and yet he lacked the will to restrain himself from robbery and murder. In *Richard Hurdis* (1838) Simms wrote, concerning John Hurdis and the killer, Pickett: "A proper education, alone, with due reference to their several deficiencies, could have saved them; and, under strict guidance and just guardianship, they had, doubtlessly, been both good men." In *The Yemassee* (1835) Richard Chorley, a criminal pirate, complained that "whenever a man becomes a bad man—a thief, an outlaw, or a murderer—his neighbors have to thank themselves for three-fourths of the teachings that have made him so."

Most of Simms's criminals were morally insane, in the sense that they gave no evidence of inherent abnormality or of a diseased intellect. As children they had been denied a properly trained moral sense. For Simms, man's basic personality was determined by a nonintellectual energy which seemed to have two tendencies of development. When the passions were nurtured and disciplined by an

[13] *Ibid.*, p. 454.

ideal family environment, they turned outward in sympathy and feeling for other people. On the other hand, an indulgent mother and a weak father could reverse this natural development of morality. As with Guy Rivers, the emotions might be turned inward to inflate the ego. This centripetal emotion produced an overbearing pride, a grasping, devouring urge to possess the world, and an unrestrained and remorseless aggression against everything that prevented a personal conquest. If a mother sanctioned and justified an assault upon the father's authority, the very source of conscience had disintegrated, and the son became a lonely outcast in a hostile world. Intellectual training and even experience could never restore the blasted foundation of morality.

We have seen that American writers of fiction generally recognized the existence of a kind of moral insanity which had been described by psychiatrists but denied by interpreters of law. Because it was an axiom of popular fiction that virtue brought rewards and evil brought destruction, the remorseless killer was inexorably doomed, though this was a metaphysical principle and not a matter of human justice. Since the depraved criminal was free to seize what he desired, free to kill his enemies, and free to compete in an unlawful way, he embodied the suppressed wishes of normal men, and was therefore too dangerous to live. On the other hand, his twisted soul was the product of forces beyond his control, and the ultimate responsibility for his evil rested on society. Law, in the last analysis, was something that was transmitted from parents to children, and unless this continuity was preserved, the sympathetic bonds of society would vanish. In a land which had rejected primary symbols of paternal authority, unity of the individual family assumed a new significance.

PART THREE

The Fundamental Motive

NOW we know everything—except why the murder was actually committed. —Sigmund Freud

Reason is the conscious explanation a man makes for himself or an outsider makes for him before, during, and after a deed. *Motive* is the real driving force which is at least partly unconscious and which can be understood only as part of a continuing and developing process. In the medico-legal discussions and proceedings of this case these two terms were constantly confused.

—Frederic Wertham

Chapter VI

THE MYSTERIOUS POWER

OF SEX

THE strange relation between sexual reproduction and the desire to destroy is certainly one of the oldest subjects in the world's literature. When writers turn to the delicate and beautiful theme of human fertilization, they seem to be irresistibly drawn to the wild, unpredictable emotions of an animal mating season, to the bloody combat for the possession of a quivering female, or to the spiderlike tendency of a wife to eliminate her husband, once his primary function has been fulfilled. This association of sex and aggression is at least as ancient as the *Iliad*, but it received a new emphasis with the spread of the novel and with a widening of interest in romantic love in the second half of the eighteenth century. In America, from primitive tales of seduction and stirring adventure to the dime novel, the imaginative life has been increasingly dominated by the linked images of sex and violent death. For reasons which have never been satisfactorily explained,

147

however, literary descriptions devoted more care and realism to sudden death than to the sexual relation. This curious disproportion between fiction and reality has been so thoroughly accepted that it has seldom been questioned or analyzed.

As a necessary preface to this question of sex and violence, it should be observed that between the mid-eighteenth and mid-twentieth centuries there occurred a sexual revolution with implications as far reaching as any political or religious transformation. Social historians have expressed interest in the movement of female emancipation, but the actual changes in woman's social status and the consequent effects on child-rearing and national character have been only dimly suspected. In this study we can only suggest that the transformation of woman's economic and social position was accompanied by psychological tension, reflected in fiction by the heightened association between sex and death.

If the legal status of English and American women did not change significantly in the seventeenth and eighteenth centuries, it is obvious that their actual role had become less certain by 1800. The increasing agitation for reform and liberation, especially after the French Revolution, is ample evidence of the fact. Social attitudes toward sex and marriage were necessarily influenced by an expanding population, the growth of cities, the use of women in primitive industry, the enlistment of men into large armies, and the emigration of many unattached males to distant colonies or frontiers. With the rapid emergence of the textile industry, it was evident that strong forces were pushing the sexes toward a common role as undifferentiated units of labor.

In America there were special circumstances which delayed the integration of women into the economy but did not thereby reduce the uncertainty associated with social change. The ability of a young man to support a wife and children, together with a general shortage of women, gave the weaker sex a dignity and power they had not possessed in Western culture since the days of Rome.[1] It is a commonplace of history that colonial America was distinguished by early marriages, large families, the absence of dowries, a high degree of feminine choice, a concept of marriage as a civil contract, and a stern attitude toward adultery and mistress-keeping.

Since the scarcity of women undoubtedly both increased their value and enhanced the institution of marriage, Americans were especially susceptible to the kind of romantic love celebrated in sentimental fiction. In America a woman's prestige and power were greatest in those brief, adolescent (or postadolescent) years when she exercised free choice and enjoyed the luxury of comparing and contrasting suitors. The emotional life of a girl's late adolescence was something to be cultivated, treasured, and relived, for it was often her most meaningful experience. Whatever status, whatever happiness she was ultimately to achieve would be determined, according to theory, by the quality of those early emotions.

American attitudes toward sex in the late eighteenth century were also strongly influenced by English moral philosophy with its emphasis on the balance, order, and unity of nature. Although some lawyers continued to talk as if the principal evil of seduction lay in its depreciation of a woman's market value, it was obvious to enlightened minds that women could no longer be regarded as mere livestock, to be fattened and preserved in chastity for a profitable sale in marriage. Francis Hutcheson, who advocated equal property rights for women, thought that sexual indulgence without regard for tender and generous

[1] Arthur W. Calhoun, *A Social History of the American Family from Colonial Times to the Present* (New York, 1917), II, 11–27.

passions would bring about a weakening and disintegration of the mental powers as a result of violating natural law. Nature made mankind "capable of more frequent gratifications than most other animals, as a compensation for the superior toils of educating their offspring. But . . . nature has pointed out the method of gratification which is consistent with all the moral sentiments of the heart." [2] Since adultery was a crime against the harmony of nature, it should therefore be punished with death.[3] Although William Paley held that men "will not undertake the incumbrance, expence [sic,] and restraint of married life, if they can gratify their passions at a cheaper price," he stated that illicit sexual relations depraved the mind and moral character more than any other vice,[4] a belief which also found expression in the more materialistic writings of David Hartley.

It is interesting that the philosophers who equated morality with an innate sense or with the rule of expediency, who stressed the dependence of mind on body, and who supported a more liberal view of women's rights, also identified corruption and sin with sexual transgression. Thus the very thinkers who tended to undermine traditional Christian morality also tried to preserve the ancient doctrine of sexual sin. When such an orthodox theologian as Timothy Dwight discussed the subject of lewdness and adultery, he found himself in the curious position of quoting from William Paley, whose beliefs on other matters he found quite unacceptable.[5] Obviously embarrassed by analyzing a subject which, he said, had been

[2] Francis Hutcheson, *A System of Moral Philosophy, in Three Books* . . . (London, 1755), II, 153–154.

[3] *Ibid.*, p. 176.

[4] William Paley, *The Principles of Moral and Political Philosophy*, 7th ed. (Philadelphia, 1788), pp. 193–194.

[5] Timothy Dwight, *Theology; Explained and Defended in a Series of Sermons* . . . (New Haven, 1836), III, 414–415.

practically banished from religion, Dwight echoed the writings of Benjamin Rush and other semimaterialistic students of human pathology: "To all these must be added the putrefactive influence of impurity itself; which, as the pestilence through the body, diffuses mortification and rottenness throughout the soul; and converts it into a mere mass of death and corruption." [6] We may take Dwight's acceptance of Paley as an authority on sex as a symbol of the increasing tension over woman's changing status. Despite their many differences regarding the source of morality, most philosophers and theologians in the first decades of the new century were united in their effort to preserve traditional sexual standards in the face of a changing society.

As the nineteenth century progressed, Americans grew even more uncertain over the future of marriage, divorce, birth control, and female employment. Radical reformers offered shocking theories, frontier settlements were often distressingly far from minister or magistrate when time was of the essence, growing cities made it difficult to enforce traditional sexual restrictions, ugly rumors emerged from the South concerning the sexual side of slavery, and newly educated or newly prosperous classes attempted to achieve respectability by a purification of language and custom. The quaint New England practices of bundling and of mass confessions of fornication were distinctly out of fashion. [7]

As the fear of sexual corruption increased, certain offenses were omitted from a liberal criminal code for a curious and most interesting reason:

Because, as every crime must be defined, the details of such a definition would inflict a lasting wound on the morals of the

[6] *Ibid.*, p. 416.

[7] Calhoun, *Social History*, II, 151. Bundling lingered in a few remote areas and among the Dutch and Germans in rural Pennsylvania.

people. Your criminal code is no longer to be the study of a select few: it is not the design of the framers that it should be exclusively the study even of our own sex; and it is particularly desirable, that it should become a branch of early education for our youth. The shock which such a chapter must give to their pudicity, the familiarity their minds must acquire with the most disgusting images, would . . . be most injurious in its effects.[8]

If Edward Livingston had "not polluted the pages of the law" by mentioning abnormal sexual crimes, he had no fear that the omission would encourage such outrages in America:

Although it certainly prevailed among most of the ancient nations, and is said to be frequently committed in some of the modern, yet, I think, in all these cases it may be traced to causes and institutions peculiar to the people . . . which cannot operate here; and that the repugnance, disgust, and even horror, which the very idea inspires, will be a sufficient security that it can never become a prevalent one in our country.

Yet Livingston did not consider the details of murder injurious to the minds of youth, nor did he think that the horror and disgust inspired by the idea of murder would be "a sufficient security that it can never become . . . prevalent . . . in our country." The conception of a crime too horrible to deserve either trial or punishment was something new in jurisprudence and was not unrelated to the tension over woman's changing status.

While there is little evidence that the early colonists were especially troubled by questions of marriage and sex, these had become deadly serious issues by the 1840's and 50's. From a fairly uniform acceptance of early marriage and large families, American sexual experience had moved in a variety of conflicting directions. Tradi-

[8] Edward Livingston, A System of Penal Law, for the State of Louisiana . . . (Philadelphia, 1833), p. 17.

tionalists complained about the increasing number of
working women, the celibacy of Shakers and Catholic
clergy, the mounting number of prostitutes, the alleged
immorality of convents, the mistresses of the rich, the
spread of birth-control information, the high number of
divorces in western states, the rumors of free-love communities, and the polygamy of the Mormons. Social and
political issues were dramatized in sexual terms. According to *De Bow's Review* in the South and to Mormon
critics in the West, each defending their own "peculiar
institutions," moral decline in the North had reached a
point unrivaled by Rome in its days of greatest de-
bauchery.[9] In 1859 a writer in *The New Englander* declared that Anglo-Saxon superiority rested in the race's
"hiding power" of chastity and in that deeply felt "reverence for woman" which had enabled Saxons and barbarians to conquer England and Rome. America's position
as a leader of the superior race was now seriously threatened by six thousand New York prostitutes, by Washington society where "the reputation of a harlot scarcely
impairs the standing of a wife and a mother," and by the
fact that adultery was not punished as a state offense. When
the public morals were not protected by law, "we are not
surprised when the popular sentiment sustains the wronged
husband in taking summary vengeance on the guilty, who
have embittered his home and disgraced his innocent
babes. The wife, who violates her vow . . . merits severe
punishment." [10]

Literature reflected this tension and this self-consciousness, provided an outlet for both social and personal conflicts, and attempted to reassure the discontented. Order
and balance could be maintained by a sentimental alle-

[9] Calhoun, *Social History*, II, 157; Orson Pratt, *Masterful Discourses*,
comp. by N. B. Lundwall (Salt Lake, n.d.), p. 52.
[10] "Unchastity," *New Englander*, XVII (May 1859), 471–488.

giance to motherhood, by a deification of respectable woman, and by an unrestrained assault on seduction, lechery, prostitution, and adultery. No longer was sex to be a subject for literary humor or casual reference; there was nothing amusing about it.

Two tendencies, which were not entirely separate, may be discerned in the literary treatment of sex from the early 1820's. On the one hand, there was a persistence of such eighteenth-century ideals as chaste maidenhood and the romantic selection of husbands. In Daniel Jackson's popular version of *Alonzo and Melissa* (1811), terror and death were associated with an unfeeling father's thwarting the course of romantic love. After 1830 the feminine ideal included an increasingly sexless motherhood which curiously resembled Catholic doctrine. Thus George Lippard described the young wife of a wicked and licentious Protestant minister as the image of "holy chastity." With a babe at her breast, this blissful mother was the goddess of beauty and purity except to the kind of man who degraded the "holiest impulse of our nature, into a bestial appetite," the miserable wretch whose "heart is foul with pollution at the very mention of woman." [11]

The other development was both stranger and more complex. A popular fascination for science, particularly medicine, coincided with the concern for purifying love. Newspapers in the 1830's and 40's were full of advertisements for remedies, "revealed truths," and pamphlets on personal medical problems. Common people were becoming conscious of some mysterious relationship among the animal passions, physical organs, and specifically human powers. The new physiology pointed to certain disturbing similarities between men and animals, yet civilization seemed to demand that these likenesses be minimized. It

[11] George Lippard, *New York: Its Upper Ten and Lower Million* (Cincinnati, 1853), p. 136.

was altogether possible, men reasoned, that the chief distinction between human intelligence and animal crudity lay in man's control over his sexual impulse, just as the Anglo-Saxon's superiority might be attributed to his liberation from the tyranny of sex. Ancient religious conceptions of chastity as a purification of a corrupt and evil body acquired a new validity from science. Doctors proved that sexual expression drained human energy from loftier and nobler pursuits. Along with the increasing circulation of pseudomedical literature, there were such innovations as the "bachelors' guides," which urged self-discipline and threatened young men with insanity and death if they submitted to licentious habits. Even Benjamin Rush advised young men that they might remain chaste "by never looking directly in the face of a woman," and recommended cold baths, supplemented by vegetable and salt-free diets to reduce the sexual impulse.[12]

It is doubtful, of course, that licentiousness constituted a greater problem in America in 1830 than it had in 1730. But there is reasonable evidence that in the early nineteenth century ministers, doctors, and writers of fiction were increasingly troubled by sexual immorality. The spread of political and social democracy reminded conservative gentlemen of the ominous predictions by European arisocrats: popular government would lead inevitably to anarchy and thus to unrestrained sexual indulgence. In the eyes of most Americans who had heard of the lascivious courts of Europe, this was obviously aristocratic prejudice. On the other hand, a nation which lacked rigid social controls and a central ecclesiastical authority had to prove that liberty was not an excuse for profligacy. The excessive prudishness of Americans was partly a manifestation of this self-mistrust. In fiction, the identifi-

---

[12] Benjamin Rush, *Medical Inquiries and Observations upon the Diseases of the Mind* (Philadelphia, 1812), pp. 352–354.

cation of sex and death was the psychological result of
the tension between fear and freedom.

II

From the sentimental tale of the 1790's to the yellow-
backed novel of the 1850's there was a constant and monot-
onous repetition of the theme that seduction meant
homicide. In 1794 Mrs. Susanna Haswell Rowson presented
America with a simple expression of this idea, and Americans thereafter showed their gratitude by reprinting the
book at least seventy-seven times before 1848. Such success
naturally encouraged other gentle souls to imagine the
possibilities leading up to, and resulting from, seduction.
In the category of consequences, in spite of Parson
Weems's maxim that "the greater her depravity and
misery, the greater be your pity and '*labour of love*' for her
recovery," there was only death, almost always in childbirth, and destitution, or the life of a street-walker, which
was considered living death.

The "wages of sin" theory was not new, of course, but
there was something new in the shrill insistence that sexual
error, violence, and murder were parts of one inexorable
process. A girl had the choice of blissful, sublimated love
and holy motherhood or disgraceful and painful death.
A man could be a vigorous, alert, altruistic gentleman or
a depraved, disintegrating lecher. If one were to judge by
fiction, an alarming proportion of both sexes made the
wrong choice.

So obsessed were American writers with the importance
of rape and seduction that by 1823 these were discovered
to have been the real causes of the American Revolution.
According to John Neal, who was of course eccentric about
many things, it was only when rape became an issue that
the Revolution really got under way: "Men of America!
—will ye ever forget it? . . . These things, at last, drove

us mad. We arose, as one people—a nation, about to offer up its enemies in sacrifice." [13]

Twenty-four years earlier, Charles Brockden Brown's ideal heroine in *Ormond* was willing either to commit suicide or to sacrifice her persecutor for the preservation of female honor; but an uncertainty of sexual values was expressed in the rational arguments of the villain in the same book. Ormond did not appeal to animal magnetism, since he possessed the power of reason:

How shall I describe it? Is it loss of fame? No. The deed will be unwitnessed. . . . Thy reputation will be spotless. . . . All that know thee will be lavish of their eulogies as ever, their eulogies will be as justly merited. . . . It is neither drudgery, nor sickness, nor privation of friends.

Having already killed two men during his courtship, Ormond now proposed that Constantia surrender to him beside the corpse of his latest victim. Without an appeal to reason, she declined and threatened to stab herself. This was to insult Ormond's logic:

So! thou preferrest thy imaginary honor to life! To escape this injury without a name or substance, without connection with the past or future, without contamination of thy purity . . . thou wilt kill thyself. . . . Die with the guilt of suicide and the brand of cowardice upon thy memory. . . . Thy decision is of moment to thyself, but of none to me. Living or dead, the prize that I have in view shall be mine.

Constantia solved her problem by the simple expedient of killing Ormond and thus saved her feminine purity. In this incident, however, there are several suggestions which have great importance for a study of sex and homicide. The dominant theme is an association between death and sexual intercourse: the villain's sexual desire had been the direct motivation for murder; the heroine proposed to

[13] [John Neal], *Seventy-Six* [anon.] (Baltimore, 1823), I, 66–67.

kill herself to escape possession; the sexual act itself would have been a symbolic death, beside the body of a murdered man; and this implication was reinforced by Ormond's rather surprising suggestion of necrophilia. (This same linking of death with illicit sex was very strong in Matthew Gregory Lewis' *The Monk,* which was published four years before *Ormond,* but the combination was more common to the nineteenth than to the eighteenth century.) A clear reflection of the Enlightenment is perhaps to be seen in the villain's logical reasoning. There were few nineteenth-century seducers who, like Brown's villain in *Wieland,* would attempt to persuade a girl by saying, "Even if I execute my purpose, what injury is done? Your prejudices will call it by that name, but it merits it not." Even for the purpose of dramatic effect, such talk was increasingly dangerous.

That any death was infinitely preferable to the loss of chastity was one of the most frequent literary clichés. When a family missed their beloved daughter, they might worry slightly about murder, but they could not even face the possibility of a lost virginity: "It was terror enough for them to know that their child was gone; but that she was dishonored! Better than to tell them this would it have been to pour molten lead on their quivering eyeballs!" [14] Better that twenty bullets pierce a girl's heart than for her to lose her chastity in an unholy union.[15] Even when a friend's life was at stake, virginity was triumphant: "Although the life of my friend is dearer to me than my own, I will never consent to save it by a dishonored allegiance with the son of a pirate!" [16]

[14] George Lippard, *The Quaker City; or, The Monks of Monk-Hall* (Philadelphia, 1845), p. 355.

[15] Robert Montgomery Bird, *Nick of the Woods; or, The Jibbenainosay, A Tale of Kentucky* . . . , ed. by Cecil B. Williams (New York, 1939), p. 260.

[16] Benjamin Barker, *Blackbeard; or, The Pirate of the Roanoke: A Tale of the Atlantic* (Boston, 1847), p. 48.

By the 1840's the question of seduction had become infused with social consciousness. In the preface to the twenty-seventh American edition of *The Quaker City* (1844), George Lippard pompously defended the sexual rights of the lower classes:

The seduction of a poor and innocent girl, is a deed altogether as criminal as deliberate murder. It is worse than the murder of the body, for it is the assassination of the soul. If the murderer deserves death by the gallows, then the assassin of chastity and maidenhood is worthy of death by the hands of any man, and in any place.[17]

Unlike the Brown villain of the late 1790's, a rich young seducer of the 1840's did not rely upon rational argument. Since he wanted to arouse the primitive and savage nature of a woman, he talked excitedly of shimmering lakes, green valleys, and untouched forests. Even the most innocent maid was unable to depend on principle and enlightened education when the talk was charged with images of sublime nature: "Her bosom rose no longer quick and gaspingly, but in long pulsations, that urged the full globes in all their virgin beauty, softly and slowly into view. Like billows, they rose above the folds of the night robe, while the flush grew warmer on her cheek." Mary Arlington was not a Constantia Dudley who could coldly assert her feminine independence and kill the dastard threatening her honor, yet death was more closely associated with the delicate, submissive girl of the 1840's!

Despite her passion and her throbbing bosom, Mary resisted the evil and aristocratic Gus Lorrimer not for herself but for the purity of their love. The incident was symbolic of the diverging conceptions of romantic and sexual love. Sex was described as murder, as a brutal struggle, as rape in the dark. It was something that even a licentious brother must avenge with a triumphant and

[17] Lippard, *Quaker City;* this preface is between pp. 206–207.

joyous killing. But though Mary had been dishonored against her will, she was irretrievably ruined:

The crime had not only stained her person with dishonor, but, like the sickening warmth of the hot-house, it had forced the flower of her soul, into sudden and unnatural maturity. It was the maturity of precocious experience. In her inmost soul, she felt that she was a dishonored thing, whose very touch was pollution.[18]

Outside the mysterious and ambiguous relation in marriage, sex brought a rotting, a decomposition of human virtue and dignity. If a girl had natural warmth and passion, even a single sexual experience made her capable of any crime.[19] A combination of "fat, greasy churchmen" and an unjust wage system might be responsible for prostitution, but once a girl's soul had been "murdered," she had no chance for recovery. Regardless of her age or experience, a lost woman was marked with a "bold, brazen expression" which could never be assumed by the virtuous nor lost by the damned.[20] If man's nonintellectual nature was the source of his semidivinity, the feelings and passions had to be preserved from contamination by animal sexuality. There was no room for a partial or temporary corruption; only death could atone for a ruin so total and absolute.[21]

The frontier presented special opportunities for seduction, since there an isolated population was often careless in the confidence they granted to strange men, and frontier girls might be dangerously discontent or unenlight-

---

[18] *Ibid.*, p. 124.

[19] [George Thompson], *Dashington; or, The Mysteries of a Private Mad-House* by Greenhorn [pseud.] (New York, n.d.), p. 21.

[20] [Edward Zane Carroll Judson], *The G'hals of New York: A Novel,* by Ned Buntline [pseud.] (New York, n.d.), p. 148.

[21] Edgar Allan Poe, "Politian," *The Works of Edgar Allan Poe,* ed. by Edmund Clarence Stedman and George Edward Woodberry (Chicago, 1894), X, 56.

ened. But according to William Gilmore Simms, the men were "exquisitely alive to the nicest consciousness of woman" and were quick to avenge seduction with extreme fury.[22]

It was in New York City, however, that the theme of seduction and homicide received its fullest elaboration, especially after 1840. In the great metropolis the Madam Sitstills and Madam Resimers engaged in a lucrative "trade of *murder*," in the "vilest crime known in the annals of Hell," where science and vice combined in "a traffic which, in its incredible infamy, has no name in language." [23] Nothing excited the indignation of popular novelists so much as the "dens of abortion," of which there were countless tales describing the "three-fold murder" of a deluded girl's chastity, her body, and her unborn child. The villain was usually a wealthy, aristocratic youth whose success was insured by the moral blindness of indifferent and impersonal neighbors.

III

On Saturday night, April 9, 1836, a young prostitute named Dorcas Doyen, known in New York as Helen Jewett, was murdered with an axe at Rosina Townsend's "Palace of the Passions." The criminal had attempted to prevent detection by setting fire to the luxurious bed, but the body of Miss Jewett, in her *dishabille,* was but slightly burned. On Monday, James Gordon Bennett reported the case in his New York *Herald* as "one of the most foul and premeditated murders, that ever fell to our lot to

[22] William Gilmore Simms, *Charlemont; or, The Pride of the Village: A Tale of Kentucky* (New York, 1856), pp. 9–10.

[23] [Edward Zane Carroll Judson], *The Mysteries and Miseries of New York: A Story of Real Life,* by Ned Buntline [pseud.] (New York, 1848), p. 100; Lippard, *New York,* pp. 123–124. The abortion theme also received a sensational treatment in such pamphlets as *Wonderful Trial of Caroline Lohman, Alias Restell, with Speeches of Counsel, Charge of Court, and Verdict of Jury* (New York, 1847).

record." [24] During the next few weeks Helen Jewett and her alleged nineteen-year-old slayer, Richard P. Robinson, were principal subjects of conversation on the sidewalks and wharves, in family circles, taverns, and barbershops. The recently established *Herald* launched a new era in journalism by increasing its circulation threefold in little more than a week.[25] Like Edgar Poe, Mr. Bennett had a curious attachment to dead, beautiful women:

The body looked as white, as full, as polished as the purest Parian marble. The perfect figure, the exquisite limbs, the fine face, the full arms, the beautiful bust, all surpassed, in every respect, the Venus de Medici, according to the cast generally given her. . . . For a few moments I was lost in admiration of the extraordinary sight, a beautiful female corpse, that surpassed the finest statue of antiquity. I was recalled to her horrid destiny by seeing the dreadful bloody gashes on the right temple.[26]

The editor examined Miss Jewett's "elegant" room and discovered there a small library of poetry, novels, and monthly periodicals: "There hung on the wall a beautiful print of Lord Byron as the presiding genius of the place. The books were Byron, Scott, Bulwer's works and the Knickerbocker." What could be more exhilarating for the romantic imagination than a literate prostitute whose figure surpassed the Venus de Medici! Mr. Bennett continued knowingly: "She has seduced by her beauty and blandishments more young men than any known in the police records." The demand for "human interest" increased as the editor studied Miss Jewett's personal correspondence: "Not a fulsome expression nor an unchaste

[24] Quoted in H. R. Howard, *The Lives of Helen Jewett and Richard P. Robinson, by the Editor of the New York National Police Gazette . . .* (New York, n.d.), p. 121.

[25] Willard Grosvenor Bleyer, *Main Currents in the History of American Journalism* (Boston, 1927), pp. 181–183.

[26] Howard, *Helen Jewett*, p. 122.

word is from her in any of these letters. They contain apt quotations from the Italian, French and English poets. . . . Her hand writing is uncommonly beautiful."

She was, in short, a creature of refined sensibilities, an ideal of feminine attraction, who mysteriously combined the attributes of a genteel woman with the undisguised sexuality of a prostitute. She was fascinating and, at the same time, upsetting. Harlots were supposed to be depraved, diseased streetwalkers, not accomplished goddesses of Parian marble who read the *Knickerbocker*, lived in luxurious suites, and wrote with elegance and learning. But if Helen Jewett challenged certain American assumptions about refinement, she also reinforced the association between sex and death. On the surface, here was simply a demonstration that sexual sin resulted in horrible murder. Psychologically, however, the case furnished a symbolism clearly expressed in the morbid writing of James Gordon Bennett. Like many other Americans of his time, Mr. Bennett used the image of statuesque nudity to evoke erotic interest. From Vanderlyn's "Ariadne" to Hiram Powers' "Greek Slave," classical nudity was curiously identified with daring sexuality. But, as Mr. Bennett observed, there was a disturbing similarity between a cold, sculptured ideal of Venus and a cold, naked corpse, helpless and frozen before the gaze of men.

The symbolism of sex and death was enhanced by the burning bed in which Helen was discovered. She represented, for the more sensational-minded, a sleeping princess of sin, rescued at the last moment from the retribution of a ravaging, masculine fire. Even when the poor girl's body had been buried there was an inevitable and final association between death and illicit sexuality. Americans of the mid-twentieth century pride themselves on their worldly attitude toward sexual perversion, but it is doubtful if even the earthiest of moderns could help wincing at the strange nineteenth-century obsession with corpses.[27] After Helen Jewett had been buried, there was great excitement over the rumor that resurrectionists had found her grave and had taken the body to doctors for dissection: "The sensitive shuddered, and the hardened laughed at the relation, and in mixed circles, the shudder mingled with the obscene jest." [28] Thus the tension over death and forbidden sexuality was resolved into the typically adolescent rebellion of obscene humor. The psychological formula for such an attitude might read as follows: Helen Jewett's sexuality is attractive but taboo, therefore she must die; but in death she is even more appealing and even more forbidden, therefore she must be subjected to the supreme indignity.

It was not enough, however, to dismiss the sensational case with an obscene jest. For men who believed in inevitable moral progress, it was necessary to explain why a pretty, cultivated girl of twenty-two should have chosen the path of sin; why a hard-working, nineteen-year-old clerk with a good family and a promising job should have frequented houses of ill fame. The Jewett case was an American tragedy of the younger generation which demanded interpretation.

H. R. Howard, the editor of the New York *National Police Gazette,* wrote in 1848 what was probably the most careful study of Helen Jewett. According to Howard's account, Helen had been a spirited and intelligent girl whose passions were precociously aroused by romantic literature. Had she benefited from gentle paternal guidance, she might have married happily, but tyranny and social

[27] See especially, Bernard DeVoto, *Mark Twain's America* (Boston, 1932), pp. 152–153. DeVoto referred to American humor, especially in the West, as "a violent humor, appropriate to violent life. . . . Death in picturesque, horrible, or exaggerated forms was a source of laughter, Bodies of the lynched, the murdered, and the grotesquely killed are stock devices."

[28] Howard, *Helen Jewett,* p. 124.

injustice forced her into sin and prostitution. Her young lover and murderer, who had been reared in the "quiet routine of country life," was a victim of "the intoxicating pleasures and dazzling temptations of this great Babel of enjoyment." The problem, then, bore a striking resemblance to the issues involved in moral insanity, although Howard emphasized social and institutional evil more than faulty childhood training. Intelligence and education could not protect the moral sense from corruption, nor could good intentions bring redemption when society condemned an erring girl to hopeless slavery. After studying the facts of the Jewett case, a reformer might conclude that prostitutes and teen-age murderers were helpless victims of injustice, but American writers of fiction were not yet prepared to accept the values of *Sister Carrie* and *An American Tragedy*.

Seven years after the murder, the indefatigable Joseph Holt Ingraham, who wrote seventy "novels" between 1840 and 1849, unlimbered his machinelike pen for the inevitable subject of Helen Jewett. *Frank Rivers; or, The Dangers of the Town* (1843) is not a good novel, but it is interesting as a fictional "explication" of a well-known murder. In the Ingraham version, everything was simplified by the devices of contrast and accident. The principal contrast was between masculine nature, always capable of both sexual error and repentance, and feminine nature, which was either pure or totally depraved. Related to this traditional division was the strong contrast of the virtues of the country with the "dangers of the town." The other primary difference from Howard's version was that the seduction, the murder, and the trial, all involved accident.

Hart Granger, a senior at a "time-honored University" on a beautiful New England river, was an ideal American boy. He was rich, popular with his fellow students, respected by the faculty, and had never been in love. Ellen, an orphan girl with a tyrant aunt, informed him that no good could result from their friendship, since her station was below his; but such frankness and self-distrust only aroused Hart's passion. Ellen might be a sweet, innocent girl, but "Professor" Ingraham argued that only careful education and the correct example of a mother could protect society. It was Ellen's sin to be unloved and unguided.

Against her protests, Hart succeeded in persuading Ellen to climb into his boat for a ride on the river. When the boat tipped over, he valiantly rescued the girl, taking her half-unconscious body to his college rooms. The weaknesses of these innocent teen-agers had brought them to the brink of sex and death, but the accident of the boat pushed them to their fall.

After losing her virginity, Ellen became an entirely different person. In New York City, where Hart for a time provided elegant rooms, expensive clothes, and jewelry, she resolved to achieve power and rank at any cost: "How seldom is the first error in woman followed by penitence and cessation from guilt. . . . With reckless facility she plunges deeper and deeper into error, till vice is personified in her."

Frank Rivers was another ideal American youth from New England, working as a confidential clerk in a New York mercantile house. Just before he sailed for Madeira, and after she had been abandoned by Hart Granger, Ellen skillfully seduced the young clerk. Thinking her a pure and virtuous girl, Rivers was overwhelmed by his guilt, offering marriage to retrieve her from ruin. Even the lost Ellen could not think of so deliberate a falsehood, however, and she confessed in a letter that she had been a sinful woman. "Thank—thank God!" Rivers breathed, "I am at least free from the guilt of the seducer. . . . I have now only to bleed for my own fall." He resolved not to see her again and wrote a letter urging her to be pure.

But Ellen was now free for a life of unrestrained indulgence: "She looked to the sacrifice of her person, with a sort of proud satisfaction, as if thereby she should avenge herself upon Granger. . . . She felt a kind of joyous despair, at the contemplation of the scenes of guilt into which she was about to plunge." After an affair with a naval captain, Ellen took the plunge by visiting the third tier of the theater on the night of Fanny Kemble's benefit, the third tier being informally reserved for the purchase of feminine charms: "Her beauty was her power, and she triumphed in it. She felt a sort of revenge against the other sex, and used every art to seduce and ruin young men. . . . To tempt and to ruin became with her a system, and hundreds were slain by her."

Meanwhile, Hart Granger, a candidate for orders at Trinity Church, was about to marry beautiful Adaline Langdon, daughter of the governor. Upon discovering such news, Ellen wrote to Hart, threatening to reveal his past as well as his paternity of a child unless he broke off the engagement. Hart, now thoroughly reformed, was shattered by this information: "Adaline's happiness must not be wrecked. . . . She must not know my shame and guilt. It would kill her; and better this base woman perish."

But banishing the thought of murder, Hart proceeded to Madam Berryton's, in the hope of persuading Ellen to remain silent. In the meantime, Frank Rivers had returned from Madeira and, unable to resist the charms of his seducer, had been living with Ellen at Madam Berryton's. He had just departed for the theater, leaving behind his cloak and a hatchet, which he carried to ward off the watchman's dog. When Hart Granger was unsuccessful in persuading Ellen to suppress the disturbing past, he grabbed up the hatchet in a fury and struck her. He was horrified, yet relieved, when he found he had killed her: "Be it hers to answer for it, not mine! She brought it upon herself by

her obstinacy. Now for escape, and afterwards a life of
remorse and horror for this dark deed of a moment!"
Frank Rivers was then unjustly arrested and tried for the
murder; though acquitted, his existence had been ruined
by Ellen. Hart Granger fled to Europe, where he presumably led a life of remorse.

Compared with the facts of the Jewett case, the Ingraham story becomes a jumble of confused values. The central contradiction, implicit in any defense of the double
standard, arises from the belief that men are both freer
and less guilty than women. Men conform to a traditional
morality which holds that faculties are separate and distinct and that the capacity for virtue is unaffected by
accidents of experience. If Hart Granger and Frank Rivers
were susceptible to seduction and to outbursts of passion,
they also underwent the strain of inner conflict which
finally resulted in remorse and repentance. A man may
sin, so the theory goes, but he never loses his basic moral
nature. Precisely the same assumption may be found in
the jurisprudence based on Locke and Blackstone, and,
as we have seen, it was this conception of a universal moral
capacity which was challenged by the theory of moral
insanity.

The fictional study of Helen Jewett thus brings us back
to the distinction between two systems of ethics, but in
this case the division is made along sexual lines. A woman,
Ingraham argued, was like a machine, which could either
be steered and directed by parents in the direction of holy
virtue or be allowed to run free and unattended in the
broken fields of chance. The delicate moral machinery
of woman was easily warped and sprung beyond repair, so
that total destruction was the only possibility. But this
was to say that moral capacity was determined by external
circumstances which were, in themselves, amoral. We
have previously seen that Simms's villain, Guy Rivers,
once he was corrupted by his mother, waged ruthless war

on society. In a similar fashion, Ingraham's Ellen, once seduced, became a Sensual Woman who lived only to ruin virtuous men and subvert the social order. Like the victim of moral insanity, the dishonored woman experienced no inner conflict and therefore lacked the capacity for remorse and redemption.

In tracing changing conceptions of human nature, we saw that Locke's "capacity for suspending desire" became a "moral sense" for the Scottish philosophers and that this "sense" was increasingly identified with physical passion and emotion, which might be nurtured or corrupted by social forces. We have suggested that there was a close association between this romantic moral sense and libidinal energy, whose discipline depended upon parental guidance. Because popular novels tend to simplify moral issues and to provide arbitrary conclusions, this association became complete with the stereotype fallen woman. By assigning different moral natures to men and women, popular novelists were able to accept the traditional belief in freedom and responsibility, while, at the same time, they recognized a woman's moral dependence on her environment. But if external forces shaped woman's moral capacity, this was because she possessed an undivided nature, no part of which lay beyond the influence of early experience. The essence of this nature was, of course, sexuality; and since all evil was ultimately the result of sexual corruption, which was synonymous with corruption of the moral sense, it was inevitable that Sensual Woman should die. Whereas rational man was guilty because he failed to suspend desire according to his inner law, a fallen woman, like the morally insane, embodied positive evil and was thus condemned as one alienated by metaphysical necessity. In other words, men were under a rational covenant with society, their guilt and punishment being determined by the degree of their willful moral alienation. Men might choose but could not actively generate evil: Hart Granger was dangerous only as a bad example to other men. But woman, being inherently more subversive, was either within or totally outside society. She had no other choice: the feminine alien was a breeder of contagious evil.

The fictional version of Helen Jewett's history ignored both the gradations in her fall and the social responsibility for prostitution. By having the original seducer commit the murder and by stressing the fortuitous nature of both the seduction and killing, Ingraham absolved the males from genuine guilt, identifying aggression and death with feminine sexuality only. Nothing could so clearly reflect an anxiety concerning the changing and ambiguous position of woman in the early nineteenth century.

IV

Motives for actual homicide are numerous and complex, but prior to the occasional flashes of realism in Mark Twain, it was a rare fictional killing that did not involve sexual conflict. Some of the exceptions to this rule will be discussed in later chapters, but it is interesting to note that two of the most vivid nonsexual murders in American literature—the killing of old Boggs in *Huckleberry Finn* and of Claggart in *Billy Budd*—did not appear until well after the Civil War.

Most American writers before 1860 (and, indeed, before the 1880's), were not primarily concerned with a spectator's factual report of an interesting event; rather, they attempted to condense reality by constructing artificial plots. Like dreams, nonrealistic fiction relied more on emotional association than on logical causality. To increase this emotional involvement, writers often exaggerated the familial relationship of characters, so that stepbrothers fought for the hands of cousins, good brothers uncovered the villainy of the bad brothers' fathers, and

good sons rescued hidden mothers and cleared the reputation of murdered good fathers. Moral values were simplified and clarified in this literature by a disproportional
emphasis on family ties and sexual attraction. Thus, in an
1840 version of Mark Twain's Sherburn-Boggs murder,
one might expect to find that Boggs was actually Colonel
Sherburn's half-brother and heir to the Sherburn estate,
that the dastardly Colonel had seduced Boggs's daughter,
an act which led to Boggs's drunkenness and insults. This
gave Sherburn the opportunity to kill the rightful heir
and to win the daughter as his mistress.[29]

It must be remembered that the line separating women
from property was still not distinct in the first half of the
nineteenth century. A woman might be a very special kind
of property, but she was still essentially a possession. As a
scarce and desirable commodity, the beautiful heroine
was therefore often a symbol of wealth and status. Nothing
was so common in popular fiction as the hero who struggled simultaneously for his father's estate and for the
heroine's hand. Sexual conflict could symbolize all conflict
between human egos, every contest between men for possession and power.

In this respect American literature of the early nineteenth century merely continued an ancient tradition of
Western culture. But in the Victorian era a heightened
sensitivity to sexual morality gave different connotations
to actual possession, especially to illicit possession. Increasingly, the complete mastery of a woman was associated with guilt and death, an association not unrelated to
a changing attitude toward the human body.

For such ancient ascetics as St. Bernard and St. Odo of
Cluny, the love of a woman's body was inconceivable,
since it was composed of blood, mucus, and bile: "Man is

[29] If this seems far-fetched, one has only to read Theodore S. Fay's *The
Countess*, 3 vols. (London, 1840).

nothing else than fetid sperm, a sack of dung, the food of worms." [30] By the nineteenth century such contempt for man's animality was no longer confined to the writings of philosophers and religious ascetics. A protest against the indecency of the human body became a major theme of popular literature in England and America.[31]

Science and the new power of industry seemed to give man, especially American man, an opportunity to rise above his former status, and to progress toward godhood. But if science provided the means for escaping the limitations of animal nature, it also furnished concepts and a vocabulary with which man might describe his degenerate and ephemeral body. Many writers expressed their disgust for the human body in an often-repeated image of a corpse in water. Only in the science-obsessed nineteenth century could a *poet* write:

The result of decomposition is the generation of gas, distending the cellular tissues and all the cavities, and giving the *puffed* appearance which is so horrible. . . . But, apart from decomposition, there may be, and very usually is, a generation of gas within the stomach, from the acetous fermentation of vegetable matter . . . sufficient to induce a distention which will bring the body to the surface. The effect produced by the firing of a cannon is that of simple vibration. This may either loosen the corpse from the soft mud or ooze . . . or it may overcome the tenacity of some putrescent portions of the cellular tissues; allowing the cavities to distend under the influence of the gas.[32]

---

[30] Quoted in Havelock Ellis, *Studies in the Psychology of Sex* (Philadelphia, 1924), VI, 119.

[31] *Ibid.*, p. 99. This aversion to the naked body apparently increased in the eighteenth century, reaching its height in the late nineteenth century, when Western peoples were outraged by the comparative nudity of savages. There is much evidence that sexual modesty was of considerably less concern in Europe before 1700. See *ibid.*, I, 1–48.

[32] Poe, *Works*, III, 125–126.

It should be added that this rather appalling comment
from Edgar Allan Poe's detective, M. Dupin, pertained to
a beautiful girl who had supposedly been seduced and
killed.

In *The Blithedale Romance* (1852) Nathaniel Hawthorne was less physiological but no less vivid in his description of the once dazzling Zenobia, whose sin was
mysterious but definitely sexual: "Her wet garments
swathed limbs of terrific inflexibility. She was the marble
image of a death-agony. Her arms had grown rigid in the
act of struggling, and were bent before her with clenched
hands. . . . Ah, that rigidity! It is impossible to bear the
terror of it." Originally Zenobia had been described as a
symbol of warm-blooded, feminine sexuality, a frank and
passionate woman whose form excited the mind of even a
finicky and fastidious bachelor: "Something in her manner, irresistibly brought up a picture of that fine, perfectly developed figure, in Eve's earliest garment." But
like Helen Jewett, Zenobia's naked sexuality had to be
reduced to the rigidity of Parian marble, if not to the
distension of "the cellular tissues and all the cavities."
The tense fascination which usually accompanied such
descriptions finally collapsed in grotesque humor; on the
American frontier the image of a beautiful Zenobia was
transformed into an ungainly Clementine, with "ruby lips
above the water, blowing bubbles clear and fine."

In the earlier tales of seduction the equation between
sexual transgression and death had been a simple causal
relation. The association became more complex, however,
when writers identified sex with the cold nakedness of
marble, or with physical decomposition. Instead of a
causal relationship, sexual sin *meant* death, and, to a certain extent, killing *meant* sexual possession.

There had been hints of this complete identification
in some of the early gothic romances, as when Matthew

Gregory Lewis' saintly abbott, Ambrosio, raped a girl in a tomb. We have also seen that Charles Brockden Brown suggested the combination of sex and death in *Ormond* (1799), but the transition is best seen, perhaps, in a surprising story by Washington Irving, which followed *Ormond* by twenty-five years.

"The Story of the Young Robber" in *Tales of a Traveler* comes as a decided shock after Irving's sirupy and conventional tales of weeping maidens and marital bliss. In this narrative, after murdering the prospective groom of sixteen-year-old Rosetta, a jealous Italian boy escaped from justice by joining a gang of bandits. The bandit leader, however, captured Rosetta. Because of his former attachment, the young lover pleaded that the girl be spared, but the gang encircled him and cocked their carbines. Horrified, he watched the captain rape Rosetta and then abandon her to the repeated rapings of the troop.

"I perceived," said the young Italian, "that the captain was but following with strictness the terrible laws to which we had sworn fidelity." When the bandit leader sent a note to Rosetta's father, demanding ransom, that kindly gentleman answered that a dishonored girl was not worth a ransom. According to the laws of the troop, this meant inevitable death. "I felt," the young lover said, "that, not having been able to have her to myself, I could become her executioner!" He explained to his comrades that he could do the act more "tenderly" than anyone else.

Rosetta, in a stupor from the numerous rapings, did not know who guided her to a thicket. She slept in her rejected lover's arms. "There was a forlorn kind of triumph," he thought, "at having at length become her exclusive possessor." Significantly, he plunged a poniard into her bosom. In this startling tale, the only "good" character was thus raped by a gang and murdered, although nothing happened to the gang or to the murderer.

The young Italian bandit learned not only that sexual desire can motivate a murder, as in the case of the rival groom, but also discovered that sexual possession and murder could be identical. Desire could only be realized by tenderly inserting a poniard into the breast of an unconscious girl.

It has often been observed that the feminine ideal was curiously ethereal from the time of Scott and Irving to that of Hawthorne and Tennyson. The perfect woman was a wispy dove-girl, a formless, buoyant spirit, whose delicate life was sustained by a pure and sexless love, a being incapable of either the drudgery of household chores or of the degrading, unfeminine work of a factory girl. Such an ideal might soothe masculine anxiety over the status of woman in a changing economy, but it had the disadvantage of being far removed from the reality of sexual desire, marriage, and procreation. Since sexual possession stood for the dissipation of ethereal womanhood, the unhappy male was faced with a choice between ascetic love and a spiritless, dying body. In a curious paradox, then, the strictly sexual ideal was often transformed into an image of a dead naked woman.

Regardless of how far one wishes to analyze Poe's symbolism, his imagery of death often bears an obvious sexual connotation which does not require the extremes of Freudian theory for understanding. The tombs, chimneys, crypts, pits, and the damp "interior recess" between "two colossal supports" which envelop his hapless characters may or may not be definite sexual symbols, but that Poe identified sexual love with death and decomposition cannot be doubted. If sexual contamination did not result in total death, mesmerism provided a useful substitute in the concept of a hypnotic trance, which well symbolized a spiritual and moral death. In a state of hynotism or catalepsy a woman was without will and might be more desirable, but the line between mere physical existence and decay was very fragile; without consciousness and moral power, a man's body could crumble and rot away to "a nearly liquid mass of loathsome—of detestable putridity." [33]

Poe's friend, George Lippard, was more direct in his combination of catalepsy, sin, and sexual desire. In one of his novels a character named Marion Merlin had been forced into an unholy marriage by her father. But the beautiful, sensitive, and well educated girl planned to commit suicide before submitting to her middle-aged and sensuous husband. He drugged her, however, and her sexual fall, like that of the fictional Helen Jewett, occurred when she was incapable of resistance. Once her moral sense had been destroyed, she pushed the villain husband into Niagara Falls. Thereafter she seduced many men, including a young minister, and when Marion encouraged a friend to rape the minister's fiancée, the now fallen divine cursed and struck his former mistress. Thinking she was dead, a "celebrated" doctor took her to his garret for an orgy of dissection, which gave Lippard his chance for the favorite, breath-taking description of a completely naked and beautiful woman, with ivory limbs and marble breasts. But since Marion was only in a state of catalepsy, she was finally able to seduce and ruin the "celebrated" doctor.[34] Only death itself could destroy the latent power of sex to corrupt man's passions.

---

[33] *Ibid.*, 334. Although it is dangerous to give a sexual interpretation to all of Poe's tales or to attempt to prove certain symbolic relationships by a reference to the sketchy facts of Poe's life, it seems fairly clear that the lovers' suicides in "The Assignation" and the death of Roderick and Madeline Usher are symbols of simultaneous sexual union and decomposition.

[34] Lippard, *New York*, pp. 212–228.

V

We have seen that in American fiction, at least, the total moral alien was thought to deserve swift and certain death. Completely lacking in benevolent impulses, in an emotional sense of right and wrong, and thus in sympathetic identification with his fellow men, this victim of moral insanity was an embodiment of the evil principle. But such a concept of total depravity implied a conflict in American values, since, according to the liberal tradition, a man was guilty only when he consciously chose evil. By definition, the total moral alien was a man without the capacity for good actions and was hence incapable of moral choice.

It might be argued, of course, that a totally depraved heart was the result of willful disobedience to universal moral law. The total moral alien was the final product of a *process* of moral alienation which began with a conscious rejection of sympathy and responsibility. Yet such an explanation left unanswered the ancient question concerning the origin of corruption.

If morality depended on the control of passion by reason, physical and moral alienation were clearly distinguishable, since man was held responsible as long as his reason suffered no impairment. But when philosophers transferred the locus of responsibility from reason to the senses, they made possible a theory of moral alienation which in fiction was based on the fascinating yet corrupting power of sex. Right action was the result of emotions refined and purified by the various senses, which were themselves disciplined or distorted by experience. Sexual stimulation perverted the senses and aroused the passions so that the mind, in spite of its rational knowledge of consequences, could not prevent an undermining of the moral faculty. Hence in ultimate terms there was no difference between physical and moral alienation. Writers of fiction affirmed this point by the theme of the evil woman whose original fall had been involuntary. But because all men were subject to sexual contamination against which reason was no defense, evil had to be destroyed by the irrational and absolute rule of moral survival.

Chapter VII

JEALOUSY AND

THE IMMORAL WIFE

FROM the 1790's to the twentieth century, European travelers expressed astonishment at the scrupulous fidelity of American wives. They were often puzzled by a seeming paradox: whereas American daughters were permitted greater freedom than were European girls, wives accepted more restrictions. Public opinion, as well as the courts of law, regarded even a casual extramarital adventure as a serious and heinous offense. American society, exclaimed one bewildered Frenchman, *"c'est le paradis des maris!"* [1]

[1] Francis J. Grund, *The Americans in Their Moral, Social, and Political Relations* (London, 1837), I, 35–45; Moreau de Saint-Méry, *Voyage aux Etats-Unis de l'Amérique, 1793–1798,* ed. by Steward L. Mims (New Haven, 1913), pp. 304–311. Since adultery was not punishable at common law, American statutes were ultimately based on ecclesiastical law, which, unlike Roman statutes, severely punished offenders regardless of sex (Francis Wharton, *A Treatise on the Criminal Law of the United States* [Philadelphia, 1874], II, 821–822). Such states as Missouri and Alabama punished adultery only by fines, reserving more brutal penalties for crimes against property. In New Hampshire, however, as late as 1805 an adulterer

According to Alexis de Tocqueville, democracy loosened traditional social ties, but at the same time strengthened the natural bond between man and woman. If the absence of a settled population and social hierarchy meant that various members of a community were farther apart, the same mobility and economic pressure brought the husband and wife closer together.[2] In modern terms, the individual was unconditionally attached to the smallest ingroup and was more concerned with the preservation of its moral values, while much of the neighboring community acquired the status of an out-group. The more meaningful human relations, such as sexual love, became intensified as they were restricted in area.

De Tocqueville argued that social democracy destroyed the conditions which might justify illegitimate love in an aristocracy, since a man was theoretically free to choose a girl from any class for his wife, and women enjoyed the liberty of entering a marriage which was a freely chosen civil covenant. Like a voluntary political covenant, a democratic marriage might be subject to theories of secession, but while the union endured there was a heightened sense of obligation.

Should an American wife desire an occasional diversion, the lack of an artistocracy meant a comparative lack of idle, roving men. During the working day, the two sexes were effectively separated by the universality of labor, after which time wives were expected to enjoy the com-

---

might be fined one thousand pounds, receive thirty-nine lashes on the bare back, be set upon a gallows with a rope around his or her neck for one hour, and be confined in prison for one year (*The Revised Statutes of the State of Missouri* . . . [St. Louis, 1835], p. 306; *A Digest of the Laws of the State of Alabama* . . . comp. by John G. Aikin [Philadelphia, 1833], p. 108; *Constitution and Laws of the State of New Hampshire* . . . [Dover, N.H., 1805], p. 279).

[2] Alexis de Tocqueville, *De la démocratie en Amérique* (Paris, 1868), III, 310–319.

pany of their own husbands. De Tocqueville found that public opinion successfully enforced strict values concerning marital obligation; hence the freest people in the world submitted willingly to the most rigorous and restrictive sexual code.[3]

If the heroine in American fiction proclaimed that she would accept death before dishonor, it was a natural corollary for the hero to justify murder as the punishment for dishonor. For most crimes it was sufficient to permit the execution of justice by civil authorities. The social compact meant that each individual surrendered his primitive right of retribution to the governmental power, thus acknowledging that he belonged to a state and that the entire nation constituted an in-group. But the American family, as De Tocqueville observed, transcended all other social relations and obligations. If the so-called unwritten law had an ancient history, stemming from prenational clans, tribes, and totem groups, it persisted in America as a concomitant to the democratic family.

The right to defend one's person, property, or habitation was, according to Locke, founded in the law of nature and could not be superseded by the law of society. Thus English jurists ruled that a woman may kill in the defense of her chastity, thereby preventing the felony of rape; yet adultery, which was only a trespass, could not justify homicide on the part of an injured husband, though it reduced the crime from murder to manslaughter.[4] American courts in the first half of the nineteenth century generally ac-

[3] *Ibid.*, pp. 345–347. He also noted that the punishment of most sexual offenses was far stricter than in France. Rape, for instance, received only light and uncertain punishment in France, but Americans, who considered nothing "de plus précieux que l'honneur de la femme," usually punished rapists with death.

[4] Foster's C.L. 274, 299; 1 Hale's P.C. 445, 486, 489; 1 Hawkins ch. 28, s. 23. Quoted in Nathan Dane, *A General Abridgment and Digest of American Law with Occasional Notes and Comments* (Boston, 1834), VII, 224–228, VI, 649.

cepted the English precedent that when a husband kills
an adulterer, a distinction between murder and manslaughter depends on "whether the killing was in the first
transport of passion or not." [5] When accompanied by
sufficient provocation, such as adultery, "hot blood" was
supposed to reduce the magnitude of guilt. A man who
delayed his vengeance was deemed to have entered a "cooling period" enabling him to resist his murderous impulses; but if a husband witnessed his wife's dishonor and
killed the seducer in a heat of passion, he was "entitled to
the lowest degree of punishment, for the provocation is
grievous," and in one case the court directed that the
burning off of an avenging husband's hand (the traditional
punishment for manslaughter before the 1820's) be "gently
inflicted, because there could not be a greater provocation." [6]

Some states, such as Missouri, ruled that homicide was
excusable when committed "in the heat of passion, upon
any sudden and sufficient provocation, or upon sudden
combat without any undue advantage being taken." [7] And
in practice, courts tended to expand the period when a
"heat of passion" justified homicide, so that Edwin M.
Stanton was able to tell the jury in the Sickles case (1859):
"What, then, is the act of adultery? It cannot be limited
to a fleeting moment of time. That would be a mockery;
for then the adulterer would ever escape." [8] Even when
injured husbands were convicted of manslaughter, however, there were many governors like I. Basset of Mary-

[5] Francis Wharton, *A Treatise on the Law of Homicide in the United
States: To Which is Appended a Series of Leading Cases*, 2nd ed. (Philadelphia, 1875), pp. 322–326.

[6] *Ibid.*, p. 322; Wharton, *Criminal Law*, II, 45.

[7] *Revised Statutes*, p. 168.

[8] Quoted in John Graham, *Summing Up of John Graham, Esq., to the
Jury, on the Part of the Defence, on the Trial of Daniel MacFarland* . . .
(New York, 1870), p. 47.

land, who was quoted as saying, "*Matrimony, gentlemen, matrimony is everything. . . . So all important . . . is the purity of the marriage bed, that I shall, probably, never refuse a pardon to the man who kills the villain that violates it.*" [9]

There were certain psychological factors in the American attitude toward adultery which De Tocqueville failed to analyze. Although he noted that economic vicissitudes threw a husband and wife closer together, he ignored the connections between economic opportunity, a heightened conception of the self, and a fear of sexual dispossession. It is proverbial that American men were ambitious, especially in the decades of expansion after the War of 1812. It is also a commonplace that Americans were extremely individualistic and self-conscious. As William James later said, the self may include a man's possessions, talents, social prestige, ideals, and ambitions. American social and economic conditions increased this widened sense of the self, a sense of private expansion and of escape from the early limitations of childhood. Obviously, a wife was an essential part of a man's self, especially when few opportunities existed for other intimate social relationships. Nothing could be so shattering to an expansive ego as the discovery of an intruding rival self in the unsuspected and sheltered heart of a man's proudest possession. Though American courts were haunted by the authority of English precedent, they were forced by public opinion to consider adultery as something more than a simple trespass.

Even in popular literature, there was scarcely a trace of the European tradition of humorous cuckoldry. The pompous, ridiculous husband, whose buxom wife made him a village joke, was not considered to be funny by American writers. If a husband set out to kill his wife's

[9] Quoted in Mason L. Weems, *God's Revenge against Adultery, Awfully Exemplified in the Following Cases* . . . 2nd ed. (Philadelphia, 1816), p. 20.

lover, it was not a humorous affair of clumsy chases and hidings under the bed. Readers grimly expected that infidelity would lead inevitably to the death of one or both offenders.[10]

II

Mason Locke Weems, who considered the passion of sex as a God-given instinct, "so fascinating as to require all the aids of religion to preserve it within its proper limits," traced the inflexible dialectic of sin, adultery, and murder. He concluded that when the wife of a tavern keeper had been "shamefully neglected as to her mind," when a spirited and handsome gentleman "was infected with that most shameful and uneasy of all diseases, an incurable lust or itching after strange women," and when religious and moral scruples disintegrated before the perverse logic of Thomas Paine, the combination could only lead to misery and to death.[11] In Weem's interpretation, which was typical of the late eighteenth and early nineteenth centuries, corruption arose from the acceptance of false ideas; a rejection of revealed religion brought a "contempt of all sacred obligations," providing passion with an opportunity to unseat reason; sexual transgression provoked retaliation, but since the order of nature had been shattered, even an avenging husband was doomed to

[10] It is interesting to note the persistence of social opinion and the change of individual values in twentieth-century literature. This conflict over the seriousness of adultery is perhaps best expressed in a story by Barry Benefield called "Blocker Locke" (1926), in which Blocker, an Arkansas tombstone cutter, is undisturbed when his wife runs off with a boarder. He enjoys his new freedom and the opportunity to play with the children. Public opinion, however, rises against him. When a Negro kills a wife and lover, Blocker is stung by the remark: "Even a damned nigger these days can show some white men how to protect their honor." He is finally forced to go to Little Rock, where his wife had moved, to avenge his unoffended honor. He kills the wrong couple, however, because his wife had moved again (*Short Turns* [New York, 1926]).

[11] Weems, *Adultery*, pp. 4–8.

a brooding loneliness and death. Sin, in other words, ignited a chain reaction of violence and disintegration. God's revenge against adultery was a built-in mechanism in the great design of nature.

A generation after Weems's analysis, a novel was published which discussed adultery and jealousy in terms of a gradual, developmental process. Disturbed by many of the tendencies in American society which De Tocqueville had perceptively described, William Gilmore Simms reflected a different intellectual world from that of Parson Weems. Simms felt that a murder, instead of resulting from an acceptance of false ideas or a rejection of religion, might be precipitated by an individual's isolation from the guidance of traditional institutions, by a weakness of paternal authority, and by an exaggerated emotional dependence on marriage.

Edward Clifford, in Simms's *Confession* (1841), had been orphaned at an early age and could only barely remember "the caresses of a fond mother." His uncle and aunt were called very good people because they attended the most popular church, paid their debts, and helped send missionaries to Calcutta and Bombay. But the uncle was the kind of man who demanded the latest news from the Liverpool cotton market when he returned from church. He sent his own son to the best academy, whereas Edward attended the charity school. The boy grew up, consequently, feeling unloved, insecure, and burdensome.

Simms always placed great emphasis on family environment and social education. Unlike Guy Rivers, who had been morally warped by an indulgent mother, Edward Clifford was an example of the boy who has been ignored and unindulged. He was brooding, lonesome, and uncertain: "I had no society—knew nothing of society—saw it at a distance, under suspicious circumstances, and was myself an object of suspicion."

If Guy Rivers had been incapable of genuine love, Edward was inclined toward an excessive love and friendship for the few individuals who showed any interest in him. William Edgerton saved him from bullies in school; William's father later helped him to become a lawyer; and Julia Clifford, the daughter of his unfeeling aunt and uncle, loved Edward as a boy and finally married him.

Even as a husband and lawyer, however, Edward Clifford was isolated and unhappy: "My feelings were too devoted, too concentrative, too all-absorbing, to leave me happy, even when they seemed gratified." As a man who had never loved before, Edward's attachment to his wife resembled De Tocqueville's description of the American husband: "My love—linked with impatient mind, imperious blood, impetuous enthusiasm, and suspicious fear— was a devotion exacting as the grave, . . . as jealous of the thing whose worship it demands as God is said to be of ours."

Edward was delighted when William Edgerton, who was poor lawyer but an able artist and musician, discovered that Julia had talent at sketching and proposed to give her lessons. Although he encouraged the hobby by converting a room into a studio and by buying the necessary materials, Edward's self-confidence had been fragile since boyhood, and he found, to his surprise, that Julia's praise of her new instructor was disturbingly unpleasant.

Finding that he had become slightly isolated from his wife, Edward feared that she would think him jealous if he mentioned his discontent. At first he merely brooded over the affair, taking long walks into the country whenever the strain became unbearable. As Edgerton increased the number of his visits, however, Edward lost self-control and began to spy on the couple. This brought a deep sense of guilt, since he had always trusted his friend, to say nothing of his beloved wife: "The shame I already felt; but, though sickening beneath it, the passion which drove me into the commission of so slavish an act, was still superior to all others."

When there seemed to be evidence that Edgerton was actually falling in love with Julia, Edward gave them every opportunity to be alone. Meanwhile, Julia was growing uncomfortable and vainly pleaded with her husband to spend more time at home. This stage of spying and miserable doubting ended when Edward read a letter from his aunt, Julia's mother, urging her to enjoy the privileges of a European wife. As soon as he surmised that his wife's infidelity was common gossip, reaching even the ears of her mother, Edward decided that his rival must die. But it was only when his sensitive ego had been wounded by the remarks of his hated aunt that he moved from obsessive thought to compulsive action.

One evening Edward found his former friend playing a flute outside Julia's window. Although he had a pistol and was about to shoot, the action was frozen by an image from the past. As a boy Edward had once seen his worst bully lying unprotected in the grass beneath a great oak. He found two bricks and slowly crept into position, until he was able to throw with deadly aim. He saw the brick flying in the air, the blood spurting from the boy's head, and the boy's bewildered rise and collapse. Though seriously injured, the bully did not die, yet the agony and horror of the scene, recurring in Edward's imagination, now kept him from killing Edgerton.

Somewhat later, after Edward had intercepted another letter from the aunt, informing Julia that "so far you've played your cards nicely," he felt compelled to leave the couple alone, so that he might spy on their activities. They were playing a quiet game of chess when Edgerton leaned across the board, grabbing Julia's hand; she blushed, whereupon the villain pushed the table aside, grasped her waist, and dragged her to his knee. The scene was too much for Edward's excited emotions. He fainted and saw no more.

When Julia failed to report the insult, there seemed to be no question of her unfaithfulness. Edward now felt a calm tenderness toward her, because he knew that she was soon to die. First, however, he took a friend and the unsuspecting William Edgerton to the woods for a duel. But Edgerton, when suddenly presented with a pistol, refused to fight. Edward Clifford was furious:

You must not refuse me the only atonement you can make. . . . You have violated the rites of hospitality, the laws of honor and manhood. . . . These offences would amply justify me in taking your life without scruple, and without exposing my own. . . . But my soul revolts at this. I remember the past —our boyhood together—and the parental kindness of your venerated parent. . . . If life is nothing to you, it is as little to me now.

Edgerton admitted his guilt, proclaimed his readiness to die, but still refused to fight. Edward was about to shoot him unopposed when his friend knocked the pistol away, declining to witness a murder. Finally, Edgerton agreed to a duel on the condition that he be given time to write to his father.

At home, impatient at the delay in his vengeance, Edward waited anxiously for Julia to confess her sin; but when she did not, as the time for the duel approached, he poured poison in her cup of tea: "I never did anything more firmly. Yet I was not the less miserable, because I was firm. My nerve was that of the executioner who carries out a just judgment."

Arriving at Edgerton's lodging house, Edward discovered that his enemy had hanged himself to save his former friend from committing murder. In a long letter Edgerton confessed that he had loved Julia but had struggled against unholy desires: "the indulgence of fond parents had gratified all my wishes, and taught me to expect their gratification. I could not subdue my passions even when they were unaccompanied by any hopes." He added that he had been encouraged by Edward's neglect of his wife but that all advances had been repulsed; thinking that he noticed signs of coldness between the married couple, he had tried to embrace Julia at a chess game, but she had been outraged by his conduct.

Since Edward had already killed his wife, he tried to convince himself that Edgerton's confession was merely an attempt to cover Julia's guilt. At his law office, however, he found a letter Julia had hoped he would read before any crisis arose. He was horrified to discover that has wife had actually hated Edgerton and had been insulted by her mother's letters: "for your sake I have borne much; for the sake of peace, and to avoid strife and crime, I have been silent—perhaps too long." After doctors attributed Julia's death to apoplexy, a friend convinced Edward that he should not surrender himself to justice. Only by living, Simms concluded, could he atone for his crime. If, according to the rule of the law, Edward lacked sufficient provocation for homicide, his motives, at least, were acceptable to a large segment of American society.

It is significant that Simms did not subject his hero to formal justice. Edward Clifford was legally guilty of murder, yet he had acted neither from maliciousness nor from hasty passion. Again and again Simms emphasized Clifford's severe conscience, his inner conflict, and his hesitation. But if Edward's motives were approved by many Americans, Simms indicated that his crime was more than one of simple error. Here we may note a resemblance between the case of Edward Clifford and that of a monomaniac like Wieland, who also killed for worthy motives.

In literature, motives were seldom isolated from the rest of a personality. Unfounded suspicions, like hallucinations, were not merely accidental.

The importance of Simms's tale lies in its portrait of an American marriage and of a jealousy which originated in essentially American conditions. The actions of both Clifford and Edgerton were determined by an interplay of chance and childhood training. The precise nature and time of a murder might be subject to accident, as were the specific impressions which seemed to confirm Edward's suspicion of his wife's infidelity. But the basic motivation, the inclination toward jealousy and self-torture, was a part of Edward's total personality. His development as a child had turned his emotions inward so that, incapable of genuine love and friendship, he remained an outcast from family and society. Yet he was not a moral alien, for he accepted the standards of marriage, virtue, and friendship, and it was this conflict that led to the self-punishment of suspicion. Simms made it clear that this inclination toward jealousy was further stimulated by the isolated nature of American marriage and by social values which stressed the danger of adultery and condoned the avenging husband. In one sense, *Confession* is a moralistic tale exhorting husbands to have more faith in their wives, but it is also an attack on a society which throws men into emotional isolation.

III

Our interpretation of Simms's *Confession* was presented within a sociological framework, in the sense that attitudes toward jealousy and violence in fiction were related to the nature of American marriage and to American values concerning adultery. But the fictional treatment of jealousy and the immoral wife cannot be explained by sociology alone. If novelists sometimes expressed interest in such problems as the changing status of women, they discussed these problems at the imaginative level, combining in a language of symbols both conscious and unconscious attitudes. In Chapter Six we considered the symbolic association between sex and death, a half-conscious relationship which appealed to imaginative poets and writers in many ages. To understand the full implications of murder inspired by jealousy, we must return to this symbolic connection between dying and sexual fulfillment. Consequently, we may move from a sociological to a psychological mode of analysis.

The plot of Richard Henry Dana's "Paul Felton" bears a striking resemblance to Simms's *Confession,* but it also contains overtones requiring a different critical approach for clear understanding.[12] At present, the status of Freudian theory in literary criticism is by no means clear, since the dubious products of reckless Freudian enthusiasts have quite naturally raised serious questions concerning the validity of any psychological study of art. On the other hand, some literary works are better suited for psychological analysis than others. In "Paul Felton," Dana assumed or implied a psychology similar to Freudianism in several important respects. It must be stressed, however, that we are not trying to prove that writers in the early nineteenth century anticipated modern theories. Rather, we wish to use modern concepts as tools for the clarification and interpretation of symbolic language.

Specifically, the romantic psychology, as expressed in most of Dana's tales, had six basic assumptions which parallel some of the principles of Freudian theory: first, the passion of love, including the sexual desire and a need

[12] "Paul Felton" appeared in Dana's *The Idle Man* in the 1820's and was published in book form in *Poems and Prose Writings*, 2 vols. (Philadelphia, 1833) (Evert A. Duyckinck and George L. Duyckinck, *Cyclopaedia of American Literature* . . . (New York, 1856), II, 90). Simms's *Confession* was published in 1841.

for affection and approval, was man's supreme motivation; second, a mother's love was an essential factor in shaping and determining a personality; third, although a man's ideas could be changed in later life, his emotions and actual psychic behavior were determined in childhood; fourth, an individual's perceptions and impressions of reality were subjective and, in effect, only a reflection of his particular psyche; fifth, both the moral sense and imagination were related to the basic passion of love; sixth, repression or perversion of the love impulse could obliterate the effects of moral training and result in open aggression and death.

It is obvious that the conservative elder Dana did not think of love in Freud's sexual terms, yet for him romantic love was never entirely disassociated from sex. If the game of symbol-hunting can lead to futile extremes, there are also occasions when sexual symbols clarify important beliefs concerning human nature and violence, beliefs which are implicit in the six assumptions just enumerated. In this discussion we shall therefore confine our purpose to the discovery of imaginative associations between sex and aggression, avoiding any impulse to dwell on symbols for their own sake.

Unlike Simms's Edward Clifford, Paul Felton was not an orphan. His mother had died, however, leaving Paul and his sister with an isolated and grief-stricken father. In a household darkened by persistent silence and the melancholy of death, Paul became reserved and pensive: "His character was of a strong cast; and not being left to its free play among equals, it worked with a force increased by its pent-up and secret action."

Less quick tempered than Edward Clifford, Paul was also more philosophical, brooding, and romantic. His father, who had no use for the "modern system" of educating an encyclopedic mind, encouraged Paul to read slowly and deeply in the great books. An antirationalist who scorned the pretensions of science, Paul considered the universe as an immense and exciting mystery: "Material became intellectual beauty with him; he was as a part of the great universe, and all he looked upon, or thought on, was in some way connected with his own mind and heart." In other words, Paul's perceptions were partly a reflection of his own psyche, which endowed impressions from the material world with beauty and mystery.

Paul Felton was isolated from society like Simms's character, but for different reasons. The Federalist Dana could sympathize with Paul's distaste for the crude and uncouth townsfolk, "who had, for the most part, that rough and bold bearing which comes from a union of ignorance and independence." Yet isolation brought self-doubt and self-torture. Overly conscious of his awkward appearance and morbid character, Paul longed for love and understanding, for someone's recognition of his depth of soul, and for moral reassurance. Like his father, he yearned in silence for the lost mother.

In such circumstances, it was only natural that Paul should fall in love with Esther Waring, the daughter of his father's friend, who had come to visit his own sister. During a highly emotional courtship, Paul experienced undulating states of mania and despair; and his brooding unhappiness did not disappear with marriage. In an extreme depression, he even doubted if his bride genuinely loved him: "She found that her kindness touched me and made me happy, and this stirred an innocent pride within her, and she mistook it all for love. And, fool! fool! so did I."

Esther had once had a suitor named Frank Ridgley, who now returned from abroad. She had grown up with Frank and had always liked him, but she had never felt a trace of deeper affection. Frank, who had easily recovered from Esther's rejection, was a gay, cheerful young man, whose handsomeness and amiability made Paul Felton feel insecure and inferior. With no knowledge of his wife's past, Paul began to suspect that she had once loved another man, perhaps more deeply than himself.

As Frank Ridgley's visits became more frequent and as Paul's suspicions of his wife's past increased, a new character appeared who clarified the origins of his jealousy. Abel, a wild boy who lived in the woods, was persecuted by the superstitious villages. They accused him of selling his soul to the devil. On one of his brooding walks Paul discovered the half-crazed Abel, pitied him, and fed him; and thereafter the boy became the constant companion of the jealous husband. Since Dana had already indicated that Paul's perceptions were often projected images of his own heart, there can be little doubt that Abel was intended as a symbol. Like Paul, Abel was isolated from society, yet the mature husband, if vaguely envying the villagers' happiness, took refuge in his conviction of superiority. Abel, on the other hand, had not voluntarily rejected his neighbors.

Abel's story is especially significant in Freudian terms. Once he and a group of other boys were walking through the fields in search of crows' eggs. None of the boys had ever dared to enter the dark woods beyond the fields, but Abel saw the crows flying toward a particular tree. When he went in pursuit, his superstitious companions, horrified by his boldness, did not follow. After climbing to the crows' nest, where he gathered some eggs, Abel was discovered by the devil, who was referred to as "He." Attempting to flee with the eggs, Abel finally collapsed to the ground, where the other boys found him later with broken eggs in his hand: "See his hands; they are stained all over!" Abel accepted the boys' belief that the crow was an agent of Satan. By entering the forbidden woods, by stealing the eggs, and by polluting his hands, Abel felt he had enslaved himself to the devil, and despite his remorse, he was forever isolated from human society.

Now the search for crows' eggs was clearly a symbol for a boy's seeking the mystery of reproduction. All of the other boys were interested, even fascinated, but only Abel dared to violate the taboo of the forest. The outraged father in the form of a devil, the stained hands, the physical collapse, and the overpowering guilt, suggest that Abel had discovered the secret of both sexual orgasm and of parental intercourse. He was mysteriously enslaved by a power (sex) which he identified with the devil, yet he was so terrified and guilt-ridden that he could not think of entering the devil's forbidden hut. It is significant that when Paul listened to the pathetic story of Abel's submission to the devil's power and subsequent isolation from society he felt both sympathy and personal guilt. Paul's strange feelings tended to identify Abel with his own boyhood.

Although his wife was reluctant, Paul persuaded her to attend a gay ball in the village without him. Later, feeling lonely and distraught, he arrived at the hall, blinded and confused by the flare of lamps, the whirl of skirts, and the babel of sounds. Weak and sick at the sight of Esther springing and laughing in a dance with Frank, Paul overheard a group of men raving about his wife's beauty. They described her marriage as "a sort of Vulcan and Venus match," observing that she probably regretted not marrying her former suitor. One man, adding that Frank had been stupid to believe her refusal, since everyone had known her to be a coquette, concluded that she had married "Vulcan" only to annoy the amorous Frank Ridgley.

As Paul moved toward the dancing couple, he heard people around his wife joking about himself. Then Esther saw him and shrieked. When the crowd rushed up to her, she said, "I know not. . . . 'T'was a—a spider!—some horrid creature on me!"

"Ugly things!" Paul whispered to her, as he half supported her body, "that lie hid in corners, with meshes spread for silly flies. Beware, for they draw the blood, and leave their prey hanging for the common eye."

According to Abel, the devil lived in a little hut by the woods. Though he was haunted and persecuted by the devil, Abel had never dared enter the cabin. Half-crazed by the affair in the ballroom, Paul Felton next wandered across the fields and, scorning Abel's dire warnings, entered the hut. Once inside, he noticed that the ceiling was broken, so that when the rain began, it fell in a regular rhythm on the tattered roof and on the floor. As Paul suffered a mounting agony in the cabin, reliving the ballroom scene, he felt the ground rock and pitch, while the small room darkened, the floor shook intensely, and the walls began to enlarge. He was seized by a fainting convulsion, and his hand "swept down the side of the hut where it struck against the handle of a rusty knife that had been left sticking loosely between the logs." "When he began to come to himself a little," Dana wrote, "he was still sitting on the ground, his back against the wall. His senses were confused. He thought he saw his wife near him and a bloody knife by his side." As Paul's mind cleared, the image of his wife disappeared, but the real knife remained.

Like Edward Clifford, Paul spied on his wife during Frank's visits, with the hope of catching her in a compromising position. Increasingly, however, he spent his time in the hut, scraping rust from the knife and sending Abel to the house as a spy: "Paul sat, as he had done each day before, in the same spot, passing the knife slowly over the stone, then stopping and feeling it, and looking it over. . . . When Abel came up, he did not, as usual, conceal the knife. Abel knew it instantly, though now bright and sharpened. All his horrors rushed upon him; his knees knocked against each other, his hands struck against his thighs. . . . 'The knife! the knife! hide it! hide it!' "

Abel erroneously reported that Esther's father, who had come to soothe and comfort his abandoned daughter, had left the Felton home. Consequently, when Paul looked through the window and saw his wife embracing another man, he supposed it to be Frank Ridgely. Later, after creeping into Esther's bedroom, he stood for a long time, watching her sleep. He finally placed the knife's point on her heart, and with one hand against his eyes, he sank the blade between her ribs. In the morning, they found him senseless at her side. When awakened, he looked upon his wife's murdered body and died himself. Abel was found dead on Paul's grave.

As we have noted, the plot of this melodramatic story resembles Simms's *Confession*. A lonely, brooding husband, inclined toward jealousy by his childhood environment, tries to end his previous isolation by an unconditional devotion to a woman. A chain of accidental circumstances push him through the fires of jealousy and suspicion, until he murders his once-beloved wife. Simms's story, more detailed and plausible, relied on social factors and accident. Hence Simms's protagonist was less involved in guilt and did not have to die.

If Abel's original experience symbolized a boy's discovery of his parents' sexual relation and of his own sexual nature, then Paul Felton's aggression was primarily a revolt against this knowledge. Yet he could not escape: "Perhaps there are no minds, of the highest intellectual order, that have not known moments when they would have fled from thoughts and sensations which they felt to be like visitants from hell." Because Paul could not flee, his "natural superstition" persuaded him that his passions "were good or evil spirits which had power to bless or curse him."

In his marriage with Esther, Paul had hoped to recover the original, sexless love of a mother's adoration. He could not, however, forget his discovery that his mother had been contaminated and that he himself had the masculine power to contaminate. The recurring image of Abel was a reminder of both the first horrifying knowledge of sex (the symbol of eggs and the stain on the hands) and of the guilt which this knowledge brought to the memory of his own tender love for his mother. The sexual aspect of marriage meant that he could never again experience the pure and unquestioned love from a mother, especially when his wife was attractive to other men. Frank Ridgely's harmless and innocent friendship raised the haunting thought of the possession of his mother by his father. Perhaps, he thought, Esther, too, had once been possessed. In the emotional crisis at the ball, he re-experienced the crushing discovery that a mother might divide her affection in different ways, that a woman's love is not, as a child assumes, unconditional.

Unlike Abel, the image of his frightened and guilt-ridden boyhood, Paul was not afraid of the father-devil. As a man, he was capable of facing directly the facts of sex, of entering the forbidden hut, where the symbols clearly expressed the sexual relation. Abel, who could not enter the hut because he was a boy, was terrified and shocked by Paul's open display of the knife, which has traditionally signified male potency. Abel had not yet recovered from the stigma of stained hands.

But if Paul was able to enter the cabin and discover the knife, he could not thereby remove the guilt and sense of fatality which accompanied his decision. Once he had found the knife, an act which represented his surrendering all hope of recovering a stainless and idyllic love, Paul felt that his wife's death was inevitable. Like the devil-father, he could enter the broken, rain-defiled hut, he could pull the knife from the wall and scrape it clean, he could even imagine the figure of his wife beside him after the convulsive agony, but his wife, in the image, must be dead.

As in so much of the popular literature, sex might be supremely realized only in the moment of death. In murdering his wife, Paul Felton expressed the conviction that a total possession, such as a child's illusory possession of his mother's affections, could, in reality, be achieved only in death. He was killing not only his wife and himself, but his mother, woman, and sex, in a frantic attempt to prevent the alienation of the most intimate and total love.

Dana probably intended his symbolism to have religious significance, which would provide a different, but by no means unrelated interpretation. Like many of Dana's contemporaries, Paul Felton was a religious enthusiast, who attacked the "idols" of reason and "Idea." God, he argued, was an infusing, passionate spirit, not an abstract principle or a universal intelligence. Thus the story might be explained as a dramatization of religious enthusiasm, of the problem of how enthusiasm might be controlled, without sacrificing vital religion. The strictly religious discussions, however, seem to have been added as an afterthought. Related to the question of enthusiasm, and more integral to the story, is the problem of how to control sexual desire without sacrificing love.

If Paul Felton was more like a creation of Emily Brontë than like a typical American husband, this should not conceal the fact that Dana's theme developed the implications of what De Tocqueville observed concerning the

American family. Paul Felton was doomed by the very factors which De Tocqueville described: social isolation and emotional dependence on a wife. In a fluid society, lacking the security of fixed status and reciprocal obligations, a husband and wife were thrown closer together, and love became the most private and exclusive part of life. Sex therefore acquired a heightened seriousness, which was reflected in the American attitude toward adultery.

According to the principles of rationalistic law, "hot blood" weakened the power of calm reason and thus mitigated the guilt of homicide. In the eyes of many Americans, it was only natural that an injured husband's blood should remain hot until revenge was complete. But here we meet with a contradiction which is related to our previous discussions of alienation and responsibility. The legal theory of hot blood followed by a cooling period was based on an assumption that the moral faculty was rational and that hot blood was a kind of partial physical alienation, stimulated by external causes. When a man discovered that his wife had been dishonored, his calm reason was temporarily overpowered by animal passions. Since he was then unable to suspend desire, he was not a responsible agent. If, however, the moral faculty was identified with a man's fundamental inclination, expressed by senses and passions, it was irrelevant to talk of hot blood as preventing calm judgment. When morality was the product of purified emotion, when virtue was independent of intellect, it was clear that an act committed in passion must reflect either a good or an evil heart.

The moral-sense philosophy thus raised a question which traditional jurisprudence had successfully ignored. It was not sufficient to dismiss the case of a husband who killed his wife's lover on the ground that passion had overpowered reason. Legally, this might be the only defense, but there was a strong tendency in America to excuse the vengeful husband as an agent of triumphant virtue. If matrimony was indeed "everything," as Governor Basset said, then Americans were justified in pardoning a husband whose outraged moral sense drove him to homicide. The highest values were not to be maintained by reason, but rather by righteous emotion. Yet, as Dana sensed, there was a disturbing ambiguity concerning "moral passion." When an aggressive impulse was so closely linked to sexual passion, it was difficult to distinguish virtue from evil. Hot blood was related, after all, to sexual jealousy, which might itself be the hidden result of excessive isolation and of a yearning for unconditional love.

IV

De Tocqueville shared the view of many foreign travelers that Americans were unique in their respect and admiration for women. It was also true, however, that many American men were unhappy over the extreme idealization of the fair sex, which inevitably brought restrictions for men. Sentimental writers might glorify motherhood, but mothers also exercised more power in America than in most other countries; society might extol the virtuous, independent maiden, but the independent maiden could turn a man down, regardless of his qualifications. Observers from abroad reported that American wives had special talents for spending and planning to spend money. We have noticed the frequent blame attached to coddling mothers, and to wives who usurped their husband's authority, in fictional explanations of crime.

Especially during the 1840's, American literature seemed to express an increasing consciousness of the evil in woman. Convention demanded that the heroine be pure and altruistic, yet the erring wife was no longer pictured as a frail, deluded soul whose heart had been turned by the deceptive tongue of a skillful rake. After 1840, readers of popular literature encountered an increasing number of women who were coldhearted, dishonest, and mortally seductive. Perhaps this new interest in the wicked woman reflected a deeper sexual hostility, engendered by the feminine restriction upon, and frustration of, boys and men; perhaps it was hostility that lay behind the obsession with the female corpse. At any rate, the concern with adultery and feminine evil was clearly a result of the progressive uncertainty over woman's status and of the ever-widening gap between the ideal and reality.

In both *Confession* and "Paul Felton" jealous husbands murder virtuous wives. This would seem to imply that even a wife's virtue was not sufficient to remove lingering doubts concerning feminine evil. Although the murders were precipitated by simple mistakes in factual information, inference, and deduction, feminine evil was in one sense responsible for even these circumstantial errors and for the resulting jealousy. If certain murdered wives proved to have been faithful, universal woman still bore the subtle stain of Eve's first sin. A husband's suspicions might be irrational, groundless, and even tragic, but if wives were universally virtuous, there would be no jealous husbands. Dana and Simms may have been conscious of this ancient concept of a universal nature, at once ideal and sexually corrupt, but they placed the actual burden of guilt on the deluded husbands. During the 1840's, as the problem of feminine status became more acute, writers increasingly portrayed the woman with the poisonous heart.

There has long been a curious paradox in the male attitude toward woman's nature. Popular literature in Western nations has traditionally separated the virtuous and innocent damsel from the willful hussy. On the other hand, there has been a persistence of what might be termed "the Colonel's lady and Judy O'Grady theory." Doubtless this latter view has roots in medieval scholasticism and in philosophical realism. If the universal of man was inextricably involved in Adam's fall, the universal of woman was just as inescapably associated with sexual passion. Since woman *was* sex, society might be justified in rigorously determining a single status and position for all women. Well before the nineteenth century, of course, men had shown an increasing discrimination among various feminine stereotypes. The ideal heroine, by her refinement and delicacy, transcended the limitations of a universal sex. Even in popular literature, however, the relation between the Colonel's lady and Judy O'Grady was never totally obscured. Sometimes, indeed, the contrast between the two feminine characters only served to accentuate the dual potentialities of single, universal woman.

Moralists who condemned novels as the "nerve and arm of the Duelist and the Murderer" issued a stern warning to girls who thought of themselves as refined heroines: "In *your* opinion, the delicacy of your feelings, the high estimate which you have formed of the female character, the restraints which are imposed on you by custom; will effectually guard you against the force of temptations which have called forth the depraved dispositions of the opposite sex." Yet human history proved that female nature, despite its capacity for refinements, was easily as wicked as was the male: "Ambition, pride, revenge, cruelty, envy, and contempt for God, are the dispositions which human nature uniformly displays." [13]

[13] T. East, *The Memoirs of the Late Miss Emma Humphries, of Frome, England, with a Series of Letters to Young Ladies, on the Influence of Religion, in the Formation of Their Moral and Intellectual Character* . . . (Boston, 1819), pp. 70–72.

Ned Buntline, whose autobiography reads like the memoirs of a Victorian Casanova, created several hundred of the purest, most conventional heroines. But his experience also contributed to a general skepticism regarding Woman:

A dog will lick away the sores and wounds of another of its own kind; man, tried himself in the crucibles of . . . suffering and temptation, has still some sympathy for a fallen brother; but woman, ever liable herself to error, and yielding to a mean spirit of selfishness . . . can find in her heart . . . no feeling for the fallen or erring of her own frail sisterhood.[14]

In the cheapest novels of the 1840's and 1850's, there was little restraint in the treatment of wicked women. One refined English woman, who made a hobby of collecting the reports of celebrated murder trials, loved to ask her friends in a soothing and delicate voice, "Did you never feel that it would be a joy to die?" When her husband contemplated the lynching of some robbers, she suggested, "If we could only bring them all together at one grand barbecue, and poison them!" [15] A beautiful damsel named Emily Walraven, who must have been inspired by Poe, caressed and kissed her would-be lover as she pushed him slowly backward toward a pit of death.[16] Even some wealthy New York sisters, "dressed in all the flaming gorgeousness of fashion," could express surprising sensibilities for the weaker sex. When the servant brought a handsome young man into the house after he had collapsed on their steps, they fought over the honor of seducing him: "I'll teach

[14] [Edward Zane Carroll Judson], *The G'hals of New York; A Novel*, by Ned Buntline [pseud.] (New York, n.d.), p. 147.

[15] [Alfred W. Arrington], *The Rangers and Regulators of the Tanaha; or, Life among the Lawless. A Tale of the Republic of Texas*, by Charles Summerfield [pseud.] (New York, 1856), pp. 65, 70.

[16] George Lippard, *The Quaker City; or, The Monks of Monk-Hall* (Philadelphia, 1845), p. 59.

you, Miss Impudence, that I'm not only mistress of the house, in father's and brother's absence, but of you, also!" The other sister ripped a poniard from a morocco case, and said, "I'll rip your black heart out." [17] When the young man recovered, they made a compromise and both "showed him the elephant," as it was euphemistically termed in 1850.

On a more serious level, Hawthorne repeatedly suggested the feminine potentiality for evil, especially in such tales as "Rappaccini's Daughter" (1846) and "Young Goodman Brown" (1837). Nor should it be forgotten that in *The Marble Faun* (1860) Miriam's sexual power, combined with her subtle and mysterious propensity for evil, drove Donatello to murder. After Donatello committed the act, Miriam embraced him in a way that made the crime resemble seduction:

It was closer than a marriage-bond. So intimate, in those first moments, was the union, that it seemed as if their new sympathy annihilated all other ties, and that they were released from the chain of humanity; a new sphere, a special law, had been created for them alone.

But if Miriam and Donatello were temporarily saved from the "icy loneliness of virtue," Miriam came to realize that "an individual wrong–doing melts into the great mass of human crime, and makes us,—who dreamed only of our own little separate sin,—makes us guilty of the whole." Like Eve, who also unwittingly corrupted a natural man, Miriam knew that she must bear the guilt of all women.

That the great mass of human crime was generated by woman's sexual power was a theme which underlay the general treatment of adultery and homicide in fiction. It is important to remind ourselves that in 1850 Hawthorne chose adultery as the classic symbol for moral evil. The

[17] [Judson], *G'hals,* p. 84.

date is significant because some of the most widely read novels in the late 1840's and early 1850's showed an increasing interest in adultery, as opposed to the more traditional theme of sentimental seduction. In the cheaper tales, however, there were few Hester Prynnes to arouse a reader's sympathy. In George Lippard's *The Empire City,* published the same year as *The Scarlet Letter,* Gulian Van Huyden discovered his wife in the bushes with his brother. She confessed that she had only married to suit her father. Gulian, who was not a dramatic character like Roger Chillingworth, did not plot subtle revenge. He simply let his wife die unattended in childbirth while he enjoyed a Christmas revel.

Lippard was perhaps more concerned with adultery than was any other popular writer before the Civil War. If part of his immense success resulted from his Gothic sensationalism, he must also have reflected certain popular interests and attitudes. He never tired, and his public apparently never tired, of the portrait of an incredibly evil wife whose original fall had been determined by circumstance.

In *The Quaker City* (1844), his adulteress had been forced to sacrifice a marriage of love for one of wealth. Her husband loved her tenderly and dearly, but she soon proved to be unfaithful. Once fallen, her pure evil became manifest in a plot to murder her husband and in her willingness to sleep with anyone who might help her in that cause. In the end, the righteous husband gloated as he refused to give an antidote to his poisoned, pleading wife.

There can be no doubt, however, that in 1853 Lippard created one of the most evil women and achieved one of the most grotesque combinations of sex and death in all literature. In *New York: Its Upper Ten and Lower Million,* he carried Poe's favorite theme to completion.

In the manner of the gift books and annuals, the hideous chapter was entitled, "The Bridals of Joanna and Beverly." Beverly Barron had seduced Joanna Livingstone after giving her a fabricated account of her husband's amorous affairs. When Eugene Livingstone discovered the deception, Barron killed him in a duel. Essentially, then, Joanna was a loyal wife and mother, whose fall had been engineered only by false insinuations and by spurious letters.

Some time after the duel, when Barron called on his lovely mistress to persuade her to accompany him to Europe, she greeted him in a flowing, snowy robe, with every detail of her voluptuous bust and figure revealed. After discussing future plans, Barron asked for a glass of old Tokay; so, with a smile, the beautiful Joanna brought a decanter and goblet of scarlet Bohemian glass. As they walked side by side, hand in hand, she leaned her head on his shoulder, allowing her breast to throb against his chest. Reviewing the history of their romance, Joanna suddenly added that if Eugene's letters had been forged, then "you and I would be guilty, O, guilty beyond power of redemption, and Eugene would be an infamously murdered man." Barron assured her that the letters were authentic and that Eugene had been unfaithful.

In a passionate embrace, he whispered something in her ear. At first she refused, but in response to his kisses, she submitted: "Come then," she said at last, "come, husband—." Joanna led him to the bedroom, where a magnificent bed was draped by a white canopy: "Trembling, but beautiful beyond the power of words,—beautiful in the flush of her cheeks, the depth of her gaze, the passion of her parted lips,—beautiful in every motion of that bosom which heaved madly against the folds which only half-concealed it,—trembling, she led him toward the bed."

Remarking that her first marriage bed had been polluted by a false husband, Barron promised to love her faithfully until death and then he pulled back the folds of the curtain. " 'Our marriage bed, love,' " Joanna said. " 'Why are you so cold?' and again she laughed." As Barron stared in horror at Eugene's now rotting corpse, the voluptuous Joanna laughingly told him that the wine was poisoned. Thinking that she lacked the nerve to murder him, Beverly Barron escaped from the house and staggered along Broadway, where crowds hooted at him as a drunk. Between a pile of bricks and boards, in a dark corner behind the Tombs, Barron collapsed on his last, frozen, bridal bed.

Apart from the vulgar sensationalism of this tale, which is embarrassing to modern readers, there are two ideas which deserve consideration. First, there was a close association between death and expected sexual fulfillment. As we have seen, this relationship was common in the sentimental theme of seduction, but for Lippard, it was the sexual woman who brought death. Lippard's desire was obviously to shock his readers, to describe preparations and events leading to an expected realization of sexual passion, approaching the point of pornographic detail, only to resolve the growing tension by a sudden shift to murder and death.

Second, the immoral wife was pictured as a uniquely evil being who, though not responsible for her original fall, was capable of a cunning and subtle aggression exceeding the worst treachery that a man might devise. In most stories, except in the case of a monomaniac, the development of a male criminal was generally described as a slow process; but the descent of a woman into adultery and crime was a sudden event, determined by circumstance. Any wife, the reader might conclude, if she were unprotected and unsupervised, might fall into the clutches of a Beverly Barron, in which case one's innocent and modest spouse would be instantly transformed into a cold-blooded, murderous demon.

This portrait of the wicked woman undoubtedly represented a growing fear of adultery, which, in turn, reflected a general anxiety over the changing status of women. In the 1830's De Tocqueville had provided an explanation for the seriousness with which Americans regarded marital fidelity. He optimistically observed that American wives cheerfully accepted a more restricted and servile role than that of their European sisters. But by 1850 there were discernible forces which seemed to threaten woman's traditional position of subservience. On the one hand, the literary ideal of feminine perfection had become inflated to a point beyond even the dreams of realization. At the same time, a changing economy undermined the sources of masculine authority in the home. It is significant that popular writers expressed their fear of change in specifically sexual terms. A husband's loss of prestige and power could best be symbolized in the outrage of sexual dishonor. Social disorganization could be represented in its ultimate form in the union of sex and death.

Chapter VIII

THE THIRST FOR VENGEANCE

THROUGHOUT this study we have dealt explicitly or implicitly with the subject of revenge. Most of the fictional homicides discussed thus far have involved this motive, and we shall consider the social implications of vengeance in our later treatment of dueling, lynching, and capital punishment. But before we turn to the general subject of homicide and society, it is important that we examine the assumptions concerning motivation and guilt in several typical cases of fictional revenge.

When William Ellery Channing analyzed the causes of war in 1816, he also touched upon the sources of revenge and crime. His benevolent view of human nature notwithstanding, Channing was aware of man's "passion for superiority, for triumph, for power." He told the Congregational ministers of Boston:

The human mind is aspiring, impatient of inferiority, and eager for pre-eminence and control. . . . Were this desire restrained to the breasts of rulers, war would move with a sluggish pace. But the passion for power and superiority is universal; and as every individual, from his intimate union with the community, is accustomed to appropriate its triumphs to himself, there is a general promptness to engage in any contest by which the community may obtain ascendency over other nations.

Nineteen years later he found the elements of war in the very heart of the social order:

It may be said that society, through its whole extent, is deformed by war. Even in families we see jarring interests and passions, invasions of rights, resistance of authority, violence, force; and in common life, how continually do we see other men struggling with one another for property or distinction, injuring one another in word or deed, exasperated against one another by jealousies, neglects, and mutual reproach. All this is essentially war, but war restrained, hemmed in, disarmed by the opinions and institutions of society.[1]

All of this had been said before, of course; the argument, or a very similar one, had been used by Hobbes to justify an authoritarian state which might restrict an individual's will to power. It is important, however, that the truculence of western "war hawks" in 1812 and the increasing violence of the Jackson era should prompt such remarks from a kindly disposed and tenderhearted Unitarian. It is important that Channing, disturbed by the spirit of aggression and revenge in American life, looked for an explanation in man's nature and, ultimately, in the original family conflict.

If, as Channing said, an act of war represented something more than the mere rivalry of nations, then a vindictive murder might also be occasioned by something greater than a simple conflict of interests. The difference between "normal" revenge and monomania would be only one of degree. For some reason, a particular private enmity

[1] William Ellery Channing, *The Works of William E. Channing* (Boston, 1899), pp. 647–654.

might be chosen as a symbol of all restriction, as a concentration of every frustrating force from parental authority to the first sexual rival. An act of murder would then be a triumphant release from all bondage and a vengeance against every power that had ever dared to challenge an ascending ego. After a period of frustration and self-deception, all oppressive forces might crystallize in the image of one supreme enemy, who seemed to threaten not only the freedom of the subject's ego, but the entire extended self, in the form of an in-group or family. If the hated person became alienated, in spite of a sometimes intimate relationship, the vengeful murder would then be essentially an act of righteous war.[2]

During the first half of the nineteenth century, the questions of revenge and personal honor were not academic problems for Americans. Political democracy, combined with fluid and uncertain social conditions, reopened the ancient debate over the boundaries of personal and public wrongs. The frequency of duels and of mob violence presented a problem of public lawlessness and of private justice which, centuries before, had been compromised by the emerging power of European kings. When writers of fiction turned to the general subject of vengeance, there was a new urgency in their attempt to explain the sources of an aggression which was everywhere apparent.

That these American writers often traced the origins of revenge to family conflict is the principal argument of this chapter. If the motive for retaliation was rooted in original family loves and hatreds, vengeance was not unrelated to woman's sexual power or to primary social

[2] This psychological process of alienation is evident in many actual cases of vengeful homicides. See especially, Andreas Bjerre, *The Psychology of Murder: A Study in Criminal Psychology*, trans. by E. Classen (London, 1927), p. 119; Frederic Wertham, *Dark Legend: A Study in Murder* (New York, 1941), p. 179.

restrictions. In discussing the approbation or condemnation of revenge in fiction, we shall therefore continue to develop themes considered in Chapters VI and VII. Vengeance was, after all, the supreme fulfillment of the "fundamental motive"—man's "passion for superiority, for triumph, for power."

II

In Dr. William Alexander Caruthers' *The Knights of the Horse-shoe* (1845), there is an interesting discussion concerning the murder of John Spotswood, son of Virginia's colonial governor. All circumstances pointed to the guilt of Henry Hall, who was really the aristocratic hero, Frank Lee. Ellen Evylin could not believe that Henry was guilty, because he appeared to be a well-mannered gentleman. Although her father, Dr. Evylin, was one of the few who stood by Hall in his trying hour, he told his daughter that English records of state trials proved that some "innocent" gentlemen and even noblemen had been guilty of horrible crimes. Good character, it seemed, was not enough: "It is not that upon which I found my confidence in his innocence, it is the absence of all motive." Later events showed that the wise doctor was correct. John Spotswood, despite his cavalier background, had possessed a weak moral character. Led astray by alcohol, he had seduced an Indian girl, Wingina, sister of the ferocious warrior, Chunoluskee. The inevitable consequence of such sexual sin was brutal murder. As Dr. Evylin sensed, revenge was the only logical motive.

Caruthers expressed a conventional literary attitude toward motive. Behind most fictional killing lay an inexorable law of revenge, which balanced a real or imagined injury with the pain of death. Yet individuals did not rationally calculate the exact degrees of injury, nor did they, as the law presumed to do, measure the punishment

in proportion to the offense. Natty Bumppo, as the Pathfinder, was not quite human when he said, in spite of his
hatred of the Mingo, "I never pull trigger on one of the
miscreants unless it be plain that his death will lead to
some good end." Such a magnanimous spirit was possible
only for a man who lived alone, close to God and natural
law.

Certainly any reasonable consideration of the greatest
social good would have furnished a more than adequate
motive for Melville's Starbuck. "But shall this crazed old
man be tamely suffered to drag a whole ship's company
down to doom with him?" Starbuck asked, while he held
a loaded musket toward Ahab's sleeping body. "Yes, it
would make him the wilful murderer of thirty men and
more, if this ship come to any deadly harm; and come to
deadly harm, my soul swears this ship will, if Ahab have
his way." In such a case, Starbuck reflected, logic would
justify a murder, as would the instinct for self-preservation: "A touch, and Starbuck may survive to hug his wife
and child again." Starbuck had every reason to kill, Ahab
had no reason to pursue the whale, yet the crazed Ahab
could never become Starbuck's Moby-Dick. In the figure
of the hesitating mate, Melville stated what many other
writers at least implied: revenge and murder were not
determined by reason. Men might justify their vengeance
with very good reasons, but the origins of violence were
nonintellectual.

If a murder resulted from a robbery or even from a
paid assignment to kill, it seldom appeared to be so serious
in fiction as did the motive of personal revenge. When a
robber killed a stranger, it was an impersonal, almost
casual relationship, something like the murder of an
Indian or foreigner. Revenge, on the other hand, was more
intimate, often implying a revolt against authority, an

undermining of official justice, and a destruction of the bonds of group loyalty.

Yet when writers examined the causes of a particular act of vengeance, they sometimes found that understanding brings sympathy. Conflicts between an established authority and a growing son (or a maturing people) were likely to suggest that the authoritative power had ignored sensitive boundaries or had violated an inner circle of self-respect.

In 1843 Cooper expressed this idea in an Indian character named Wyandotté. The relationship between an Indian and a stern English captain had many advantages for the study of vengeance, an accepted trait of Indian morality. By 1843 American writers were conscious of the discrepancy between the image of a proud and noble savage and the degenerate, half-civilized Indian of their own experience. This discrepancy could be translated into a character with a split personality, and fiction could dramatize the struggle between a persecuted ego whose boundaries were shifting and ambiguous and an unenlightened authority.

Wyandotté was an old Tuscarora chief who had become attached to the white settlers after being rejected from his tribe. As "Saucy Nick," he had been employed by the English in the war against the French, after which he had helped Captain Willoughby obtain large tracts of land. The Indian had come to look upon Mrs. Willoughby as a mother and upon Maud Willoughby as a sister, whereas his relationship with the captain was essentially that of a servant. A stern disciplinarian of the "old school," Willoughby had in the past occasionally flogged the once-proud chieftan.

When an army composed of American patriots and Mohawks attempted to drive the Willoughbys from their land, the captain, expressing mistrust in Nick's loyalty, reminded him of these past floggings. Nick sullenly replied that it was unwise to put a finger on an old sore, reviving an ancient shame. It was one thing to flog the drunken Saucy Nick, he said, but no man could whip Wyandotté and live to see the setting sun. Time had gradually worn off the Indian's craving for revenge, but after the captain had alluded to the whipping post in a threatening tone it was inevitable that he would be murdered. Cooper was not without sympathy for Wyandotté:

He believed that, in curing the sores on his own back, . . . he had done what became a Tuscarora warrior and chief. Let not the self-styled Christians of civilized society affect horror at this instance of savage justice, so long as they go the whole length of the law of their several communities, in avenging their own fancied wrongs, using the dagger of calumny instead of the scalping-knife, and rending and tearing *their* victims, by the agency of gold and power, like so many beasts of the field, in all the forms and modes that legal vindictiveness will either justify or tolerate.[3]

By 1843 Cooper had, of course, felt the daggers of calumny himself and knew whereof he spoke. Like Channing, he found that a vengeful murder was only an extreme example of the kind of aggressive behavior which seemed to characterize American society. If it was the American's "gift" to write a slanderous editorial, it was the Indian's "gift" to murder and scalp.

There are other implications, however, in the story of Wyandotté. Indians were often equated with children, and in a very real sense, Wyandotté was a grown child in the Willoughby family, differing from an actual, white son in only one important respect. The Indian's glory and self-expansion lay behind him and not ahead. A real son,

[3] James Fenimore Cooper, *Wyandotté; or, The Hutted Knoll: A Tale* (New York, 1857), p. 408.

growing in prestige and authority, might have ultimately struggled with his father for independence; yet Wyandotté had degenerated from nobility and independence, his ego gradually diminishing in area, his self-esteem disintegrating in the lowly status of a servant, until the memory of a past greatness motivated present revenge. Captain Willoughby stood for the concentrated power of civilization and restriction which had, in the Indian's imagination, brought decay and ruin on him. So long as Wyandotté was permitted to forget his former prestige, he might adjust to his servile position, suppressing all violent impulses. A sudden reminder of his fall, however, brought swift retribution, which, instead of being the act of an expanding ego claiming and possessing a new dominion, was the desperate lunge of a wounded self at bay.

The fact that Wyandotté was an Indian and that Willoughby represented callous white despotism may have minimized the murderer's guilt, yet Cooper still held that the savage must ultimately be converted to Christian morality and, after expressing appropriate remorse, must die.

III

Edward Bulwer-Lytton's deterministic study of a criminal in *Paul Clifford* (1830) had a profound influence on popular American literature. William Gilmore Simms (who, as we have seen, named a character Edward Clifford) might well have written:

We see masses of our fellow-creatures—the victims of circumstances, over which they had no control—contaminated in infancy by the example of parents, their intelligence either extinguished, or turned against them, according as the conscience is stifled in ignorance, or perverted to apologies for vice. A child who is cradled in ignominy, whose schoolmaster is the felon, whose academy is the house of correction . . . becomes less a responsible and reasoning human being than a wild beast which we suffer to range in the wilderness, till it prowls near our homes, and we kill it in self-defense.[4]

In this passage, as in the plot of *Paul Clifford* itself, Lytton set forth a fairly complete philosophy of crime, which, he imagined, would eventually aid in the reformation of prisons and penal codes. The story of a hapless boy, forced by circumstances to associate with hardened criminals, whose own career of lawlessness was a frantic revenge against a heartless society, provided a challenge to the complacency of an antiquated legal machine in an industrial age. Fifteen years after publishing *Paul Clifford*, Lytton was gratified to have seen an amelioration of the penal code and a growing impulse to rid the world of the hangman. As an artist, he felt that he had played his part:

Between the literature of imagination, and the practical interests of a people, there is a harmony as complete as it is mysterious. The heart of an author is the mirror of his age. The shadow of the sun is cast on the still surface of literature, long before the light penetrates to law.

Like Paul Clifford, Ned Buntline's river pirate, Edward Harris, was forced into crime by circumstance and by an evil father-figure. When the real father died dur-

---

[4] Edward Bulwer-Lytton, *Paul Clifford*, vol. IX of *The Novels of Lord Lytton* (New York, 1897), pref. to 1848 ed., pp. xvii–xviii. In theory, at least, this statement is strikingly similar to the assumptions of many naturalistic writers of the early twentieth century. It is interesting that the American editor of Lytton's works felt disturbed by *Paul Clifford* in 1893, to the point of writing a preface objecting to the novel's principal thesis. In America, he said, there was daily evidence that men were rising above heredity and environment. The English protagonist "must have had little moral stamina," the editor concluded. It was against this morality that the naturalists rebelled; yet their theories of crime had been anticipated by Lytton, Hugo, and Zola.

ing Harris' childhood, his mother married a villain. The future pirate was a senior at Yale when he discovered that his mother had been poisoned and that a new will had been forged by the diabolical stepfather. He killed the villain, escaped from the Sing Sing steamboat, and joined a band of river pirates. After systematically murdering relatives who were accomplices of his stepfather, Edward Harris declared war on society:

Little does the world at large know how a wronged and desperate man can cherish *revenge*. . . . If they did, more careful would they be—more cautious in *forcing* a brave, proud heart into extremes; for the more pure, noble and generous it *has* been, the more reckless, depraved and bitter will be its charge; even as a woman supremely virtuous, becomes, when once fallen, the vilest of her sex.[5]

Even without considering the fact that Judson (Buntline's real name) rebelled furiously against his own father, one can detect a theme of parricide only thinly disguised in this novel. In literature, a mother's second marriage often resembles a child's discovery of the sexual nature of her first marriage. In this tale, the mother had been dishonored and killed by an evil father-figure, yet society condemned Edward Harris' revenge. When the sight of a beautiful girl reminded him that society was also about to deprive him of sexual love, Harris resolved to escape from the Sing Sing steamboat. Later, Harris saved the same girl from rape by killing a molester who had attacked her on the street. Essentially, the rapist was another symbol of a molesting father. The girl rewarded Harris by becoming his matronly and devoted wife. The pirate and motherly wife together combatted society. Here is obviously a juvenile fantasy of a remorseless Oedipus.

[5] [Edward Zane Carroll Judson], *The B'hoys of New York: A Sequel to "The Mysteries and Miseries of New York"*; by Ned Buntline [pseud.] (New York, n.d.), p. 51.

Buntline often combined his theory of criminal revenge with a bumptious attack upon the American aristocracy. Barton, in *The G'hals of New York* (1850), was born a bastard and raised by an aristocrat:

And they paraded me, in my coarse charity livery, before them, every Sabbath, to church, to display to an admiring world the child of their *bounty*, the living evidence of their *charity!* Visitors never came to the house but I was brought up and my whole history rehearsed before them, till my knees trembled.[6]

The legitimate son of the family delighted in bullying young Barton and in referring to him as "the charity boy." When a millionaire's boy refused to compete with a bastard at school, Barton attacked him, an offense for which he was sent to prison. Forced to associate with criminals, like Paul Clifford he found upon his release that respectable people shunned him as an ex-convict. Finally, he obtained a job and by industry won the confidence of his employer as well as the heart of the employer's daughter. At the wedding, however, the father of the beaten schoolboy denounced Barton as a graduate of State Prison. The ceremony was never completed, and Barton's fiancée died of grief. On this subject, Ned Buntline became almost hysterical:

For that—for *presuming* to lay my pauper hands upon the *privileged* flesh of an aristocrat—for daring to punish the insolence of a representative of our country's aristocracy—for daring to teach him that a pauper can have intellect, feelings, and sensibilities, as well as a wealth-bloated aristocrat . . . I was, thenceforth, to be pursued, persecuted, and hunted down.

We may surmise that Buntline's audience was not composed of wealth-bloated aristocrats. On his fiancée's grave,

[6] [Edward Zane Carroll Judson], *The G'hals of New York: A Novel*, by Ned Buntline [pseud.] (New York, n.d.), p. 111.

Barton swore to avenge himself on a corrupt American society. Tracking down the wealthy families that had brought about his destruction, he murdered the men and ruined the women. At the head of a great criminal organization in New York, the hero quieted his remorse with liquor and ultimately entered the profitable business of prostitution.

If some American writers shared Lytton's conviction that circumstances shaped a criminal and that the wounded and thwarted man who avenged himself against society was no more responsible than a wild beast (this really meant that the insanity plea should be extended to the morally depraved), there was greater skepticism concerning the belief that criminal revenge could be prevented merely by reforming the prisons and the penal codes. Because Americans were not immune from violent crime even though they enjoyed the blessings of political liberty and relative prosperity, there was a widespread conviction that the roots of rebellion lay beyond the simple injustice of social institutions.

Social reform could not have prevented the villainy of Simms's Guy Rivers, who, as we have seen, was corrupted in childhood by his mother. Yet this early perversion of a moral sense provided neither a motive nor a specific occasion for criminal revenge. In one sense, Guy Rivers' moral depravity and unruly passions corresponded to Wyandotté's Indian nature: both had the capacity for revenge if the occasion was presented, one because of his nurture in a savage culture, the other because of his faulty education.

Looking forward to a promising career at law, Guy Rivers was neither stifled by an oppressive aristocracy nor persecuted by an evil father. He decided to achieve power and wealth by crime only when a wealthy and ignorant fop had beaten him in an election to the legislature and when a beautiful girl had rejected him. If, like Paul Clifford, he was tutored early in life by a professional criminal, he soon exceeded his master in brutality. Colonel Munro, the professional bandit who desired only money, asked Rivers to spare his first victim, a man who, when pleading for mercy, talked of his family, his rank, and his great possessions. But as Rivers explained:

> These were the enjoyments all withheld from me; these were the very things the want of which had made me what I was, . . . and furiously I struck my weapon into his mouth, silencing his insulting speech. Should such a mean spirit as his have joys that were denied to me? I spurned his quivering carcass with my foot. At that moment I felt myself; I had something to live for.

Guy Rivers' revenge was principally directed against all society; nevertheless he had developed an overpowering hatred for one individual, a youth named Ralph Colleton who had succeeded in winning the beautiful girl and whose horse had once kicked Rivers' face, leaving an ugly scar. Even Munro, the cold-hearted robber, could not understand the true meaning of this insult. All that Captain Willoughby's floggings meant to Wyandotté was concentrated in Rivers' humiliation over a kick in the face. Simms attempted to explain the causes of revenge in a long conversation between Rivers and Munro. Reflecting upon the popular belief in trauma, Munro said: "I was always inclined to think that circumstances in childhood . . . such as a great and sudden fright to the infant, or a blow which affected the brain, were the operating influences." But the colonel could not account for Rivers' extreme malignity by such a theory.

Rivers himself observed that his hatred for Ralph Colleton arose from a natural antipathy, which resembled the fear and disgust felt by some men for a black cat: "In this way you may understand why it is that I hate this boy, and would destroy him. He is my black cat, and his presence for ever throws me into fits." Continuing to justify his revenge, Rivers said:

It appears to me but natural to seek the destruction of that which is odious or irksome to any of our senses. Why do you crush the crawling spider with your heel? You fear not its venom; inspect it, and the mechanism of its make, the architecture of its own fabrications, are, to the full, as wonderful as anything within your comprehension; but yet, without knowing why, with an impulse given you, as it would seem, from infancy, you seek its destruction.

Later Rivers pointed out that thousands of normal citizens will travel for miles and endure privations to gape upon the execution of a fellow human at the gallows:

The same motive which provokes this desire in the spectator, is the parent, to a certain extent, of the very crime which has led to the exhibition. It is the morbid appetite, which sometimes grows to madness—the creature of unregulated passions, ill-judged direction, and sometimes, even of the laws and usages of society itself, which is so much interested in the promotion of characteristics the very reverse.

It was Simms's conclusion, then, that human nature often manifests a "morbid appetite," a desire for excitement, violence, and destruction, which should be controlled by careful parental guidance. In his portrait of Guy Rivers, Simms implied that this "morbid appetite" was a perversion of what Channing described as man's natural "passion for superiority, for triumph, for power." Faulty training or family conflict corrupted this passion for power, leaving an individual unprepared for the ordinary disappointments and frustrations of life. Revenge was that mechanism of the sick mind whereby a single hated person came to stand for the combined restrictions of society.

Yet we must not overlook the implication that retributive murder brought a kind of freedom and independence to the avenger. Wyandotté, Edward Harris, Barton, and Guy Rivers all achieved a sense of personal triumph and a liberation from self-mistrust in their respective acts of violence. Moreover, vengeance was often presented as an inevitable expression of righteous law, though writers sometimes purified their heroes' retaliation by the device of accident.[7] If we first analyze a story in which revenge was equated with inexorable law, we may better understand the association of vengeance with liberation in the literary treatments of the famous Beauchamp murder, to which we shall turn in a moment.

Edith Vernon (1845), a New England tale by Francis Alexander Durivage, merged the theme of sentimental seduction with Gothic incest, exploited hidden and implied familial relationships, and finally resolved an ambiguous conflict with an Oedipal murder. On the surface, Durivage's plot was simple, if unbelievable. Edith Vernon, a beautiful and high-born girl, befriended an old hag, who predicted, nevertheless, that Edith would become an unwed mother. The hag had a half-wit grandson named Dick Darrell, who enjoyed shooting crows because they resembled ministers. After nearly shooting Edith in the woods, Dick attempted to make love to her, though she was horrified by the idea of loving such a grotesque creature.

[7] For example, in Newton Mallory Curtis's *The Bride of the Northern Wilds* (1843) the hero killed an Indian, another Indian killed the renegade villain who was about to murder the heroine, and in this indirect manner the hero's purpose was accomplished without stain of guilt. Since Indians symbolized an impersonal evil, they were often used by writers to relieve the hero of his retributive duty.

This half-wit had a deep hatred for Colonel Miles Forrester, a local aristocrat who had once threatened to have the boy whipped for shooting birds in his orchard. Dick avenged himself by identifying Forrester with a hawk. He wounded the bird and then poked his gun muzzle against its throat, squeezing until the eyeballs popped out. He laughed deliriously when the hawk died!

Edith Vernon became engaged to Miles Forrester's virtuous brother. Miles, in turn, married Edith's gentle sister. But Edith, who lived with the Forresters while her fiancé was abroad, was ultimately seduced by her brother-in-law. After a brief but happy romance, resulting in the birth of an illegitimate child, Miles urged Edith to marry according to schedule, since his brother would never know of their intimacy. But Edith chose to commit suicide on her wedding day.

Before killing herself, Edith Vernon discovered that Colonel Miles Forrester was actually the father of Dick Darrell, the half-wit. Many years before, the old woman, who was not then a hag, had permitted her beautiful daughter to find a job in Boston. The daughter had returned, seduced by Forrester, ruined by abortion potions, and had died at the birth of Dick Darrell, the half-brother of Edith's own child. After Edith's suicide, Miles Forrester had become a pious philanthropist, hoping to atone for his past sins. But twenty years after his sister-in-law's death, he was ambushed by a robber on the highway. When he put up a fight, the young bandit killed him. Tried and executed for his unintentional parricide, Edith Vernon's bastard son was buried beside his murdered father.

One could not ask for a more direct statement of the ancient Oedipus theme. Essentially, Edith's robber son and Dick Darrell were identical figures. The half-wit's hatred for his father, his attempt to emasculate a father-image in the shape of a hawk, found realization in the final parricide. The old hag's daughter, who took abortion potions instead of poison, was a counterpart to Edith Vernon, so that the relation between the hag and the aristocratic girl was actually that of mother and daughter. Hence Dick Darrell's profession of love and his attempted seduction of Edith were but veiled expressions of a son's unnatural passion. Yet the half-wit did not know why he loved Edith nor why he hated Forrester, and, similarly, Edith's son did not know that he killed his father. In the symbolic language of popular fiction many writers traced the inevitability of revenge to an original family conflict. Yet the connotations of this conflict were disguised by such devices as hidden identities, accidental encounters, and the repetition of similar characters and incidents.

Although the plot of *Edith Vernon* may seem hopelessly contrived, Durivage implied a theory of natural law which deserves attention. In the novels of the late eighteenth and early nineteenth centuries, natural law was commonly identified with reason and with human society. Since man's moral faculty was rational, he could determine right and wrong by his natural endowments. When groups of men devised laws and punishments, these codes conformed to precepts which had been divinely implanted in the human soul. Revenge was an unnatural manifestation of the passions. In *Edith Vernon*, however, the inevitable law was not rational. Isolated, in a sense, from the rest of society, the Vernon "family" was the origin of conflicts so deep rooted and ambiguous that reason was powerless to judge or to punish. As in much of the popular fiction of the 1840's and 50's, brothers and sisters fought for sexual possession; sons irresistibly loved, hated, and killed. Out of this turmoil of passion and aggression, vengeance appeared as the only natural law for family crime. For such writers as Durivage revenge might be directed outward against such substitutions as a wounded hawk, but it moved inexorably, irrationally, to an accidental triumph on a lonely road.

IV

No matter what wrongs might afflict the ideal heroine, she seemed incapable of the vengeful spirit that characterized men. Few heroines excited such widespread admiration as Brown's Constantia Dudley, who felt no bitterness for her father's murderer:

Had the perpetrator stood before her and challenged retribution, she would not have lifted a finger to accuse or to punish. The evil already endured left her no power to concert and execute projects for extending that evil to others. Her mind was unnerved, and recoiled with loathing from considerations of abstract justice, or political utility, when they prompted to the prosecution of the murderer.[8]

In the literature from 1830 to 1860 it was almost a rule that feminine revenge sprang from sexual dishonor. A woman's retaliation was generally directed against a single man, who stood for a specific act of seduction and desertion. Only a completely fallen prostitute, like George Lippard's Bessie, could strike out against all society. She helped to seduce other girls because:

Have I not as good a right to the comforts of a home, to the smile of a father, the love of a mother, as she? Have I not been robbed of all these? . . . Is this innocent Mary a whit better than I *was*? . . . I feel happy . . . when I can drag another woman, into the same foul pit.[9]

Such a sentiment was, however, extremely rare in American literature. Women were not supposed to generalize

[8] Charles Brockden Brown, *Ormond; or, The Secret Witness,* ed. by Ernest Marchand (New York, 1937), p. 179.

[9] George Lippard, *The Quaker City; or, The Monks of Monk-Hall* (Philadelphia, 1845), p. 69.

an accumulated series of wrongs, directing their vengeance, like a man, against some symbol of authority, restriction, or rivalry. Women, as Irving remarked, lived entirely for love; only when this love was betrayed did their desire for revenge become concrete and specific.

On the night of November 6, 1825, a young Kentucky lawyer named Jereboam O. Beauchamp went to the Frankfort home of Solomon P. Sharp (a large landowner, a former United States congressman and attorney general of Kentucky, who was scheduled the next day to become speaker of the state House of Representatives) and murdered the distinguished gentleman with a butcher knife.[10] When Beauchamp was twenty-one he had married Miss Ann Cook, a sallow, desiccated woman of thirty-eight, whose appearance was marred by missing front teeth and whose reputation suffered from the fact that she had conceived a child some years before her marriage. During a bitter political struggle in 1821, Attorney General Sharp was accused of having fathered Ann Cook's stillborn child, and in the election of 1825 handbills appeared which claimed that in order to clear himself of the former charge Sharp had scurrilously insinuated that Ann Cook's baby had been a mulatto. Beauchamp had been undisturbed by the first rumor, but after hearing the mulatto story he saddled his horse and grimly rode up to Frankfort. When he returned home to his wife, there was a five-thousand-dollar reward for his arrest.

Beauchamp was convicted of murder and sentenced to be hanged. An impatient crowd stood around the gallows on July 7, 1826, anticipating the sight of triumphant justice, when the word spread that the Beauchamps had

[10] J. Winston Coleman, Jr., *The Beauchamp-Sharp Tragedy* (Frankfort, Ky., 1950), pp. 2–11. Coleman, who is also the historian of Kentucky's famous duels, has a strong bias in favor of Sharp, but he does quote and use much source material which is otherwise unavailable.

committed suicide. The crowd was greatly relieved when Jereboam Beauchamp, nearly dead from self-inflicted knife wounds, was dragged to the gallows and hanged. Ann Cook Beauchamp, who was probably the author of the suicide pact, had killed herself with the knife after failing to do so with laudanum.

According to Henry St. Clair, who in 1833 compiled *The United States Criminal Calendar: or, An Awful Warning to the Youth of America*, this sordid affair had a romantic moral. Beauchamp's martyrdom might "serve to teach a respect for the laws of honor, for revenging the violation of which he gave his life." [11] As this myth began to take form, it appeared that Miss Cook was celebrated in Kentucky for her beauty, talents, and feminine charm, that she had been outrageously seduced by Colonel Sharp, who owed his success in life to the Cook family, and that when the ungrateful Sharp wanted to marry another girl, he "forged a certificate stating that the child of his sins was a mulatto, thus degrading his victim still further." Beauchamp, according to the myth, had found the beautiful Miss Cook living in seclusion with her mother. Although she at first repulsed his advances, thinking that her "ruin" precluded honorable love, she finally consented to marriage, provided that her husband would agree to avenge her dishonor. When Sharp persistently refused to fight Beauchamp in the usual manner, the righteous husband took the law into his own hands. [12]

Thomas Holley Chivers read Beauchamp's *Confession* while still at Transylvania University and, greatly excited by the dramatic power of the story, wrote a play called *Conrad and Eudora,* in which the counterparts of Ann Cook and Beauchamp were school sweethearts. In

[11] Henry St. Clair, *The United States Criminal Calendar* (Boston, 1833), p. 284.
[12] *Ibid.,* pp. 287–291.

May 1842, Edgar Allan Poe wrote in *Graham's Magazine*: "No more thrilling, no more romantic tragedy did ever the brain of poet conceive than was the tragedy of Sharpe [*sic*] and Beauchamp." Seven years earlier Poe had used the legend of the young Kentucky lawyer in his drama, *Politian*; in 1840 it was incorporated into Charles Fenno Hoffman's *Greyslaer*; and in 1842 Simms gave the tale a more direct treatment in *Beauchampe*. The basic theme appeared in other works of drama and fiction, being even faintly suggested by Hawthorne in *The Marble Faun*.

Poe's drama, which was written ten years after the murder, did not include the racial implication. Poe's Politian was a Hamlet-like character, irresolute and procrastinating, while Alessandra was more persistent and unswerving in her desire for vengeance than were other counterparts of Ann Cook. In *Greyslaer* an evil Tory, Bradshawe, after instigating Alida's capture by an Indian, forced her to marry him to escape the licentious savage. When Alida discovered the marriage was false, she plotted revenge; but later, when betrothed to Max Greyslaer, she shuddered at her earlier desire for blood. During her fiancé's absence in the patriot army, "she gradually learned to shrink as painfully from the idea of a deadly personal encounter between him and Bradshawe, as she lately had from her own unfeminine dream of vengeance." [13] Greyslaer, too, began to forget his hatred, until Bradshawe spread the tale that Alida had conceived a child from an Indian lover.

In Simms's version, young "Anna Cooke" lived only for revenge, determining to use the unsuspecting "Beauchampe" as her instrument: **"Shall** I not use his love for my hate? What is his love to me? . . . His love, indeed— the love of a young ambitious lawyer. Is it not the perfection of vengeance that I should employ one of the tribe

[13] Charles Fenno Hoffman, *Greyslaer: A Romance of the Mohawk* (New York, 1840), I, 125.

for the destruction of another!"[14] But this scheming attitude was soon replaced by the purity and warmth of marital love. As a "ruined" girl of eighteen, Anna had contemplated sacrificial oaths and bloody altars in the woods, but as a loving wife of twenty-two, she began to pray that the terrible pledge be forgotten: "She was *now* willing that the Lord should exercise his sovereign right." The Lord moved, however, in mysterious ways. Colonel Sharpe, who turned out to be a friend of Beauchampe's, tried to renew familiarities with Anna when he was visiting the couple as a house guest. Despite her attempt to keep the secret from her husband, Anna was forced to identify Sharpe to prevent further dishonor. Observing the obligations of a southern gentleman and host, Beauchampe allowed the villain to leave in safety.

Although Anna had threatened to kill Sharpe regardless of the rules of hospitality, Beauchampe was determined to follow the gentleman's code. Yet Sharpe refused to fight as a gentleman should, thinking that a humble apology might soothe Beauchampe's growing anger. Under the rule of the code, however, only blood could atone for the insult of a guest's attempted seduction of his hostess. When Beauchampe demanded immediate satisfaction, Sharpe tried to save himself by whispering that Anna's child had not been white. Of course, no southern gentleman could imagine a greater provocation for murder than the suggestion that his wife had once loved a Negro.

According to Simms, the murder was committed in a state of temporary madness: "We may plead the madness of the criminal, and this alone may excuse what we are not permitted to justify." All discussions of moral respon-

[14] William Gilmore Simms, *Beauchampe; or, The Kentucky Tragedy* (New York, 1856), p. 109. In *Charlemont* (1856) Simms used the same characters but concentrated on the original seduction theme. In both novels Simms changed the spelling of the names, adding an "e" to Cook, Sharp, and Beauchamp.

sibility presupposed a conscience, yet Beauchampe "was laboring under a degree of excitement which makes it something like an absurdity to talk of conscience at all." Thus (as we have seen in the case of adultery) the theory of hot blood overpowering reason became a means of excusing "what we are not permitted to justify." Yet in the actual case of Beauchamp, there could be no doubt concerning premeditation, since the murderer had to travel a long distance to Frankfort to execute his purpose. Simms significantly changed the facts by having *his* Beauchampe first hear the miscegenation charge from Sharpe himself. The insult provoked instantaneous retaliation. It is extremely doubtful that the real Beauchamp would have been convicted had the murder been committed under such circumstances, but Simms was attempting to justify the impulse of vengeance without simultaneously contradicting traditional values.

Despite Simms's sympathy for the code of honor, he referred to personal revenge as a usurpation of "the sublime privilege of Deity." Beauchampe's guilt was mitigated by his temporary madness, but this did not save him from inevitable death. The conflict between private honor and public justice, between individual righteousness and divine prerogative, was, as in the case of dueling, a conflict that deeply disturbed the American conscience. Devout men could not deny that the Lord had reserved the power of vengeance for Himself, since even the mightiest of kings and governments felt it necessary to justify their right of punishment by a divine sanction which Christianity unequivocally withheld from the individual. But for men of the nineteenth century it was difficult to believe that the unrepentant seducer and murderer would be smitten by a bolt from heaven. In most regions of the United States, secular justice seemed incapable of preventing or avenging personal insults or sexual dishonor, especially since the offender could flee to a frontier area where men did not inquire closely about a stranger's past. New England ministers might darkly hint that some bloody catastrophe would destroy the nation if the spirit of revenge were not checked, yet these same ministers based their arguments against fiery tempers and personal violence upon secular considerations. When men debated in secular terms, there was apt to be a certain sympathy for the outraged or blinded husband and for the slandered statesman who but redeemed their honor.

In fiction, then, the problem could be artificially resolved by inevitable death. The wronged woman who failed to repent of her unnatural desire to kill was a generator of evil who deserved to die, usually before gratifying her desire for vengeance. Conventional morality ruled that her sexual fall, no matter how undeserved, could be expiated only by suffering and by prayer.[15] It was difficult, however, to argue seriously that a man should passively accept his lost honor and pray for forgiveness. Death might necessarily follow revenge, but this convention was little more than a concession to Christian morality.

The story of Beauchamp appealed to Americans because it dramatized the natural differences between man and woman, linking the hero's sin to the instigation of an Eve-like heroine whose frailty was originally responsible for evil. It justified the concept of private justice without directly challenging dominant values, inasmuch as the

---

[15] In a typical example of feminine revenge, Alfred W. Arrington's Lucy betrayed her criminal lover, soliciting the help of a half-breed Indian by a promise to become his wife. Unlike masculine revenge, however, a woman's desire for retribution knew no bounds: "I must see him writhe like a worm in the embers, through the long torture of years, I would protract it to ages, if I had the power. His heart must break by inches as he has broken mine" (*The Rangers and Regulators of the Tanaha; or, Life among the Lawless* [New York, 1856], p. 128). Although Lucy's vengeance was finally successful, she died without the satisfaction of knowing it. Sexual passion made the vindictive woman less sympathetic and more evil than a man.

murder was committed in a moment of blind passion and
in defense of both feminine honor and racial purity. If
Beauchamp had to die, he also approached the ideal of a
superman in his moment of action. Revenge might deaden
the voice of conscience, but it released the natural impulse from all restrictions. For one instant, at least, an
individual was totally free, free from external morality,
from public opinion, and from political justice. What was
unnatural for a woman might be supremely natural for
a man. Never could a hero be so self-reliant as in the
moment of triumphant revenge.

The actual superman, as we have seen, was generally
a villain. He fascinated writers but he could not be
justified, because he was too dangerous. The hero of
revenge, however, exemplified in Beauchamp, approached
the freedom of a superman in only one instance—he did
not rationalize his action into a general philosophy of
independence, and he accepted death as inevitable.

During the first half of the nineteenth century, American officials, especially in the South and West, were increasingly reluctant to enforce the laws against dueling
and private combat. Vengeful husbands profited by the
American jury's traditional respect for the unwritten law.
This tale of the young Kentucky lawyer who avenged his
wife's early dishonor provided an expression for these
unofficial values. Yet literature, at least in the nineteenth
century, occupied a position somewhere between the unofficial values of various social groups and the dominant
morality of religion and law. Hence the values in fiction
were shaped to bridge the disturbing space between sentiment and law, so that, no matter how glorious, the state
of freedom was felt to be ephemeral.

V

In previous discussions we have noted that the moral
sense theory, invented to preserve absolute virtue from

the contingencies of experience, broke down in the ambiguities of human passion. To escape from mechanistic psychology, men might glorify the pure, original impulses of nature, but these impulses tended to lose their innocence when translated into action. As natural man became social man, he unconsciously identified virtue with his own desire, and was thus reduced to the moral impotence of a Pierre Glendinning or a Donatello. The monomaniac and the compulsive killer were the final result of this confusion between motives and desires. But when individual desires were frankly recognized as the only basis for normative judgment, the natural man of pure feeling became a superman of amoral action. The theory of moral insanity provided a genetic explanation for such a rejection of social standards. The first two parts of this book are essentially an enlargement of this theme. When American writers described the causes and implications of homicide, their thought was deeply influenced by this dilemma of romantic psychology. The dangerous extremes of moral impotence and moral relativism were implicit in any system of ethics based on an inner sense.

We began Part Three with a suggestion that sexual desire was closely associated with corruption of the natural moral sense. The sources of jealousy, alienism, and aggression, seemed to lie in woman's sexual power. By this power man's unlimited desire for love might be transformed into a passion for hatred and destruction. Morality and social unity depended on equal friendship and identification within a group, yet sexual desire was by its nature individual and exclusive. In fiction this dangerous passion brought about a severing of social bonds, a withdrawal of natural sympathy, and, usually, an act of violent aggression.

But if evil was thus linked to a mysterious conversion of *caritas* into *eros*, the actual motive for revenge lay in a fear of ridicule, inferiority, dispossession, and isolation. In our analysis of fictional revenge we have seen that what Channing called the "passion for superiority, for triumph, for power," was often described as the effort of an insecure ego to save itself from final degradation. Ultimately this revolt was aimed at the family restrictions which had originally created the tension between aggression and the enforced acceptance of frustration. From the traditional point of view, revenge was an example of both moral confusion and moral relativism, since a specific injury was used to justify the release of cumulative aggressive desires, and, at the same time, the individual rejected the guidance of external authority and of universal law. Yet we must make a distinction between "normal" and "abnormal" revenge in fiction, even if the dividing line was seldom clear. As we have seen, the abnormal killer was in some way corrupted, perverted, or blinded; whether he was a superman or monomaniac, writers stressed his moral alienation. In this chapter we have so far discussed several cases of fictional revenge in which writers justified rebellion by a concentration on circumstances. There was no hint, for instance, that Simms's Beauchampe was in any way a moral alien. Simms made it clear that positive evil was confined to Sharpe's sensual mind, to Anna's feminine weakness, and to the persecuting mob of villagers. Hence the question posed in cases of "normal" revenge was this: how much pressure can an ordinary man resist before he rebels against traditional restrictions and declares a private war? When the pressure was great enough to justify war, the vengeful hero became a convenient outlet for the projected aggressions of society. It was comforting for a reader to know, in view of his own frustrations, that there were occasions when the Sixth Commandment might be suspended.

PART FOUR

Homicide and Society

COULD Washington and his hero-band, could the immortal throng of Signers, once more assemble, . . . what would be their emotions, as they gazed upon the fruits, which the republican tree has borne? We left you pure, they would say, we left you happy, and now we find Bribery on the Bench of Justice, the Knife and the Torch in place of Law, a people beggared by dishonest Banks, and a city disgraced by Riot, by Robbery, by Murder! Are these the fruits for which we fought and bled? Was it for this we dared the rebel's gibbet, the traitor's doom? —GEORGE LIPPARD

Chapter IX

THE CHANGING STATE

OF THE UNION

THUS far we have considered certain beliefs and values concerning moral freedom, the origin of evil, responsibility, types of alienation, sexual corruption, jealousy, and revenge. Throughout the first three parts we have been principally interested in the individual murderer, though our examination has occasionally involved a recognition of social and cultural problems. In Part Four we turn to the ancient conflict between social stability and violence, between the law of tradition and the "natural law" of individual retaliation.

Although the cultural and regional ramifications of violence are obviously complex, we must confine the present discussion to the few primary conditions of American society which writers of fiction associated with homicide. From the Revolution to the Civil War many Americans were shocked by reports of violence in the South, on the frontiers, and in the growing cities. Such outbreaks of lawlessness seemed to contradict the optimistic assumption that a peaceful and virtuous society was the natural outgrowth of political freedom. We shall therefore begin this chapter with a brief discussion of violence and the democratic state. We may then analyze attitudes toward tradition and lawlessness in America as expressed in fictional interpretations of the Revolution, of subsequent rebellion, and of violence on the frontier and in eastern cities.

II

That democracy leads invariably to anarchy and mass murder was one of the traditional clichés in Western political thought. The more conservative leaders of the Revolutionary period in America were haunted by the ominous pronouncements of such thinkers as Hobbes and Calvin, who had held the ancient fear that democracy and social disintegration were inseparable. In the 1780's and 90's many Federalists looked upon mob violence as a sign of impending disaster, since the rabble seemed to think that law had been abolished by political independence. Conditioned by the classical political philosophy of Europe, most American conservatives suspected that the Revolution had unleashed forces endangering just and orderly government. In the Constitutional Convention, in the *Federalist*, in countless sermons, letters, poems, and editorials, prominent Americans expressed concern over an increasing "spirit of faction," which, if unchecked, would result in endless civil war. Especially after the beginning of the French Revolution, conservatives appealed for unity in the critical struggle against creeping democracy, mob rule, the Illuminati, materialism, infidelity, and mass murder. The Federalist reaction was in part motivated by an irrational fear that man in his true natural state would resemble the theoretical description of Hobbes and not that of Locke.

Though Americans might exult in their liberty and prosperity, they were also sensitive to "the opinions of mankind," and it was therefore necessary to prove that they respected law, tradition, and the sacrifices required for social unity. Yet when Jefferson's election failed to produce a cataclysm, when assaults on life, property, and religion failed to accompany a gradual spread of manhood suffrage, even conservative Americans began to lose sight of the classical equation between democracy and anarchy. Whigs and former Federalists might deplore political and social change in the Jackson era, but for them the word "democracy" seldom suggested a picture of unrestrained rape, murder, and pillage. As reformers in Europe strove to remove the worst abuses of the old regime, senators proclaimed triumphantly that America was a beacon shedding the light of democracy upon a world darkened by centuries of despotism and slavery. It was the destiny of the United States to lead politically backward countries toward a millennium of liberty and prosperity, in which social order would be preserved by the moral virtue of a free and enlightened citizenry. Especially after 1830, Americans celebrated the memory of the Founding Fathers, whose unprecedented wisdom and courage had initiated this glorious march of democracy. In the nationalistic histories, in the mythology of plaster busts and Fourth of July orations, the Men of Seventy-Six were cleansed of self-interest, uncertainty, bitterness, and savagery—in short, of human passions and motives. If the plaster-cast demigods had rid the Western world of British tyranny, they had somehow fought without involving themselves in brutality or in sordid violence. Once independence had been achieved, American patriots returned to their ploughs and forges, serenely content to pursue their individual callings until another despot should threaten freedom's shores. Neither the Revolution nor democracy implied disorder, factional strife, lawlessness, or aggression.

One might reject the theory that democracy led to anarchy, yet it was difficult to maintain the belief that America was a happy, peaceful, and domestic land of friendly neighbors and unpretentious desires. During the 1830's thoughtful men were disturbed by a spirit of violence and brutality which seemed to be spreading across the nation.[1] When one looked to Europe—to the horrors of the French Revolution, to the mob violence of July 1830, to the Reform bill and Chartist riots in England— bloodshed might be explained as the natural result of corrupt and undemocratic systems. But in America, even if one expected lawless killing on the frontier, it was troubling to read of lynchings and fatal duels in the settled

---

[1] It is impossible, of course, to measure accurately the increase or decrease of violence in historical periods, since many crimes go unpunished and unreported, and such factors as the rise of cheap newspapers appealing to a wide audience intensify the public consciousness of violence which would have been unnoticed before. Nevertheless, most legal writers were agreed that crimes of violence were more frequent in America than in most other countries. Edward Livingston wrote that between 1802 and 1818 convictions for murder in New Orleans, compared with those in London and Middlesex, were in a ratio of 27 to 1, while in a seven-year period there were 154 murders punished with death in Louisiana, compared with 19 in all England and Wales (A System of Penal Law for the State of Louisiana . . . [Philadelphia, 1833], p. 30). In a fourteen-year period there were 34 convictions for murder in Pennsylvania, compared with 20 in all Scotland, and though London was nearly twice as populous as Pennsylvania in the late eighteenth century, it had far fewer executions for murder (William Bradford, An Enquiry How Far the Punishment of Death is Necessary in Pennsylvania . . . [Philadelphia, 1793], pp. 38–39). Robert Rantoul showed that murders increased threefold in Massachusetts from 1795 to 1845 (Hon. Robert Rantoul, Jr.'s Letters on the Death Penalty [n.p., n.d.; letter to the Governor of Mass., Feb. 4, 1846], pp. 8–9). The public also became more aware of violence through a series of spectacular incidents, such as the Nat Turner rebellion, the burning of convents, the Vicksburg lynchings, the Cilley-Graves duel, the Astor Place riot, the Dorr war, the antirent wars, the Mormon wars, and the riots of fire companies.

South and of mob uprisings in Boston, New York, and Philadelphia.

On August 22, 1835, *Niles' Register* lamented that "many of the people of the United States are 'out of joint.' A spirit of riot or a disposition to 'take the law into their own hands,' prevails in every quarter." [2] The next year saw the Helen Jewett murder and riots in Boston and Philadelphia. *Niles*, mourning that *"another revolutionary centennarian* [has] *gathered to his fathers,"* expressed misgivings over the new age: "We have a great flood of murders, suicides, and other acts of violence. . . . We are certainly losing character. Executions, in pursuance of law, are more numerous now in the United States ('the freest and most enlightened nation in the world') than, under the 'bloody code' of England." [3] It seemed that the glorious ideals of the Revolution would perish with the last veterans of Washington's army. Forgetting the humility and the restraint of the Founding Fathers, certain Americans appeared to lust for unlimited power. In 1846, just twenty days after General Zachary Taylor occupied Matamoros, Theodore Parker gloomily described the "Genius of New Civilization": "That stripling giant, ill-bred and scoffing, shouts amain: 'My feet are red with the Indians' blood; my hand has forged the negro's chain. I am strong; who dares assail me? I will drink his blood.'" [4] But as the "Genius of New Civilization" marched beyond the Rio Grande, a shadow from the "Genius of Old Civilization" fell from the Alps across the Atlantic, signifying the inevitable destruction of empire.

If Americans blamed aristocracy for European violence and corruption, Thomas Brothers, a hostile English

---

[2] *Niles' Weekly Register,* XLVIII (Aug. 22, 1835), 439–440.

[3] *Ibid.,* L (April 23, 1836), 129.

[4] Theodore Parker, *A Sermon of War, Preached at the Melodeon, on Sunday, June 7, 1846* (Boston, 1846), p. 43.

traveler, turned the American guns on their own institutions. Thomas Paine, he recalled, had predicted that a new era was dawning in the Western Hemisphere. Brothers acidly observed: "The promise was fulfilled, and a 'new era' came; and what are the consequences? Lynching, firing, stabbing, shooting, and rioting are daily taking place in this '*his beloved America*,' where, he told us, there was nothing to *engender riots* and *tumults*." [5]

In other words, the traditional fear of democracy had been correct, and optimists like Paine made a tragic mistake in associating peace and order with liberty. Brothers had only to quote from American newspapers to prove his point. For example, along with innumerable accounts of appalling murders, the Vicksburg *Sentinel* mourned that "shooting and cutting of throats appear to be the order of the day"; the New York *Evening Star* proclaimed, "It is the interest, as well as duty, of all to zealously aid in checking the riotous spirit which seems to affect all parts of the country"; the Boston *Morning Post* attacked the notion that a mob was a democratic assemblage and stated that America faced a crisis of violence.[6]

In the mid-1830's the United States seemed to many alarmists to be a land without peace or justice, a land where convicted murderers received executive pardon, where respected men led lynching mobs, where legislators "disagreed" with bowie knives and smooth-bore pistols, where Indians and Negroes suffered from the worst barbarity and cruelty, and where, as Brothers said,

I have seen such mobs, without any alleged cause, other than that, in their opinion, the negroes ought not to be suffered to live in a *free country*—I have seen such mobs march in order

[5] Thomas Brothers, *The United States of North America as They Are; Not as They Are Generally Described* . . . (London, 1840), p. 8.

[6] *Ibid.*, pp. 269–270, 264. A large part of Brothers' book is composed of lengthy quotations from the American press illustrating the extent and seriousness of violence.

down to that part of the city of Philadelphia, which is principally inhabited by coloured people, and deliberately set about
to murder them, destroy their houses, break up their furniture,
steal their money.[7]

Brothers argued that behind this ruthless aggression,
the burning of convents, the lynching of editors, and the
approval of homicide, there lay a double cause: republican government and universal suffrage. Freedom permitted the pursuit of wealth to go unchecked, enslaving
masses of people in a state ruled by bankers and greedy
merchants. Money was the only power in a democracy;
justice, which depended upon an impartial authority
transcending the interests and power of contestants, was
an impossibility; revolution had diseased the very cell-
tissues of American society, with the result that each individual was deprived of collective protection.

Brothers' attack was an expression of the traditional
aristocratic fear of democracy. Despite the exultant optimism of native rhetoric, Americans were sensitive to
European criticism and to the theory that the Revolution
had set in motion forces which would lead inevitably to
anarchy. American writers of fiction, who sometimes acted
as a national conscience, could not ignore the kind of
violence described by Thomas Brothers. But in so far as
they accepted dominant American values, imaginative
writers were required to show that this violence was not
an outgrowth of democracy, but was rather a betrayal of
"Washington and his hero-band." The same writers who
dealt with the two focal points of American violence—the
city and the frontier—also perpetuated the plaster-cast
mythology of the Revolution. Before analyzing the literary
interpretations of frontier and city lawlessness, we must
therefore examine attitudes toward tradition and liberty
in fiction.

[7] *Ibid.*, p. 198.

III

The most glorious event in American tradition was not the repulsion of a foreign invader nor the suppression of feudal lords who conspired against the king; it was rather a successful revolution. Writers of fiction searched for a formula to show that the rebel fathers had fought on the side of eternal law and that their violence had not been directed against legitimate authority.

During the 1820's and 1830's, novels dealing with the Revolution multiplied in number and became increasingly standardized in plot. In the fictional Revolution as it took shape, the conventional plot focused on a struggle between brothers for the possession of land and women. Armies of redcoats and Hessians served mainly as a colorful backdrop, against which patriots and Tories wrestled for the destiny of a virgin continent. American heroes had not waged war against fathers, kings, tradition, and authority, but against villainous renegades of the same age and blood. Instead of being subverted, law was being enforced against the criminal designs of Tory Americans, who had determined to capture women and wealth by illegitimate means. In popular fiction, at any rate, the Revolution seldom involved the rights of Englishmen, the abuses of an unnatural king, a state of nature, or government by compact. It was rather the glorious effort of righteous men to suppress a group of subversive outlaws and bandits, who rather mysteriously employed the aid of a foreign army for their evil purposes.

In the typical plot there were essentially five important characters: a sympathetic old gentleman, often the heroine's father, whose loyalty to king and motherland temporarily blinds him to the villain's true iniquity; a young Tory villain, usually leading a band of native cutthroats who collaborate with British officers (but are actually despised by them), fighting for unearned wealth and love without honor; the heroine, who adopts the patriot cause only when the Tory nature has been revealed (her sister or maid is often a patriot from the beginning, and is likely to be shot while defending the heroine); the hero, whose fiery radicalism becomes tempered with experience and whose rebellion is never against law or even against parliamentary abuse; and the old patriot, whose age justifies the cause, whose lands or daughter have been seized by Tories, and who is a man of calm judgment, dignity, and political wisdom.[8]

It is true in fact that the Revolution was in large measure a civil war, yet the special emphasis of popular fiction is significant. Historians, conceding that British sovereignty had existed, justified violence by a lengthy description of intolerable acts and abuses by the British. But writers of fiction did not stress political injustice; they were able to ignore both sovereignty and sanction. In these novels there were occasional interludes between the chase and pursuit of good brothers and bad brothers, when the reader glimpsed the godlike figure of a Founding Father. If he spoke, the Father's words were full of restraint and majesty, and even his momentary presence endowed the patriots' cause with benevolent justice and unquestioned legality. Since the hero fought on the side of established authority, struggling against criminal outcasts and foreign invaders, there was seldom a suggestion that the Revolution furnished precedent for further violence.

American writers might reject the classical fear of rebellion and democracy, but many novelists were never-

[8] I have drawn this summary from many tales, but the outline can be clearly seen in Newton Mallory Curtis, *The Black-Plumed Riflemen: A Tale of the Revolution* (New York, 1846), or in William Gilmore Simms, *Mellichampe: A Legend of the Santee*, 2 vols. (New York, 1836), and *The Partisan: A Romance of the Revolution* (New York, 1854).

theless disturbed by the continuing spirit of aggression
and lawlessness. How was one to interpret the resistance
of a whisky tax in Pennsylvania or the struggle against
foreclosures and rising indebtedness in Massachusetts? If
the writer of fiction upheld the dominant values of democratic tradition, he also felt an obligation to analyze the
dangers confronting America.

In 1835 Ralph Ingersoll Lockwood wrote a novel about
the lost generation of the American Revolution. A curious
variation on the patriot-Tory theme, *The Insurgents* described the tense, demoralized Massachusetts of the 1780's.
The novel was at once a plea for moderation in the interest
of national unity and an analysis of the two most divisive
dangers in a democracy.

Henry Eustace, who had been a courageous young major
in the Revolution, spent his time discussing battles with
his colonel father. Ignoring both politics and the farm,
dwelling only upon a glorious past, the two veterans
longed for excitement and action. Colonel Talbot, a youth-
ful political opportunist, finally converted Henry to
radicalism. After his natural idealism had been outraged
by the plight of rural debtors and by the government's
use of militia against angry farmers, Henry studied Milton,
Locke, and Sidney, deciding "that the governed have at
all times a right to resolve society into its original elements, and remodel their government without regard to
the form prescribed by the constitution." Taking an active
part in Shays' Rebellion, Henry Eustace identified himself with the earlier Sons of Liberty and even wrote a
utopian constitution. For Lockwood, he represented the
danger of lawless reform, however idealistic, which, if
unchecked by an absolute authority, might destroy society,
justifying aggression and private interest in the name of
freedom.

Colonel Talbot, who originally subverted Henry, was

politically ambitious. Converted to the government side by promises of a senatorial seat, he urged suppression of the rebellion by force. As families split apart and a general war loomed on the horizon, Henry prophetically asked, "In what age or what country has a civil war once kindled, its flames once burst forth, ever proved other than long, bloody and remorseless?" In Lockwood's picture the extremes of opportunism and idealism nearly threw the state into total anarchy and mass murder. Only the prudence and godlike wisdom of General Lincoln prevented a civil war and ultimately reconciled the rivals. Lincoln was essentially a Founding Father of the plaster-cast tradition, a giant of sterling integrity and kindly justice who prevented a betrayal of democratic unity. Though neither Eustace nor Talbot was a villain, Lockwood seemed to warn the struggling brothers that they might not always rely on General Lincoln to save them from their own blindness.

For Simms and Cooper, who were probably the two most important American novelists of the 1830's and 40's, the supreme issue was whether a code of morality could replace authoritarian power in the enforcement of limits and self-sacrifice. Like many of his fellow Carolinians, Simms gradually put his hope in the dream of a regulated, semiaristocracy, bulwarked by slavery and family unity. He felt, however, that this idyllic, half-Greek, half-medieval state was threatened by a widespread conspiracy of outlaws. In *Woodcraft* (1854) and *The Forayers* (1855), these bandits, plunderers, and slave-stealers were significantly former Tories, who preyed upon a society disorganized by the recent Revolution. Gangs of outlaws resembling the legendary Murrell band were pictured in the border romances, which dealt with the southwestern frontier of a later period. Essentially, however, these criminal conspirators were all Tories, renegades, and traitors, who, renouncing all social responsibility, plotted to seize governments, lands, and slaves. Freed from the restraints of effective law and social custom, their principal sin was a denial of individual limits. They strove to realize the wildest and most selfish dreams of the human imagination.

Cooper's ideal democracy depended upon a deeply felt reverence for the supreme power of God and Nature. Only in the recognition of such transcendent authorities, Cooper felt, could the members of a democracy be saved from "the foible of national vanity—that foul and peculiar blot of American character!" If Americans would escape the decay pictured in Thomas Cole's "The Course of Empire" or keep their land from sinking back into the sea, like Vulcan's Peak in *The Crater* (1847), they must recognize a greater authority than the voice of the people:

Let those who would substitute the voice of the created for that of the Creator; who shout "the people, the people," instead of hymning the praises of their God; who vainly imagine that the masses are sufficient for all things, remember their insignificance, and tremble. They are but mites amid millions of other mites, that the goodness of Providence has produced for its own wise ends.[9]

Leatherstocking might exemplify the ideal of an independent man, humble before the magnificent power and order of God's works, but Cooper's novels were also filled with characters who lacked the capacity for compromise and self-sacrifice. Dangers in the American character could be illustrated by an Ishmael Bush, the frontier squatter who made and executed his own law; by the cowardly demagogue, Steadfast Dodge, who deified the popular will, manipulating mass prejudice to satisfy his personal desires; or by Tom Daggett, whose greed for wealth and obsession with property resulted in the death of a miniature society. These men ignored the demands of a higher

---

[9] James Fenimore Cooper, *The Crater; or, Vulcan's Peak: A Tale of the Pacific* (New York, 1861), p. 494.

authority and denied the inevitable limitations of human nature. By their misuse of freedom and evasion of responsibility, they threatened to betray the promise of the Revolution.

European conservatives provided a simple and logical interpretation of American violence. Mob rule and social disintegration were the true manifest destiny of a state founded by revolution and dedicated to republican principles. American writers of fiction could not ignore native lawlessness and brutality, but for them the corrupting influence was not the Revolutionary tradition. The Founding Fathers had left to their children a happy, peaceful, virtuous land, but a new generation of renegades destroyed the unity for which their fathers struggled. Violence might be one of the evils of the growing city or the temporary result of frontier conditions, but it was also described in fiction as the betrayal of a pure and noble heritage.

IV

There was always the question of the land and people: the rich, continental land that stretched westward to sun-baked deserts; and the independent squatters, the vast migratory armies, who accepted virgin soil as a natural gift and who moved restlessly and continuously, without regard for the surveyors' invisible lines, or even for a nation's shadowy boundaries. For some men land implied law. There was the law proving ownership, the law governing settlement, and the law which maintained peace on the land. Other men looked upon unsettled country as a refuge from unjust law. They sought the power which ultimately determined law.

As American writers turned to the frontier, they described a society tending to dissolve into the most primitive units, a society torn by bitter competition, rivalry, and violence. Cooper's Ishmael Bush said that "when the law of the land is weak, it is right the law of nature should be strong." [10] But the law of nature was subject to individual interpretation. For Natty Bumppo it meant conformity to a universal balance and harmony, a law of restraint, prudence, and mutual respect. A rude frontiersman, Hurry Harry, had a somewhat different idea: "Besides, when we live beyond the law, we must be our own judges and executioners. And if a man *should* be found dead in the woods, who is there to say who slew him, even admitting that the colony took the matter in hand and made a stir about it?" [11]

One of Cooper's major themes was the conflict between those who would use land according to the law of nature, as interpreted by Leatherstocking, and those who sought to exploit land for personal power. Settlement and civilization were inevitable, but if the lonely and devout woodsman was to relinquish his claim and move ever westward, his sacrifice must not be betrayed. His sense of justice and proportion should be transmitted with the land to enlightened receivers. In their respect for a natural law of self-restraint and harmony, the woodsman and landed gentleman stood united against the ruthless hunter, the degenerate squatter, and the noisy villagers, who were led by corrupt and power-hungry demagogues. Although Cooper traced the history of this struggle from the early dispossession of the woodsman in *The Pioneers* (1823) to the final assault of Jacksonian democracy upon the very foundations of social order, his theme was essentially the same. The landed gentleman's concern for status (derived from natural endowments), his interest in family unity and morality, his devotion to a high purpose, were but reflections of the woodsman's reliance on the laws and hierarchies of nature.

[10] James Fenimore Cooper, *The Prairie: A Tale* (New York, 1859), p. 113.

[11] James Fenimore Cooper, *The Deerslayer; or, The First War-Path* (New York, 1861), p. 26.

The Chainbearer (1845), which drew from Cooper's own bitter experience in the antirent wars, dramatized these problems of land, law, and violence. An Indian named Susquesus represented the native inhabitant of the land. Still living according to his natural "gifts," he had nonetheless surrendered his authority and independence. Andries Coejemans, a veteran of the Revolution and victim of Yankee treachery, was the chainbearer for a surveyor. At the age of seventy, despite his humble occupation, he was proud, virile, and dignified. Mordaunt Little-page was the owner of a large tract of land, a fellow veteran and employer of Coejemans, and the symbol of enlight-ened aristocracy. Historically, these three men represented the legitimate and orderly creation of property.

Opposed to Coejemans and Littlepage was an immense squatter family, ruled by a patriarch called Thousand-acres, who moved his people from Vermont to Littlepage's New York estate, claiming that "what a man sweats for, he has a right to." After setting up a lumber mill and for four years exploiting Littlepage's timber, Thousandacres announced his hatred and contempt for surveyors and for legal titles. The only legitimate boundaries were estab-lished with a rifle, "which is the best law-maker, and law-yer, too, that man ever invented." Thousandacres further justified his claim by affirming that the Lord had created the earth for Adam and his posterity. Cooper, who had no love for Yankee self-righteousness, commented that "this mingling of God and Mammon is by no means an uncom-mon thing among us."

The squatter controlled the local magistrate and made a pretense of executing his own justice. After capturing Andries Coejemans, whom he detested as a symbol of property and order, Thousandacres staged a grotesque trial, relying for advice on his sons, who had once been convicted of stealing sheep. The man who measured land

and the man who took it without measurement faced each other as mortal enemies. After an involved conflict over women, who were often associated with the possession of land, the chainbearer was shot. His Indian friend, Susquesus, avenged the murder by killing Thousandacres. But Mordaunt Littlepage rescued Coejemans before the old chainbearer died, and Cooper indulged in sentimentality over the relation between master and faithful servant.

Like Leatherstocking, Andries Coejemans was a transitional figure between the noble savage and the noble gentleman. The legitimacy of succession was assured by the Indian's act of vengeance, which was justified by his own "gifts," his tribal morality being a part of the divine order. Thousandacres, allied with corrupt magistrates and vulgar townsfolk, represented the disintegration of natural law and the perversion of religion and justice. This resulted inevitably from a criminal exploitation of land, from an illegitimate succession. It was not by accident that Cooper made both Littlepage and Coejemans veterans of the Revolution. Thousandacres was a spiritual relative of the Tory bandits, of the brothers who betrayed their heritage.

For Simms the frontier represented a loosening of social ties and a regression to primitive law. Remote areas lacked the institutional barriers to crime and violence:

The planter and the farmer who dwell in the remote interior find the face of the visitor too interesting, to scrutinize it very closely. A pleasant deportment, a specious outside, a gentle and attractive manner, will win their way in our forest world, without rendering necessary those formal assurances, that rigid introduction, and those guarantees of well-known persons, which the citizen requires before you partake of his bread and salt.[12]

[12] William Gilmore Simms, *The Wigwam and the Cabin: Second Series* (Philadelphia, 1853), p. 149.

Frontier conditions might also rupture the strongest bonds of civilization. In "The Giant's Coffin" (1845) Simms described the emigration of two families from Pennsylvania to frontier Carolina in the 1760's. Although the fathers of both families were extremely close friends, their wives grew to dislike each other, despite their shared experiences and common perils. After the men had been killed in Indian warfare, the elder sons absorbed the latent hostility of their mothers, clashed in their courtship of a single girl, and ultimately took opposite sides in the Revolution. In this case, the evil Tory was brutally killed by a deformed youth whom he had wronged. It was the frontier, however, that aggravated the conflict between friendly families, destroying social unity by denying children the benefits of paternal guidance and authority. Once again, we see the pattern of dead or weakened fathers, of irresponsible mothers, and of hostile brothers, struggling for the possession of lands or women. This plot was subject to many variations, but Simms followed a convention of popular literature in saving his hero from the guilt of fratricide by the intervention of a physically deformed outcast, whose role corresponded to that of an Indian.[13]

In 1847 Joseph M. Field described a more distant frontier, in the Far West, where even heroes of the past suffered degradation. Morgan Neville had written of the legendary Mike Fink, whose exploits as a river boatman appealed to the expansive and aggressive imagination of Americans. But Field gave a new version of the hero's death, based on an account by an officer at Fort Henry, at the mouth of the Yellowstone River. In Field's story, Mike Fink had been employed by the Rocky Mountain Fur Company after steamboats had forced him to abandon the river trade. Although respected at Fort Henry for his marksmanship, Fink was also known as a terrible drunk-

[13] *Ibid.*, pp. 1–42.

ard. He enjoyed the constant companionship of a youth
named Carpenter, with whom he participated in daring
shooting matches. Attempts were made to separate the pair
by "foul insinuations" concerning the nature of their relationship, and Carpenter, who deeply resented these rumors, grew less friendly toward his former hero.[14]

Once, after a heavy drinking bout, Carpenter prepared
to shoot a can from Fink's head. The crowd taunted him,
daring him to kill the old boatman. Mike was furious
when the ball accidentally grazed his head. On the return
shot he sent a bullet through Carpenter's skull. Since Fink
had never been known to miss before, several men at the
fort called it murder. A gunsmith named Talbott was especially loud in his denunciation of Fink as a deliberate
murderer. When Mike approached him to discuss the matter, he shot the famous boatman in alleged self-defense.
In the Far West, according to Field, a great hero had died,
degraded by whisky and suspected of treacherous murder.

Social relations were described as being even more uncertain in Texas, where Charles Wilkins Webber's characters preserved the southern code of honor but lacked
the assurance of a social hierarchy. In "Adam Baker, the
Renegade" (1852) two men defended the honor of a guest
accused of treachery and murder. Williams, the guest, denied his identity as Adam Baker, a man sought by a group
of angry horsemen for the murder of a friend.[15] After a
bloody fight which resulted in the death of the chief ac-
cuser, it was discovered that Williams had actually been
lying. Those same rigid guarantees which Simms had feared
were lacking in the West might have prevented such a
subversion of the southern code. On the plains of Texas,
according to Webber, social ties were confused and am-

[14] Joseph M. Field, *The Drama of Pokerville: The Bench and Bar of
Jurytown, and Other Stories* (Philadelphia, 1847), p. 179.
[15] Charles Wilkins Webber, *Tales of the Southern Border* (Philadelphia,
1855), p. 104.

biguous, resulting in the unwitting defense of an honor
that did not exist.

The frontier might be described as an influence pro-
moting virility, self-assurance, and independence, but
American writers recognized a darker undercurrent. They
sometimes advanced a theory of progressive civilization,
explaining violence as a concomitant to growth and transition. But the West was also a place of cultural attrition,
of disintegration and of fear. If an individual's importance
increased as he moved westward, he also lost his sense of
position; when he belonged to no organized society, all
men were his potential enemies. Some writers feared that
the frontier experience might stimulate moral alienation,
since a rootless society could not preserve the bonds of
sympathetic identification which maintained a respect for
law and unity. Although Cooper and Simms differed in
their notion of an ideal society, they agreed that the American heritage could be protected only by a legitimate and
orderly creation of property, accompanied by the settlement of sober and virtuous families.

V

Every one has read those admirable works, in which Cooper,
the American Walter Scott, has described the savage habits of
the Indians, their picturesque and poetic language, and the
thousand artifices by which they fly from or pursue their
enemies. . . . We are about to place before our readers some
episodes of the lives of other barbarians, as far removed from
civilization as the savage people so well described by Cooper;
only the barbarians of whom we speak live among us, and
around us; we can elbow them, if we venture into the dens
where they assemble to plot murder and robbery. . . .

Thus begins an 1843 American edition of Eugène Sue's
The Mysteries of Paris (1842). Americans were fascinated
by this account of urban savagery, by a separate culture

within a metropolis, where men spoke a different language and observed strange laws and customs. In the works of Eugène Sue and in George Reynolds' massive *The Mysteries of London* (1845–1848) Americans might read about gloomy regions of poverty, starving families, diabolical gangs of criminals, sensuous aristocrats, and mysterious temples where secret organizations plotted treason, rape, and murder. Native writers felt that if Cooper could successfully dramatize Indians, there was no reason why they should not exploit the subject of American cities. In so doing, however, they chose to follow the formulas of Sue and Reynolds. The publishers of the cheap Jack Harrold Series explained:

Not for the mere purpose of gratifying morbid tastes for the terrible and the atrocious, but for the same reason that the skilled surgeon anatomizes the dead figure, that the causes and consequences of evil actions may read a terrible but rightful lesson. SUE and REYNOLDS, in their fearful pictures of life in Paris and London, have written similar works, from similar motives. . . . No attempt is made to soften the asperities of villainy and vice with any glitering [sic] veil of romance.[16]

Similarly, the publishers of Ned Buntline's *The Mysteries and Miseries of New York* (1848) defended the work as being of a "higher and nobler character than that of a common *novel*." Dedicated to "the Reverend Clergy of New York," the book included a letter from Buntline to George W. Matsell, New York's chief of police, thanking him for his generous co-operation. To certify further that the account was authentic, Chief Matsell's blessing was also published. It was reported that the author had actually entered the dens of vice, where he had seen the characters

---

[16] [George Thompson], *Dashington; or, The Mysteries of a Private Mad-House*, by Greenhorn [pseud.] (New York, n.d.), pref. to Jack Harrold Series.

and scenes described. That Buntline's book so closely resembled the works of Sue proved only the universal similarity of urban iniquity.

During the 1840's fictional descriptions of city crime increased to astonishing proportions. In 1853 George Lippard presented, against a general backdrop of New York poverty, prostitution, and violent death, vivid accounts of six rapes, seven adulteries, and twelve murders.[17] In the works of Ingraham, Buntline, Henri Foster, and Lippard, the "true" nature of the city was revealed to the American people. Under the bustling activity, the growing commerce, the glittering stores, and the finery of dress, they beheld an incredible social decay. If one cared to leave the main thoroughfares and walk into Boston's Ann Street or New York's Five Points, one would find a darkened area of poverty and oppression, where ragged children begged for pennies, where haggard prostitutes desperately solicited trade, where strangers suddenly disappeared, and where corpses stiffened in doorways and gutters, arousing neither sympathy nor attention. If one should discover an entire family dead in a tenement, it was

a scene incredible only to those who, unfamiliar with the ACTUAL of the large city, do not know that all the boasted triumphs of our modern civilization but miserably compensate for the POVERTY which it has created, . . . a poverty which gives to the phrase, *"I am poor!"* a despair unknown even in the darkest ages of the most barbarous past.[18]

Buntline did not find it difficult to explain why the mightiest efforts of philanthropy, religion, and law had failed to check the rising wave of crime. Self-satisfied reformers refused to combat the central causes: "Low

[17] George Lippard, *New York: Its Upper Ten and Lower Million* (Cincinnati, 1853).
[18] *Ibid.*, p. 205.

and Slowly Paid Wages, and Systematic Organizations for the Diffusion and Successful Accomplishment of Crime." [19] To prove his point, Buntline described a New York printing establishment owned by "a long-faced member of the church" who paid his one hundred employees "rat wages," withholding one-third of the payroll on the pretense of labor security, but actually using the extra capital for another business. At a time, Buntline noted, when churches were pouring money into the conversion of heathen, ten of the male employees had been arrested for criminal acts, while seventeen of the bindery girls had become prostitutes.

After the depression of 1837, America was seldom described by popular writers as a land immune from starvation and desperate crime. Some northern novelists even began to echo the South's claim that industrial slavery was worse than plantation slavery.[20] In a crude way, Lippard anticipated the economic satire of many twentieth-century writers. In *The Quaker City* (1844) an unemployed carpenter named Davis lost his small savings in a bank failure and went to the bank's president, Job Joneson, for aid. Joneson replied, "You don't mean to say that an able-bodied man like you can't get work in this enlightened city of Philadelphia? Pshaw!" Davis said that he had been unable to find a job, that his daughter was near death, and that his only capital had fallen with the bank. Advising him to make better use of his credit, Joneson refused to give even a dollar and then departed to hear an American preacher exhort his followers to discharge Catholic employees and Irish servants:

"That's the American Patent Gospel, Pope! That's the roaring of a real Buffalo a-seekin' to fight your Bull!" And then the Pope shall ask, what *is* the American Patent Gospel? As he

---

[19] [Edward Zane Carroll Judson], *The G'hals of New York: A Novel,* by Ned Buntline [pseud.] (New York, n.d.), p. 32.

[20] Lippard, *New York,* p. 206.

speaks, our answer shall thunder in his ears! Our Gospel is a patent improved Gospel; a terrifier; a scorcher; a real Locomotive-off-the-track sort of Gospel! We hold it to be a comfortable doctrine, to abuse the Pope o' Rome afore breakfast, and after breakfast, and all day long! [21]

While the banker thrilled at the words of the true American preacher, Davis returned to his tenement and killed his wife and himself.

Unemployment and economic oppression might account for a general demoralization, for the stench and filth of slums, for the armies of whores, pickpockets, bandits, and pimps that appear in the early city novels; but murder was not always so easily explained. When such writers as Buntline and Newton Mallory Curtis described Five Points and the Tombs, they did not have to rely on Sue and Reynolds. But when they embarked upon the "mysteries" of the city, they departed from their own observations.

The worst criminals, it seemed, were not the starving carpenters and machinists who faced alternatives of robbery or suicide. "The writhing criminal," Durivage wrote, "often walks abroad with the serenity of a mind at ease, and the bloom of bodily health impressed upon his face and form. . . . The very murderer may move in the social circle unsuspected and caressed." The city gave the worst villain protection and anonymity, as with Poe's "The Man of the Crowd" (1840). Beneath the surface luxury and poverty of a great city, there lay hidden conspiracies and vast criminal organizations, embracing police, magistrates, ministers, and cold-blooded aristocrats.

In the secret temples, brothels, and madhouses, the actual rulers divided their spoils and plotted tremendous crimes. Behind thick walls or in subterranean chambers, subhuman monsters practiced incredible acts of sadism at

[21] George Lippard, *The Quaker City; or, The Monks of Monk-Hall* (Philadelphia, 1845), p. 221.

the instigation of supposedly respectable masters. Readers of popular fiction knew that three groups were at the root of the mysterious horror of organized crime: aristocrats, bankers, and clergy.

Often in league with some great conspiracy were the "bloodhound" newspapers, the obscene press which "ransacks the gutters of society for new calumnies, and keeps whole legions of household spies in pay, so that it may blast reputation with a hint, and damn purity with a slur." [22]

But if the free press was merely an appendage to the underworld, if clergy supported economic suppression and conspiracy, if police received regular pay from criminals and prostitutes, then it was strikingly apparent that the entire urban society threatened to subvert America's cherished ideals. The growth of industrial cities had both confirmed Jefferson's suspicion of urban life and had betrayed the memory of "Washington and his hero-band."

Yet there was a curious complication in the treatment of homicide in city novels. Basically, these novels contained three rather separate factors: the descriptions of poverty and demoralization; the horror of organized subversion, which constituted the city's "mystery"; and a contrived plot which, it is interesting to observe, did not differ from the plots of noncity novels. The reluctance of writers to abandon a contrived plot may be seen in the literary treatment of Mary Cecilia Rogers.

Mary Rogers, a pretty girl who worked in John Anderson's tobacco shop in New York, was widely known as the "Beautiful Cigar Girl." On July 25, 1841, she disappeared. Three days later her body was found in the river. Dr. Cook, who performed the autopsy, said that she had not been drowned, but had been grossly mistreated and mur-

---

[22] George Lippard, *The Empire City; or, New York by Night and Day* . . . (Philadelphia, 1864), p. 53.

dered by a gang of ruffians. In September some boys found various clues near Weehawken, supposedly the scene of the murder.[23] The case aroused considerable excitement in New York, occasioning many demands that something be done about water-front gangs. No one ever knew, however, whether Mary Rogers had been murdered by a gang of robbers or had been killed by one of her rumored lovers. Both Joseph Holt Ingraham and Edgar Allan Poe attempted to furnish an explanation.

The actual fate of Mary Rogers is irrelevant to this discussion, but it is certainly possible that water-front ruffians captured and murdered her. In Poe's "The Mystery of Marie Rogêt" (1845) and in Ingraham's *The Beautiful Cigar Girl* (1849), however, she was spared from such a horrible end. Poe thought that the doctor who performed the autopsy was stupid, that the clues found near Weehawken had been planted, and that the girl had really been killed by a former lover.[24] Ingraham suggested that she was the daughter of an English nobleman and that she had merely been rescued from her lowly position. After many perilous adventures, during which her chastity was miraculously preserved, she was secretly taken home to England. This left the impression in New York that she had been killed, especially after the discovery of an anonymous body. Though Ingraham described criminal gangs and city evil, he based his tale on the traditional theme of sexual and family conflict.

[23] Edmund Pearson, *Instigation of the Devil* (New York, 1930), pp. 177–182. Since there was no trial, it is very difficult to locate accurate material on the Rogers case. Pearson, who said he nearly went blind searching through newspapers files, gives the best account now available.

[24] In a letter dated June 4, 1842, Poe said that he had given a new impetus to the investigation by disproving the ruffian-gang theory and by indicating how to find the true assassin. Hervey Allen adds, without citing any authority for the statement, that Mary had been murdered by a lover who later committed suicide (*Israfel: The Life and Times of Edgar Allan Poe* [New York, 1926], II, 510).

Perhaps a simple, impersonal murder by a ruffian gang was not considered to be so fascinating as a secret romance or a hidden identity. But the fictional treatment of Mary Rogers also implied an interpretation of city violence. The city might be a place of crime and danger, it might present a challenge to American values, but the villain, not social change, was the true cause of evil.

The relation of social evil to contrived plot was clearer in a trilogy devoted to urban crime by Newton Mallory Curtis. The last volume included a report, written in 1849, from New York's Chief of Police Matsell to Mayor Caleb S. Woodhull. Warning of the increasing number of "juvenile vagrants," Matsell predicted that "children who are growing up in ignorance and profligacy, [are] only destined to a life of misery, shame, and crime." [25] According to the chief of police, thousands of young rowdies were stealing goods from piers, junk shops, and warehouses, while small girls were selling nuts, fruits, and toothpicks in the low dives and counting rooms around Five Points, where they were subjected to the most "degrading familiarities."

Although Matsell's description provided an interesting comment on juvenile delinquency in 1849, it seemingly had nothing whatsoever to do with Curtis' novel, which did not concern ragged, teen-age prostitutes or hoodlum gangs, but rather the disintegration of a wealthy Dutch family. Yet the publishers obviously thought that Chief Matsell's report confirmed something that Curtis was saying.

The trilogy bore the subtitle "A Tale of Life in the Great Metropolis." Clearly the author's intention was to awaken people to the great evils and dangers of the city, which were verified by an official letter from the chief of

[25] Newton Mallory Curtis, *The Victim's Revenge: A Sequel to "The Matricide's Daughter" and "The Star of the Fallen"* (New York, n.d.), p. 91.

police. To accomplish this purpose, however, he adopted the ancient plot of family conflict. In a house "which seemed to have been preserved as a memorial of the Revolution," one brother struggled for his mother's fortune. When the good son upheld democratic principles in his marriage to a commoner, he was expelled from the house. Combining materialism with his aristocratic prejudices, the bad brother engaged in an organized conspiracy of crime, brutally killed his mother, and then attempted to incriminate the good son. Thus political corruption, prostitution, murder, and a plotted subversion of democratic society were pictured within the framework of a familial struggle.

In this trilogy, despite its artistic defects, the three strands of the early city novel were skillfully united. Chief Matsell's report should have been printed as an introduction, since Curtis was saying, in effect, that the evil city existed and demanded explanation. Matsell testified that poverty, crime, and violence posed a genuine threat to social stability. Thomas Brothers might have used this report of lawlessness to prove that democracy leads inevitably to anarchy and decay. But Curtis found his own interpretation of urban crime in the conspiracy of an unprincipled aristocracy and in the ancient drama of family conflict. In the house which was a memorial of the Revolution, the brothers were at war. The base renegade, whose aristocratic extravagance had led him to degradation and corruption, determined to secure a contested fortune by any means. The rich mother—who represented the ambiguous capacity of wealth (or of a bountiful heritage) for happiness or for conflict—finally recognized her error and blessed her democratic son. Her murder, however, symbolized a final betrayal of the old America, of the promise and ideals of the first generation.

Chapter X

WHERE THE LAW
DOES NOT APPLY

IN CHAPTER VIII we analyzed revenge in terms of motive and guilt. Although we now turn to institutionalized vengeance, this chapter is in effect a continuation of our previous discussion. We shall be primarily concerned with the motives and morality of dueling and lynching, which were two forms of revenge condoned in certain regions of the United States from 1798 to 1860. After briefly outlining the history and character of dueling and lynching in America, we may examine the literary treatment of these customs. Throughout the chapter, however, our interest will center on the justification of revenge. We shall find that while writers of fiction condemned the cold logic of dueling, which attempted to regulate homicide by reason, they showed a surprising respect for vengeance made necessary by righteous passion, an interpretation often applied to lynching. We may suggest that these values were not unrelated to the belief in a moral sense whose validity was proportionate to the intensity of a man's emotions. Thus the subject of this chapter is related to our previous discussions of romantic psychology and the doctrine of "hot blood."

II

In 1806 a prominent federalist lawyer named Thomas O. Selfridge was carrying on a feud with Benjamin Austin, a Boston Republican whom Selfridge had publicly accused of being a coward, a liar, and a scoundrel. On August 4, 1806 the two men had an altercation in State Street, resulting in Selfridge's shooting and killing Austin.[1] When Selfridge was acquitted on the ground of self-defense, the federalist was hard pressed "to elude the fury of democracy," for "the fiends of anarchy, night after night, have prompted the perpetration of the most wanton outrages against liberty, security, and the legitimate rights of man!"[2] Selfridge, who considered the honor of a gentleman "as sacred as the virtue of a woman," justified his action in a pamphlet wherein he quoted Locke on the right to kill any man who, without right and by a manner of force, declares a state of war: "May we not then take life to preserve reputation, more valuable than life itself, and without which, life itself is neither desirable to its possessor, nor useful to the community?" But by an ironic contradiction, the federalist lawyer was unable to see the relation between his own assumption of a private law and the fury of a mob which threatened to invest itself with the power of judge and executioner.

Such a violent sensitivity to insult was a peculiar characteristic of many Americans, especially in the South,

[1] Thomas O. Selfridge, *A Correct Statement of the Whole Preliminary Controversy between Thomas O. Selfridge and Benjamin Austin . . .* (Charlestown, Mass., 1807), pp. 37–45.

[2] *Ibid.,* pp. 39, 42.

where standards of gentlemanly honor were often established and preserved with smoothbore pistols, shotguns, or bowie knives. From the end of the Revolution through most of the nineteenth century, Americans of the South and West accepted two outlets for aggression which differed significantly from even the more violent and brutal customs of Europe. Dueling, which originated in the medieval Appeal and Wager of Battle to settle private wrongs, and which flourished in Europe in the form of secret and illegal combat from 1528 to the nineteenth century,[3] became, in America, an unrestrained and unregulated warfare. Unlike his European counterpart, the American duelist's principal objective was often to kill an enemy by any means whatsoever. Whereas dueling in Europe was confined to the upper classes, who were more concerned with procedures and formalities than with actual killing, dueling in America was not limited by class distinctions. In the South and West the duelist impatiently tolerated and frequently dispensed with formal rules, since his purpose was mainly to annihilate or disable an enemy with as little ceremony as possible. Although lynching has been traced back to the feudal *Vehmgerichte,* there was nothing in eighteenth or nineteenth-century Europe comparable to American lynch "law," which spread from colonial Virginia and Carolina to the south and west.[4] Both of these aggressive practices were justified by an assumption that the people had only conditionally and temporarily surrendered their primitive right of retribution to legal representatives.

[3] E. A. Kendall, *An Argument for Construing Largely the Right of an Appellee of Murder to Insist on Trial by Battle* . . . , 3rd ed. (London, 1818), pp. iii–v; Lorenzo Sabine, *Notes on Duelling, Alphabetically Arranged, with a Preliminary Historical Essay,* 2nd ed. (Boston, 1856), pp. 1–11.

[4] James Elbert Cutler, *Lynch-Law; An Investigation into the History of Lynching in the United States* (New York, 1905), pp. 1–8, 20–40.

Americans of the Revolutionary generation were familiar with John Locke's famous theory that a man who exercised unlawful power had declared a state of war which nullified the obligations of the social compact. A thief, for instance, by his attempt to steal property, a deed which would deprive the owner of liberty and power, had committed an act of war and could be legally killed by the injured man.[5] Common law had long recognized the right of an individual to defend his person or property, but when theorists began to talk of men as sovereign states, possessing the right to declare war and to suspend the limitations of the social contract, they provided an easy justification for private revenge. Thus John Lyde Wilson of Charleston needed only to paraphrase Locke in his defense of private combat: "If an oppressed nation has a right to appeal to arms in defense of its liberty and the happiness of its people, there can be no argument used in support of such appeal which will not apply with equal force to individuals."[6] Since animal nature manifested a "continual warfare for supremacy," and since "by education we make character and moral worth a part of ourselves," it was obvious that the right of self-defense included the vindication of an injured self-esteem: "When one finds himself avoided in society, his friends shunning his approach, his substance wasting, his wife and children in want around him and traces all his misfortunes and misery to the slanderous tongue of the calumniator, who . . . had sapped and undermined his reputation, he must be more or less than a man to submit in silence."[7]

In a culture where few limitations restricted the in-

[5] John Locke, *An Essay Concerning the True Original, Extent, and End of Civil-Government*, in *The Works of John Locke, Esq. . . . ,* 2nd ed. (London, 1722), II, 163–164.

[6] John Lyde Wilson, *The Code of Honor; or, Rules for the Government of Principals and Seconds in Duelling* (Charleston, 1838), p. 3.

[7] *Ibid.,* p. 4.

dividual ego, where men's ambitions were stimulated by unexpected opportunities, and where reputations, once established, were subject to the caprice of public opinion, men were especially sensitive to personal insult. When individuals thought that life was not desirable without reputation, the smallest infringement seemed to threaten the inflated ego. The existence of this heightened self could not be proved by an appeal to facts, since few reputations could go unchallenged, and the duel became a kind of judicial combat, proving by providential means the reality of an ego-ideal. Just as some men gamble to test their favor in the eyes of Providence, so the duelist reaffirmed his self-confidence by staking his life on fortune and skill.

The dueling era in America lasted from the end of the eighteenth century to a little after the Civil War. For the first thirty years duels were fought in an area extending from New York to Georgia and west to the frontier settlements, but the custom was generally limited in the second generation to the slave states and southwestern territories. By 1830 the code of honor was identified with the southern way of life.[8]

In the 1850's the South witnessed a series of splendid tournaments, complete with flashing knights and queens of beauty. But if such pageantry enchanted romantic imaginations from Maryland to South Carolina, it could not conceal the darker undercurrent of brutal violence which was often confused with chivalry. Whereas the duel in Europe had been conducted with rapiers or pistols, often ending with a superficial wound and a reconciliation and amounting to no more than a formal display of honor, there was

[8] J. Winston Coleman, Jr., *Famous Kentucky Duels: The Story of the Code of Honor in the Bluegrass State* (Frankfort, Ky., 1953), p. vii; Thomas Gamble, *Savannah Duels and Duellists, 1733–1877* (Savannah, 1923), pp. 135, 298; Oliver William Stevens, *Pistols at Ten Paces: The Story of the Code of Honor in America* (Boston, 1940), pp. 31, 50, 73.

an increasing tendency in America to use shotguns, rifles, and bowie knives and to fight under such conditions that death was inevitable.[9] In practice, the duel tended to degenerate into unrestrained personal combat, providing the professional killer, the bully, and the psychopath with an opportunity to win reputation and honor from cold-blooded murder.

The code of honor was not without extremely vocal critics, however, from eighteenth-century moralists to Mark Twain, whose ridicule is generally considered to have given the death blow to an institution already debilitated by the unexpected grimness of war. For Timothy Dwight the custom implied more deliberation and sinful intent than did most murders, since the duel often combined the sin of vengeance with the sin of suicide.[10] Lyman Beecher won his first recognition with an anti-dueling sermon given two years after the Burr-Hamilton duel had outraged New England sensibilities. Indignant at the impotence and corruption of courts which failed to prosecute the destroyer of a Christian family, Beecher urged righteous men to use political pressure to drive duelists from office. He warned that if the fierce American spirit of independence and self-importance were not checked there would be a collapse of social order and justice: "Duelling is a great national sin. With the exception of a small section of the union, the whole land is defiled

[9] Sabine, *Notes,* pp. 98–100, 144–163, 180, 184, 314; Stevens, *Pistols,* pp. 46, 89, 110, 133. It is difficult to imagine, for instance, a European duel like the one between General Armistead T. Mason, senator from Virginia, and John M. McCarty. The two cousins, provoked to a duel by gossipy friends, fought in 1818 with shotguns at four paces! Mason's gun caught in his coat as he fired, so that he only blew off McCarty's arm; Mason himself was literally blown to pieces.

[10] Timothy Dwight, *Theology; Explained and Defended in a Series of Sermons* . . . (New Haven, 1836), III, 358–367. Though Dwight stressed the aspect of suicide as a special evil, he curiously advocated the penalty of death for duelists.

with blood. . . . We are Murderers, a nation of Murderers." [11]

But with the exception of a few courageous Southerners like Charles Cotesworth Pinckney and Robert Barnwell Rhett, the enemies of dueling were confined to the North, where the practice had nearly disappeared by 1830. That laws could not suppress the crime where it was encouraged by public opinion was demonstrated by the fact that Illinois was the only state in the Union ever to hang a man for a murder committed in a duel. This one case involved deception and particular malice, which explained the jury's severity.[12] If the chivalric code, with its cold indignation and pompous self-consciousness, was finally deflated by ridicule, personal combat was more deeply embedded in American mores. Even after western gunmen had surrendered their sawed-off shotguns and six-shooters, Americans continued to glorify the memory of grim-faced duelists, who drew blood when a remark was made without a smile, who walked stiff-legged toward each other at high noon, their gloved hands poised above the curving handles of revolvers in oiled holsters.

III

If the duel was commonly thought of as a war between equal nations, the custom of lynching, which flourished in the same areas where dueling was popular, bore a closer resemblance to the punishment of a renegade or enemy spy. The victim was an alienated man, often the representative of a scapegoat group, whose very existence

---

[11] Lyman Beecher, *The Remedy for Duelling: A Sermon Delivered before the Presbytery of Long-Island . . . April 16, 1806* . . . (New York, 1809), p. 31.

[12] Stevens, *Pistols*, p. 93. Most of the southern states had severe laws against dueling, which, in practice, only served to ensure the acquittal of defendants. In 1848 Louisiana repealed an article in the state constitution which disfranchised duelists.

infuriated a mob of righteous men. When Americans endeavored to establish law and order in new regions beset by racial conflict or by social and economic uncertainty, there often was a tendency for citizens to rise in mass violence in an attempt to achieve a clear and positive expression of group cohesion, authority, and justice.

On July 19, 1834, *Niles' Weekly Register* printed a long news story under the heading: "The Law of Nature—or Self Preservation." At a spot west of the Mississippi River known as "Dubuque's Mines," which was as yet included in no particular state or territory, one Patrick O'Conner had killed a man named George O'Keefe. A group of enterprising citizens conducted an inquest, chose a jury, and tried O'Conner for murder, after which he was executed before a crowd of fifteen hundred people. The jury, conscious that they possessed no legal authority, justified their action with an interesting statement: "The security of the lives of the good citizens of this country requires that an example should be made, to preserve order and to convince evil disposed persons that this is not a place where the lives of men may be taken with impunity." *Niles' Register* considered this to be a thrilling example of democracy in action, a lesson to the nation and world in natural jurisprudence: "And as law, in every country, emanates from the people, and is, in fact, whether written or not, nothing more nor less than certain rules of action by which the people agree to be governed, the unanimous agreement, among the people to put a man to death . . . rendered the act legal to all intents and purposes." [13]

But if the people of Dubuque's Mines had acted in the glorious tradition of the signers of the Mayflower Compact and the Declaration of Independence, the virtue of popular law was not so clear the following summer in

[13] *Niles' Weekly Register*, XLVI (July 19, 1834), 352–353.

Mississippi. The citizens of Madison County were thrown into panic by a rumor that bandits and slave-stealers of the notorious Murrell gang were about to incite a slave insurrection. After hanging a group of Negroes and suspected Murrell men, the citizens issued a statement on the God-given right of self-defense. Since one of the victims was alleged to have been a Connecticut abolitionist, mysteriously associated with the Murrell conspirators, they added: "Thus died an ABOLITIONIST, and let his blood be on the heads of those who sent him here." [14] As excitement and terror spread through western Mississippi in the first week of July 1835, violence erupted in Vicksburg. The river town had long been infested with professional gamblers and prostitutes, but it was the excitement in Madison County—"the exigency of the times" —that "determined the citizens of Vicksburg to purge their city of all suspicious persons who might endanger the public safety." [15]

The affair began at a Fourth of July barbecue, when a tough gambler was captured by the Vicksburg Volunteers after he had insulted a respectable citizen. The gambler was summarily "lynched," which at that time usually meant whipping, tarring, and banishing.[16] But after administering such punishment, the citizens of Vicksburg were terrified by the thought that the gamblers might retaliate. To protect temselves, they organized a raid on the various gaming houses. In the violence of July 6 a popular citizen was killed. Aroused to extreme fury, the good people of Vicksburg hanged five gamblers "in

[14] H. R. Howard, comp., *The History of Virgil A. Stewart and His Adventure in Capturing and Exposing the Great "Western Land Pirate" and His Gang . . . Also of the Trials, Confessions, and Execution of a Number of Murrell's Associates in the State of Mississippi during the Summer of 1835, and the Execution of Five Professional Gamblers by the Citizens of Vicksburg . . .* (New York, 1836), p. 252.

[15] *Ibid.*, p. 263.   [16] *Niles*, XLVIII (Aug. 1, 1835), 381.

presence of the assembled multitude," justifying their sudden vengeance with a report which said that Vicksburg was now "redeemed and ventilated from all the vices and influence of gambling and assignation houses." It had been necessary to dispense with the forms of law because "our streets every where resounded with the echoes of their drunken and obscene mirth, and no citizen was secure from their villainy." [17] "Sickly sensibility or mawkish philanthropy" might object to lynching gamblers, but the respectable citizens of Vicksburg urged other towns to avenge their own insulted laws and to exterminate deep-rooted vice.[18]

Nine months later, in a case which gained national prominence, a free mulatto was arrested on a boat in St. Louis, after helping a slave to escape. Because the mulatto had stabbed a deputy sheriff during the scuffle, an angry mob broke into the jail in which he was later confined, dragged him outside, and slowly burned him to death. Judge Lawless (who was most appropriately named), in his statement to the grand jury, added a strange corollary to the proposition estabished at Dubuque's Mines twenty-one months before. If a man was killed by a mob of people, "seized upon and impelled by that mysterious metaphysical, and almost electrical phrenzy, which, in all nations and ages, has hurried on the infuriated multitude to deeds of death and destruction—then, I say, act not at all in the matter—the case then transcends your jurisdiction—it is beyond the reach of human law." [19] The Reverend E. P. Lovejoy, who was imprudent enough to denounce Judge Lawless, was killed by a mob in Alton, Illinois, on November 7, 1837, after his printing office in St. Louis had been destroyed by "mysterious, metaphysical powers." From the hanging at Dubuque's Mines to

[17] *Ibid.*   [18] Howard, *History,* p. 268.
[19] Quoted in Cutler, *Lynch-Law,* p. 110.

the decision of Judge Lawless, the Mississippi valley had witnessed the degradation of popular justice.

Summary justice, often referred to as "club law," had been common in back-country South Carolina during the 1760's, where "Regulators" denied the jurisdiction of Charleston courts over an area plagued by robbers. By 1817 the word "lynch," derived from the justice of Colonel Charles Lynch, had become a localism in Virginia for extralegal whipping and tarring and feathering.[20] Many of the first Regulator companies acted under conditions similar to those at Dubuque's Mines, when legitimate law enforcement was either weak or nonexistent. Gradually, however, summary punishment became an alternative to law, especially in cases where no statutory crime was involved or where public excitement made people impatient for revenge. In May 1835, two Negroes were burned to death near Mobile for allegedly murdering two children, the action being justified by an opinion that legal punishments were not severe nor painful enough for such barbarous crimes.

By 1844, when a crowd of "mobocrats" shot Joseph Smith in the Carthage, Illinois, jail, lynching had become widely accepted in the South and West as a form of democratic justice, reserved for outcasts who were beneath the dignity and patience of the law. Just as a personal insult temporarily suspended the social contract, requiring an honorable man to defend his reputation, so a mob of men could strive for unity and purpose by abrogating constitutional justice and by using violence to exorcise agents of the devil. As the people of Vicksburg said of such subversives, "no citizen was secure from their villainy."

---

[20] *Ibid.*, pp. 37–40. Cutler has good documentation for his argument that the verb "to lynch" did not mean invariable capital punishment until after the Civil War (p. 116), but during the 1830's the term gradually began to imply death, especially for Negroes and Abolitionists.

IV

In our country a great many crimes are committed to gratify public expectation. Most of our duels are fought to satisfy the demands of public opinion; by which is understood the opinions of that little set, batch, or clique, of which some long-nosed Solomon . . . is the sapient lawgiver and head. Most of the riots and mobs are instigated by half-witted journalists, who first goad the offender to his crime, and, the next day, rate him soundly for its commission! . . . All this is certainly very amusing, and, with proper details, makes a murder-paragraph in the newspaper which delights the old ladies. . . . It produces that pleasurable excitement which is the mental brandy and tobacco to all persons of the Anglo-Saxon breed.[21]

When William Gilmore Simms was not pretending to admire chivalry, he was perceptive concerning the intricate mechanisms of projected and vicarious aggression. He did not deny that there were some offenses which deserved private retaliation, yet he was deeply aware of the folly and injustice of an avenger's exposing his own life on an equal basis. In American novels from *Arthur Mervyn* (1799–1800) to Catharine Maria Sedgwick's *Clarence* (1830), and from Simms's *Beauchampe* (1842) on to Lippard's *New York* (1853), dueling was attacked for its fortuitous results, for its essential injustice, which were usually illustrated by the death of an outraged and vengeful brother or husband at the hand of a vile seducer.

In addition to what Charles Brockden Brown called the "malignant destiny" which accompanied dueling, writers were also concerned with the imagined guilt of the victorious warrior. One of William Alexander Caruthers' southern heroines wrote to her fiancé, urging him to repudiate the false code of honor: "I could never *accept*

---

[21] William Gilmore Simms, *Beauchampe; or, The Kentucky Tragedy* (New York, 1856), pp. 337–338.

that hand in marriage which had been previously stained by the blood of a fellow-being—shed in single combat and in cold blood." [22] In John Neal's *Keep Cool* (1817) and *Seventy-six* (1823) men were haunted by the memory of successful duels, even though the killings had been justified by the accepted standards of honor.

Neal sensed, however, that guilt and fear might also contribute to a compulsive need to fight. Bill Adams in *Errata* (1823) had been pampered and spoiled by an indulgent mother who had protected him, whenever possible, from the cruel discipline of the father. When his mother died, the father whipped Bill at her bedside, after discovering that the boy had crawled under the covers beside his mother's body. Terrified by his father, but trained by his mother to lie, steal, and rebel against authority, Adams grew up to be truculent and quarrelsome in order to hide his overwhelming fear. When he first drove a sword through an opponent in a duel, he was "delirious with terror," yet he would have gone mad had he not killed his enemy. Adams later said that he would give his right hand to be able to face his children and say that he had never received a blow without returning it: "Passion is madness with me. It is a whirlwind. My very blood-vessels are distended to rupture. No human strength can withstand me." Every man that Bill Adams fought was a symbol of his hated and dreaded father.

Neal's theme became clear in Adams' intensive jealousy after marriage: "A kiss! by heaven, Emma, I would as soon my wife go to bed to another man as to be kissed by him." Bill Adams suspected that Hammond, a dwarf whom he had detested since childhood, had been too friendly with Emma, and he challenged the innocent

---

[22] William Alexander Caruthers, *The Knights of the Horse-shoe: A Traditionary Tale of the Cocked Hat Gentry in the Old Dominion* . . . (New York, n.d.), p. 371.

man to immediate combat. Although the dwarf refused to fight, Adams shot him and fled to Europe. Finally, Adams was driven insane by the discovery of Hammond's innocence and of his own wife's tragic death. By applying a version of the ancient Oedipus myth to an impulsive duelist, Neal explained the desire to kill in terms of childhood fear and jealousy.

In fiction the duel was seldom caused by a simple and rational desire to preserve social unity through the defense of individual honor, which was the theory advanced by southern apologists. Even the punctilious observance of the rigid code duello, whose niceties resembled the elegant procedures of an aristocratic courtship and marriage, could not conceal the sordid motive of revenge. Instead of trying to defend morality, the fictional duelist was attempting to prove something to *himself*. As we have seen, this psychology of vengeance was essentially a rebellion which sprang from insecurity and fear.

Hence the duel was related to all human aggression and was merely an extreme example of a larger struggle. George Lippard introduced a dueling scene on the heights above Hoboken by referring to this struggle for survival:

Standing by one of these huge rocks, encircled by the trees, and steeped in the quiet of the place, you gaze upon the distant city, like one contemplating a far off battle-field, in which millions are engaged, and the fate of empires is at stake. A sadder battle-field, sun never shone upon, than the Empire City, in which millions are battling every moment of the hour, and battling all life long for fame, for wealth, for bread, for life.[23]

The hero in Theodore Sedgwick Fay's *The Countess* (1840) anticipated Dreiser when he mused:

[23] George Lippard, *New York: Its Upper Ten and Lower Million* (Cincinnati, 1853), p. 197.

This sweet forest, so fair to view, is but a scene of continual massacre. The microscope that discovers animalcule invisible to the naked eye, finds them killing each other. I have surely been led away by idle theories of human excellence. I have set myself apart, as better than my fellow-beings. . . . I do not wish to be. God made us mortal. I will kill this man.[24]

Later, however, the same hero reverted to eighteenth-century doctrine, when, impressed by the blissful serenity of Nature, he decided that God did not intend us to kill in passion.

If dueling was related to the general struggle for survival, the fictional duelist was himself usually a ruthless aggressor and thus an unfair competitor. In much of the antidueling fiction, the villain was an atheistic and murderous ruffian, often traveling in America with a counterfeit title of nobility which dazzled impressionable women, but which aroused the suspicions of patriotic American men. Like Count Clairmont in Fay's *Norman Leslie* (1835), he might temporarily pervert American justice, winning esteem and reputation from the gullible populace, yet exposure and death were inevitable and were generally associated with a repudiation of the unchristian code of honor.

Few writers of fiction openly defended dueling, though Simms often echoed the southern argument that the code protected feminine honor, raised the general tone of society, and prevented bullying and calumny. Alfred W. Arrington, who described cases of heroic generosity and courtesy among duelists on the frontier, defended the practice as a test of true physical bravery, of the same prowess which had made the demigods and heroes of mankind since the dawn of history. If the duel sometimes caused suffering,

[24] Theodore S. Fay, *The Countess* (London, 1840), II, 204.

what are all material tortures in comparison with the crucify-
ing pangs of the mind, murdered in its dearest memories, . . .
brightest hopes? How many of the rich, in the gay capitals of
commerce show mercy to the breaking hearts of the poor,
ground into the dust by their cunning monopolies! . . . The
greatest eulogist on urban civilization, to be candid, must
confess that there are other competitions more fearful than
battles with revolvers, and the willful homicide of happiness
and reputation is the worst species of possible assassination! [25]

In the West, however, there was a stronger tendency
to treat the duel with humor. Emerson Bennett described
an Arkansas bad man named Kelser, the leader of a gang
of bullies, who had killed six men with a bowie knife.
Kelser hated many things, but he especially hated Yan-
kees; and when a blue-eyed New Englander arrived in
town, Kelser was determined to fight.[26] After repeated
insults, the Yankee accepted the challenge, but proposed
terms whereby one loaded and one empty pistol should
be placed under a cloth, and at the signal, the two men
should draw and fire at point-blank range. Kelser, who
"swore that nobody but a Yankee would ever have thought
of such a heathenish way of doing business," turned pale
for the first time in his life. He pulled his pistol before
the signal was given, and, finding it unloaded, grabbed
the second weapon before the Yankee could reach it.
When Kelser discovered that the other pistol was also
harmless, that the whole affair was a joke, he rushed at
the Yankee with his trusty bowie knife. Fortunately, the
New Englander was prepared for all contingencies; after
shooting the bully with a small pistol which he had con-

[25] [Alfred W. Arrington], *The Rangers and Regulators of the Tanaha; or,
Life Among the Lawless: A Tale of the Republic of Texas,* by Charles
Summerfield [pseud.] (New York, 1856), p. 357.

[26] Emerson Bennett, *Forest and Prairie; or, Life on the Frontier* (Philadelphia, 1860), p. 148.

cealed in his pocket and being excused by a verdict of justifiable homicide, the "blue-eyed stranger resumed his journey as if nothing had happened."

Joseph M. Field's "The Great Small Affair Duel" (1847) is one of the best examples of the kind of frontier humor that deflated the code of honor and reduced the duel to a farce. Dr. Slunk and Mr. Fitzcarol, a singer who was locally known as "the feature," were going to have a duel over Miss Fanny Wilkins, an itinerant actress. Jake Bagly, who was well known for his hoaxes, had suggested the duel to Dr. Slunk as a means of winning Miss Fanny. Most of the town knew that it would be a mock duel only, that neither pistol would be loaded with ball, but that Dr. Slunk would fall as if he were dead, whereupon the crowd would threaten to lynch "the feature." Fitzcarol would rush from town in terror, so the plan went, leaving Miss Fanny wide open for Dr. Slunk: "It was to be none of your sneaking, shivering break o' day duels, but a sociable meeting for the benefit of all." [27]

Although Slunk and Bagly haughtily went through the preliminaries, the surgeon standing by in preparedness and the crowd bobbing up and down for a better view, "somehow or other the 'feature' had not shown the least uneasiness or alarm, so far, and there was nothing to laugh at." Then the pistols were discharged simultaneously, Slunk dropped his weapon to the ground and staggered backward: "Taking his hand away from his side, there appeared a dismal blotch of blood, and now, in the act of 'biting the dust,' he suddenly arrested his fall and stood up again, as if looking for a *clean place*; for, as has been remarked, the cows had been there." Finally, Dr. Slunk found a place where the cows had not been and fell like a murdered man. But it was too late. A scream of laughter

[27] Joseph M. Field, *The Drama of Pokerville: The Bench and Bar of Jury-town, and Other Stories* (Philadelphia, 1847), p. 83.

shot from the crowd, as the sentiment suddenly turned in favor of Fitzcarol. They shouted, "Can't bluff you, old hoss," and even urged him to follow through and actually kill Dr. Slunk. But Fitzcarol had enough sense of humor to know that his triumph could not be more complete.

Although dueling was frequently used as a dramatic device in American fiction before the Civil War, it was generally attacked as a form of vindictive revenge, disguised by a deceptive etiquette. A few southern novelists made a theoretical defense of the code of honor, yet the duel itself was seldom chosen by the fictional hero as a method for defeating the villain. Indeed, it was an accepted formula to have the villain kill a stubbornly brave young man and then die himself in unexpected and unregulated combat. Clearly there was no protest against homicide as such in American literature, since admirable characters like Edgar Huntley and Leatherstocking killed their enemies in battle. But if triumph by single combat was to be allowed, it was necessary that it be sudden, unrestricted, and, as with the Deerslayer's first killing, in harmony with the rhythms of nature. Even in the humorous ridicule of dueling, protest was confined to the pretensions and hypocrisy of *regulating* murder. In Emerson Bennett's tale, the Yankee burlesqued the code by his choice of weapons and conditions, but ultimately, he killed the bully under the "natural" conditions of unplanned combat.

V

In Sir Walter Scott's *The Heart of Midlothian* (1818) an Edinburgh mob killed Captain Porteous after governmental authorities had refused to punish the captain for ordering his men to shoot into a rebellious crowd at a public execution. This incident resembled the American conception of lynching more closely than did most European descriptions of summary justice, yet Scott thought of mob violence in terms of insurrection against estabished authority. In American fiction before the Civil War, lynching occupied a position of curious respectability, often being defended as a necessity of frontier life or as a fundamental expression of democracy. As late as Owen Wister's *The Virginian* (1902), there was in the popular novel a lingering sympathy for lynching.

Summary punishment began, according to most writers, during the first American civil war, when Tory atrocities provoked revenge from angry farmers and backwoodsmen. In John Pendelton Kennedy's *Horse-shoe Robinson* (1835) the hanging of Tory prisoners was justified by the fact that the Tories themselves had killed prisoners. American Skinners and British Cow-Boys hanged one another in Cooper's *The Spy* (1821), which vividly described the cool execution of the Skinner chieftain, who wanted to desert to the British side, by a group of Cow-Boys in an abandoned barn.

Even after the Revolution, Captain Porgy's partisans, in Simms's *Woodcraft* (1854), felt it necessary to lynch renegades and outlaws in a backwoods area disorganized by war. Simms commented:

The morals of law always will, and should, sustain what are the obvious necessities of society. In this you have the full justification of the code of regulation; a code which is, no doubt, sometimes subject to abuse, as is the case with the law itself, but which is rarely allowed to exist in practice—among people of Anglo-Norman origin—a day longer than is absolutely essential to the common weal.[28]

This was a strange statement for a Southerner to make in the 1850's. Seventy years was a long time for summary justice to be "absolutely essential to the common weal."

[28] William Gilmore Simms, *Woodcraft; or, Hawks about the Dovecote: A Story of the South at the Close of the Revolution* (New York, 1882), p. 154.

Yet the sympathetic Captain Porgy clarified the theory of lynching when his prisoner, Norris, challenged his right to make and to execute the law: "The good citizens of a country must always constitute a standing army for the purposes of public justice and public security." [29] This was, of course, the assumption of the *good* citizens of Vicksburg, who thought of themselves as a standing army, prepared at any moment to declare war against subversives.

The victims of fictional lynching were nearly always traitors or criminal outcasts, like Miccajah Harpe in James Hall's *The Harpe's Head* (1833), whose atrocities and settled revenge against mankind "for some fancied injury," vindicated the righteous men who placed his head on the fork of a tree; or like Rashton Moody in Emerson Bennett's *Kate Clarendon* (1848), who became a renegade with the Indians after being rejected in love and who was justly lynched in the wilderness because his captors thought it too much trouble to take him to a Cincinnati court.

The law of the frontier might be occasionally treated with humor, but unlike dueling, it was seldom ridiculed. Captain Ralph Stackpole, a comic character in *Nick of the Woods* (1837), was bound and placed upon a horse he had stolen. The halter was strung from Stackpole's neck to the limb of a tree, so that when the horse moved, the captain would be hanged: "There was a kind of dreadful poetical-justice in thus making the stolen horse the thief's executioner," Bird wrote. "It gave the animal himself an opportunity to wreak vengeance for all the wrongs received." Stackpole's frantic pleas to the hero, who stumbled accidentally upon the lynched man, were presented as being hilariously funny. The hero, observing a sign that said "Judge Lynch," refused to help the Captain: "He is hanged according to Kentucky law; a very

[29] Simms, *Woodcraft*, p. 154.

good law, as far as it regards horse-thieves, for whom hanging is too light a punishment." Only the heroine, who might be excused for her sentimentality, could save a man condemned by summary justice.

When writers chose Texas as a setting, it was a rare story that did not include lynching as a matter of course. According to Alfred W. Arrington, mob violence was a natural remedy for lawlessness in an "epoch of strife, turbulence, and general combat—the state of nature, which is always a state of war, when sanguinary crimes provoke still more sanguinary punishments." When a disgruntled suitor poisoned a bride and groom at the wedding, for instance, it was only natural in Texas that he should be found dangling from a tree three days later.

But if Texas was a state of nature, populated by a diversity of social classes exhibiting varying degrees of morality, "as if the ideal perfection of Democracy, so long doubted as a political myth, had been at last realized," it was for that reason vulnerable to the uninhibited violence of mob action: "All prudence, pity, and generous sympathy abandon such a crowd." After a respectable family had been robbed and murdered, a furious mob, stirred on by a preacher who yelled that "universal lynching would herald the Millennium," might hang a small boy with shouts of "Kill the young rattle-snake!" and "Blood for blood!" [30] While Arrington felt that lynching might be justified in the interest of security, he warned that a mob attracted the worst ruffians, who extracted confessions by torture and who chose victims without discrimination.

Charles Wilkins Webber also described the horror of the bloody Regulator Wars which disrupted Texas in 1839. In a story which was pirated and circulated through the western press in many versions, Webber analyzed the various social groups in frontier Texas. A small class of

[30] [Arrington], *Rangers*, pp. 187–188, 264.

wealthy planters was often dominated by a larger group
of small landholders, who cultivated patches between the
great plantations but who kept fine horses and depended
on crime for livelihood and excitement. A third group of
restless, migrating hunters fought to preserve their own
independence and dignity.[31] A cutthroat named Hinch,
the leader of a band of Regulators, had subjected the
entire country to fear, extracting rent for "protection"
from the rich planters and terrorizing the simple hunters
with lynching parties. Hinch developed a grudge against
Jack Long, one of the "wild turkey breed" of hunters
who first crossed the Appalachians, an independent, Boone-
like man who "had never thought it at all essential to ask
leave of any government as to how or where he should
make himself a home." Unaware of the fact that no one
ever tried to beat Hinch in a shooting match, Jack Long
surpassed the lyncher in a public contest and further
aggravated the insult by refusing a challenge to combat.
Thinking of his wife and children in their snug log cabin,
Jack was unmoved by the Regulators' sneers and taunts.

Hinch retaliated by planting a stolen horse near Jack's
cabin, and by shooting other horses and cows through
the eye, for Long had once boasted that he killed deer in
this manner. When this outrage was made known, the
populace applauded the Regulators when they went to
Long's cabin, stripped and bound the hunter to an oak,
and whipped him senseless before his own family. Before
he fainted, however, Jack calmly gazed on his persecutors,
memorizing each face. Finding the hut deserted the next
day, Hinch assumed that Jack had died and that his family
had fled.

Four months later rumors circulated among the common
farmers that a tall, gaunt creature with a beard and blaz-

[31] Charles Wilkins Webber, *Tales of the Southern Border* (Philadelphia,
1855), pp. 10–11.

ing eyes had been seen roaming the forests with a long rifle. When two of the Regulators were found dead, shot through the eye, Hinch and his company swept and raged through the country, arresting and lynching all suspicious or undesirable men: "Public sentiments justified extreme measures, for the general safety seemed to demand that the perpetrator of these secret murders should be brought to light, and great as was the license under which he acted, Hinch yet felt the necessity of being backed by some shadow of approval." Inoffensive men were hanged, revived, and hanged again, in an attempt to force confessions, but Hinch could learn of no definite conspiracy. When the third Regulator fell, the rumors gathered momentum: "Now he was to be seen mounted, careering like a form of vapor past the dark trunks of the forest aisles, or hurrying swiftly away like a rain-cloud before the wind across the wide prairie, always hair-clad and gaunt, with a streaming beard, and the long heavy rifle on his shoulder."

Because Hinch noticed that only the emigrant hunters spread the rumors, he suspected a plot against his company and instituted a reign of terror, lashing and lynching hunters until one of his Regulator's wives saw Jack Long rise from a bush and shoot her husband through the eye. Now the common people, feeling secure from personal danger, sat back to enjoy the destruction of the Regulators, who no longer held their support. One testy hunter said, "I let you know Jack come of a Tory-hatin', Injunfighten' gineration, and that's a blood whar's hard to cool when it gits riz. Them stripes has sot his bristles up, and it'll take *some* blood to slick 'em down agin."

Though the Regulators searched the woods for Jack, they could not escape the deadly bullets that flew from the most unexpected places, always striking a man's eye. After seven of his comrades had been murdered, Hinch became nervous and jumpy and decided to leave the region.

He made a desperate ride to the Red River, where, wait-
ing for the boat, relieved that he had escaped, he heard
the click of a rifle. As he turned in horror, a bullet smashed
through his eye; and Jack Long galloped away to do what
he had not done since the night of the fatal lynching. He
could now look his wife in the eyes. As Webber moral-
ized: "Powerful elements sometimes slumber in the breasts
of quiet men; and there is in uncultured breasts a wild
sense of justice, which, if it often carry retribution to the
extremest limits of vengeance, is none the less implanted
by Him who gave the passions to repose within us." [32]

In the popular story of Jack Long the code of individual
honor triumphed over the code of group violence. Yet the
theory which vindicated Jack Long in his deliberate and
vengeful extermination of the Regulators was essentially
the same theory which justified an execution by rope or
faggot. Jack Long did not send a formal challenge to his
enemies, nor was his revenge regulated by a rationalized
code. It is significant that hot blood "whar's hard to cool
when it gits riz" was considered to be an admirable and
manly possession, associated with a "wild sense of justice"
which was implanted by God.

We thus reach, with the subject of lynching and dueling, an association of ideas which we have traced in preceding chapters. The basic moral sense is identified with
passion, its validity being proportionate to intensity of
emotion. This leads to a curious reversal of the common-
law doctrine of hot blood. When morality was associated
with rational judgment, hot blood meant a temporary
suspension of responsibility, followed by a "cooling period"
in which a man regained moral capacity. We have seen
that this theory had been traditionally applied to husbands
who killed their wives' lovers in moments of blind passion.
But when the locus of morality was transferred to the

[32] Webber, *Tales,* p. 44.

passions themselves, then hot blood became the expression of "a wild sense of justice" which bore a universal and transcendent truth. That which could not be excused in a state of cold rationality, when moral values were only dimly perceived, became supremely virtuous when determined by righteous passion. It was essentially a Lockian psychology which justified summary punishment in a state of social insecurity, when, as the people of Dubuque's Mines said, "an example should be made, to preserve order." But when an insult went beyond the province of objective reason, violating the fundamental moral sense, then people were "impelled by that mysterious metaphysical, and almost electric phrenzy," which, according to Judge Lawless, transcended the jurisdiction of human law.

Chapter XI

THE IMMENSURABLE

JUSTICE OF DEATH

THUS far we have examined certain beliefs and values concerning the nature and causes of homicide which have been expressed in sixty years of American fiction, together with related assumptions in a roughly contemporary intellectual environment. Most of the problems that we have discussed reach a practical culmination with the disturbing question: what is to be done with a man guilty of culpable homicide?

At a time when most crimes were capital, though subject to the benefit of clergy and to a capricious pardoning power, the question of a murderer's status involved little debate. If an Englishman had killed in a heat of passion, and if he had the good fortune to be literate, he received a burn on his hand and was dismissed; if he had murdered with stealth and deliberation, he was hanged, along with petty thieves, forgers, and poachers. According to Lockian jurisprudence, which was generally accepted in America,[1] every man had ceded his natural right of retribution to the state, which, as his legal agent, was duty bound to execute every "noxious Creature."

By 1800, however, a group of enlightened thinkers had challenged the criminal codes of France, Italy, and England, pioneer psychiatrists had widened the conception of insanity, explaining many morbid and aggressive actions in terms of mental disease, and a pietistic religious spirit had encouraged men to sympathize with their depraved brothers and to endeavor to reform the outcasts of society. Especially in liberal intellectual circles, there was a growing uncertainty regarding the justice and efficacy of retributive punishment. It was principally the Lockian psychology which contributed to a theory of punishment as social expedience, and if utility justified Bentham and Paley's arguments for swift and harsh penalties, Beccaria combined the sensational psychology with the moral-sense philosophy and concluded that capital punishment was repugnant to "the indelible sentiments of the heart of man." [2]

During the first half of the nineteenth century a basic conflict arose between those who thought of a murderer as a moral alien—a renegade from the human species, whose death secured virtue by destroying one more nest of evil—and those who considered the murderer as a physical alien, at least as a man alienated by physical causes, still capable of penitence and salvation. The arguments of Beccaria were soon accepted and expanded by Quakers, liberal Unitarians, and social reformers, who

[1] Nathan Dane, *A General Abridgment and Digest of American Law, with Occasional Notes and Comments* (Boston, 1824), VI, 626–637.

[2] Cesare Beccaria, *An Essay on Crimes and Punishments, Translated from the Italian; with a Commentary Attributed to Mons. De Voltaire . . .* (London, 1767), pp. 8–11, 43, 102, 112.

often found in phrenology and the moral-sense theory arguments against retributive punishment. But whether men attacked the death penalty as a vestige of barbarism or defended it as essential to the security of society, they evidenced emotions disproportionate to the rational arguments involved. It is doubtful that the preservation or abolition of capital punishment would greatly affect the security of society, were the issue confined to the fate of a small number of convicted murderers. Yet the debate over the penalty of death was soon confused by such considerations as the metaphysical struggle between good and evil, the ultimate source of justice, the degree of human responsibility, the fallibility of the courts, the progress or decline of society, and the authority of the Bible. The occasional hanging of a murderer seemed to have psychological implications tending either to unify or to disintegrate society, especially in a democracy destined to lead the world to moral perfection.

Psychologically, the punishment of death was a ritual demonstrating a united hatred of evil, the murderer being generally chosen as a symbol of the most wicked and depraved disposition that men could imagine. As a ritual the penalty was reassuring to normal, virtuous men, for it vindicated their own consciences, strengthening their self-imposed restraints and efforts to suppress aggressive impulses, not because average men feared a similar punishment, but because they identified themselves with a righteous cause. At the same time, a public hanging provided an approved outlet for collective revenge. The death of a criminal was a sacrifice which ensured the virtue of society, justified mankind in the eyes of God and all other paternal authorities, and allowed each frustrated individual to fortify his own antibodies against private aggression by a vicarious act of murder.

Yet executions could serve such a convenient purpose
only so long as men believed in concrete, uncaused evil
which might totally contaminate a member of the tribe.
If a man murdered because of a warped disposition, itself the product of oppression, poverty, trauma, or faulty
training, then, as Bulwer-Lytton's Paul Clifford said,
"circumstances make guilt. . . . Let us endeavor to
correct the circumstances before we rail against the guilt!"
The debate over the death penalty was, in short, one of
the most significant points of conflict between empirical
thought, with its skirmish line of social reformers leading
the assault, and a great body of traditional values, which
relied for support on the vulnerable outpost of capital
punishment. At issue was not merely the disposal of undesirable criminals, but the preservation of public order
and virtue, the responsibilities of society to its members,
and the innocence or guilt of a time-honored method of
releasing surplus aggression through the public hanging
of a scapegoat.

From the 1820's to the Civil War, philosophic and
religious theories of punishment were converted into a
sustained social and political agitation for the abolition
of the death penalty. The arguments of Edward Livingston, Thomas Upham, and Martin H. Bovee were based
upon the premise that moral evil has external causes and
is not the result of conscious and willful choice. Since man's
passions were more powerful than was his reason, executions would not serve as a deterrent, but would rather
stimulate more impressionable minds to similar violence:

If the sight of one capital execution creates an inhuman taste
to behold another; if a curiosity, satisfied at first with terror,
increases with its gratification, and becomes a passion by indulgence, we ought to be extremely careful how . . . we lay
the foundation for a depravity the more to be dreaded, because, in our government, popular opinion must have the

greatest influence . . . and this vitiated taste would soon be discovered in the decisions of our courts and the verdicts of our juries.[3]

It is clear that this theory identified the will and moral sense with the passions, which, requiring careful nurture in a sheltered environment, would be only corrupted by spectacles of violence. In a society which offered individuals the opportunity for moral improvement, it was unthinkable to allow exhibitions that contaminated the more delicate feelings of humanity. According to Robert Rantoul in 1849, the United States had reached the "proud pre-eminence" of being able to realize Beccaria's prophecy that hanging must disappear as soon as the mass of citizens had been raised from ignorance to enlightenment: "In the present state of refinement, every infliction of the Death penalty is a foul and frightful crime." [4]

Before 1830 there had been a gradual reduction in the number of crimes punishable by death in most American states. Many legislatures followed Pennsylvania's unique system, established in 1794, of dividing murder into two degrees, which further limited the use of capital punishment.[5] If a man's intellect had been only temporarily sub-

[3] Edward Livingston, *A System of Penal Law, for the State of Louisiana* . . . (Philadelphia, 1833), p. 27.

[4] *An Exercise in Declamation; in the Form of a Debate on Capital Punishment. At the Boston Latin School, Public Saturday, March 3, 1849* (Boston, 1849), pp. 3–4.

[5] Francis Wharton, *A Treatise on the Law of Homicide in the United States: To Which is Appended a Series of Leading Cases*, 2nd ed. (Philadelphia, 1875), p. 171. Some states went still further and defined four degrees of manslaughter, which, along with excusable and justifiable homicide, allowed eight different interpretations of killing. Second-degree manslaughter included killing in a cruel and unusual manner, but with no design of effecting death; and third-degree manslaughter included unintentional killing with a dangerous weapon (*The Revised Statutes of the State of New York Passed during the Years One Thousand Eight Hundred and Twenty-Seven . . . and Twenty-Eight . . .* [Albany, 1829], II, 660–661; *The Revised Statutes of the State of Missouri . . .* [St. Louis, 1835], pp. 168–170).

verted, or if he had acted from great provocation, there was hope that he might be saved. But when a murderer's entire personality had consented to the crime, it was evident that his moral sense had been completely destroyed, making him too dangerous to live.

Critics of capital punishment were not content, however, with a compromise which saved those who killed from anger, excitement, or drunkenness, but which condemned men suffering from physical or moral disease. During the 1830's and 1840's, the reform movement nearly triumphed in New York, Massachusetts, and New Hampshire,[6] while Maine succeeded in making executions depend on an executive warrant, to be issued at the discretion of the governor one year after the date of sentence.[7] Finally, Michigan in 1847 became the first governing state in modern times to abolish the death penalty permanently for all murder, though Rhode Island and Wisconsin followed her example in the early 1850's.[8]

Although advocates of capital punishment usually began their argument by citing Old Testament authority

---

It is fairly obvious that if malicious intent could not be inferred from killing in a cruel and unusual manner, nor from the use of a deadly weapon, it would be very difficult to prove in any case of homicide involving a sudden "heat of passion." There can be little doubt that the purpose of the degree system was actually to remove several types of murder from the list of capital offenses.

[6] John L. O'Sullivan, *Report in Favor of the Abolition of the Punishment of Death by Law, Made to the Legislature of the State of New York* . . . (New York, 1841), pref.; *Journals of the Senate and House, June Session, 1842* [New Hampshire] (Concord, N.H., 1842), pp. 284–289; [Commonwealth of Massachusetts], *House* [document] no. 149, *Report of a Joint Special Committee on Capital Punishment* (April 24, 1851), pp. 3–5.

[7] Tobias Purrington, *Report on Capital Punishment, Made to the Maine Legislature in 1836* . . . , 3rd ed. (Washington, 1852), pp. 41–42.

[8] *Journal of the Senate of the State of Michigan, 1846* (Detroit, 1846), pp. 241–357; *Journal of the House of Representatives of the State of Michigan, 1846* (Detroit, 1846), pp. 498–515, 548, 575, 599, 613; Purrington, *Report*, p. 47.

and by denying historical progress,[9] the legal profession found a more persuasive doctrine in a new philosophy of justice. In 1843 George Barrell Cheever spoke of "intrinsic justice" and of "moral necessity," which required that murderers be punished invariably with death: "There ought to be such a penalty, high, awful, distinctive, to mark this crime in its *retribution*, as it stands in its *guilt*, paramount to every other." [10] Compared with the arguments of Locke, Paley, and Beccaria, this was a new note, deriving the right of retribution not from an individual's delegated right of self-defense, but from the moral dialectic of Being. When Francis Wharton later defended the death penalty, he pointedly rejected the theories that punishment was intended primarily to prevent crime, to reform offenders, or to incite terror. The justification was simple and absolute; government was the vindicator of Right, crime was a violation of eternal moral law, and "crime as crime must be punished." [11] In the philosophy of Kant and Hegel, Wharton found vindication for a theory of punishment as categorical imperative, demanded by the laws of reason. Penalties, as Hegel had said, were agencies with which to annihilate wrong in its continual effort to annihilate right.[12] Hence man was to be given a power which heretofore had been at least theoretically

[9] William Theodore Dwight, *A Discourse on the Rightfulness and Expedience of Capital Punishments* . . . (Portland, Me., 1843), pp. 8, 19.

[10] George Barrell Cheever, *Capital Punishment: The Argument of Rev. George B. Cheever in Reply to J. L. O'Sullivan* . . . (New York, 1843), pp. 42–43.

[11] Francis Wharton, *Philosophy of Criminal Law* (Philadelphia, 1880), pp. 2–12. Wharton's monumental *Treatise on the Criminal Law of the United States* was published in 1846, and many of his other works appeared in their first editions before the Civil War. His later summary of legal philosophy is therefore pertinent to this discussion, since his views were largely a comment on the debate of the 1840's and 50's.

[12] Wharton, *Philosophy*, p. 14. Wharton modified the absolute theory to some degree; he also interpreted the law as the united will of the people.

reserved for God, the measurement and negation of absolute guilt.

By a strange irony in the erratic course of ideas, the moral-sense theory, which had at first reinforced the efforts of reformers to reclaim their deluded and erring brethren, had now been expanded into an inherent and absolute knowledge of right and wrong, justifying the infliction of punishments graded in exact proportion to guilt. With the rejection of the sensational psychology in favor of intuitive knowledge and complete moral freedom, men achieved in theory the power to punish those who were alienated, not from God's law, nor from the social compact, but from the universal rules of transcendental mind. As soon as the will was separated from the passions and inclinations, becoming an immaterial and autonomous force, the most depraved criminal was responsible for his acts, and there could be no protest against the intrinsic justice of death.

But it was not only a new moral philosophy which temporarily defeated the movement to abolish the penalty of death. The reform impulse was still vigorous, and legislatures in many northern states were still debating the question of capital punishment when the Civil War broke out. Martin H. Bovee, who had been primarily responsible for the Wisconsin law and who later fought for the cause in Illinois and New York, was convinced as late as 1860 that reasonable men could be persuaded to follow the enlightened example of Michigan, Rhode Island, and Wisconsin. Just before the war he finally completed a comprehensive treatise against capital punishment, a book which seemed to refute every possible argument of the opposition. The publication date had originally been set for the year 1861, but the book did not appear until 1876. Bovee later confessed, explaining why his treatise had not been published earlier, "To have presented a work of this kind during the continuance of such a struggle, would have been 'ill-timed' to say the least." [13] It was difficult to arouse sympathy for a few murderers when the attention of sympathetic people was focused increasingly on a different and more numerous group of outcasts. It was difficult to preach against the violence of capital punishment when reformers themselves advocated the shedding of blood.

II

We may summarize the debate over capital punishment as a struggle between reformers who emphasized the effect of environment on moral behavior, arguing that criminals should be cured instead of being punished, and traditionalists who finally abandoned the rationalistic theory of deterrence and fell back upon a doctrine of intrinsic and absolute justice. American fiction in the second quarter of the nineteenth century reveals a curious synthesis of these two positions. It is probable that most popular literature has always tended to present morality in absolute terms, since virtue inevitably triumphs at the expense of evil. But if American writers accepted this ancient formula of intrinsic justice, they refused to extend its meaning to courts of law and to legal executions. Despite minor differences of opinion, early American novels show a surprising unanimity in their criticism of judicial procedure, of the corruption of justice by public prejudice, and of a system which forced innocent men to rely on accident for vindication. Much of this criticism was similar to the arguments of reformers who opposed the penalty of death.

We have already seen that many fictional accounts of murder and crime stressed environmental determinants,

[13] Martin H. Bovee, *Reasons for Abolishing Capital Punishment* (Chicago, 1876), p. viii.

which would seem to imply that the death penalty was based on a false theory of freedom and responsibility. If a murderer's disposition had been corrupted by an indulgent mother, it was absurd and unjust to defend his execution as a warning to other potential killers. Yet this acceptance of environmental causes did not lead automatically to a theory of reformation and forgiveness. In previous discussions we have noted that the superman, the monomaniac, and the morally insane were generally considered too dangerous to live.

It might be a rule of fiction that the villain could escape neither exposure nor defeat, but, as Cooper observed, the courts assumed that a guilty man was virtuous if he could not be legally convicted.[14] Whereas reformers used the fallibility of human justice as an argument against irredeemable punishment, imaginative authors enjoyed the advantage of attacking judicial imperfections without thereby endangering the inevitable triumph of virtue. Hence the attack was direct and unrestrained. If we may draw a composite picture of American justice from works of fiction, we find that jurors were usually gullible, ignorant men, who, if not susceptible to bribes, were easily swayed by subtle misrepresentation, sensationalism, and demagoguery.[15] Public opinion, stirred to excitement by gossip and newspapers, was quick to condemn the innocent or to justify the guilty without adequate evidence.[16] Al-

[14] James Fenimore Cooper, *The Ways of the Hour: A Tale* (New York, 1855), p. 48.

[15] *Ibid.*, pp. 83–84, 94, 105, 217; Edgar Allan Poe, *The Works of Edgar Allan Poe*, ed. by Edmund Clarence Stedman and George Edward Woodberry (Chicago, 1894), III, 199–204.

[16] William Alexander Caruthers, *The Knights of the Horseshoe: A Traditionary Tale of the Cocked Hat Gentry in the Old Dominion* . . . (New York, n.d.), pp. 220–248; Joseph Holt Ingraham, *Frank Rivers; or, The Dangers of the Town* . . . (New York, n.d.), pp. 92–93; Charles Fenno Hoffman, *Greyslaer: A Romance of the Mohawk* (New York, 1840), II, 231–237;

though judges were often kindly and well-meaning old
gentlemen, they were powerless before the cunning of
unscrupulous lawyers and the prejudice of juries.[17] Since
state governors were primarily concerned with political
realities, they showed a tendency to abuse the pardoning
power, so that a man with proper connections was safe
even if convicted by an honest jury.[18] But probably the
most important agreement between writers of fiction and
such legal reformers as Edward Livingston was their
common belief that capital punishment corrupted the
taste of the public and aroused violent passions in the
spectators.

According to John Neal, the masses longed for excitement and revenge and looked upon executions as thrilling
spectacles, rather than as vindications of divine and universal law. One day the mob would cheer at the hanging of
a felon, and the next day plead for another's pardon. "I
have seen ten thousand people in tears because some
handsome boy was to be executed; and I have seen the
officer who brought his pardon, hooted and pelted from
the ground, by a part of the same mob." [19] But this public
weakness did not mean that criminals should not be killed.
One of Neal's characters argued that there should be no
reprieves and that executions should be private, though
conducted at night with torch light and tolling bells, so
that the people might be properly impressed. Newton

Newton Mallory Curtis, *The Victim's Revenge: A Sequel to "The Matricide's
Daughter"* . . . (New York, n.d.), pp. 72–77; Cooper, *Ways,* pp. 135–142,
152–153, 220, 323–338.

[17] George Lippard, *The Quaker City; or, The Monks of Monk-Hall* (Philadelphia, 1845), p. 492; Nathaniel Hawthorne, *The House of Seven Gables,*
in *The Complete Novels and Selected Tales of Nathaniel Hawthorne,* ed.
by Norman Holmes Pearson (New York, 1937), p. 431; Cooper, *Ways,* pp.
131–134.

[18] Lippard, *Quaker City,* pp. 408–410; Curtis, *Victim's Revenge,* p. 83.

[19] John Neal, *Logan: A Family History* (Philadelphia, 1822), II, 9.

Mallory Curtis described a mob shouting for an innocent man's death,[20] and a crowd in George Lippard's *Empire City* (1850) was furious when a hanging was canceled because the prisoner had supposedly died: "shocking, shocking—what an example lost!" [21] Lippard suggested repeatedly that executions aroused the public's taste for blood, increasing the incidence of violent crimes.[22]

For Simms capital punishment presented a sordid contrast to the chivalric ideal of immediate revenge: "You hear the cry of 'Murder!' Do you stop, and resume your seat, with the comforting reflection that, if John murders Peter, John, after certain processes of evidence, will be sent to the state prison or the gallows, and make a goodly show, on some gloomy Friday, for the curious of both sexes?" [23] Simms observed that all killing was contrary to divine law, since human life was sacred, yet homicide was partly justified if it avenged "a crime beyond it, . . . the shedding of that vital soul-blood, its heart of hearts, life of all life, the fair fame, the untainted reputation." [24] Simms might doubt the ultimate legitimacy of capital punishment, yet he thought that "there are some honest impulses, in every manly bosom, which are the best of all moral laws, as they are the most certainly *human* of all laws." Hence young Beauchampe's private revenge was an expression of "the best of all moral laws," but his execution was an example of perverted justice, dominated by public passion: "Strange, that men should delight in such a spectacle—the cruel death, the miserable exposure,

[20] Newton Mallory Curtis, *The Star of the Fallen: A Tale* (New York, n.d.), p. 84.

[21] George Lippard, *The Empire City; or, New York by Night and Day* . . . (Philadelphia, 1864), p. 186.

[22] Lippard, *Quaker City*, pp. 317, 430–434, 452.

[23] William Gilmore Simms, *Beauchampe; or, The Kentucky Tragedy* (New York, 1856), p. 342.

[24] *Ibid.*, p. 343.

of a fellow-man!—that they should look on his writhings, his distortions, his shame and pain, with composure and desire!" [25] In other words, vengeance was not something that could be rationally planned and regulated, as in a duel or legal execution. One might excuse only that violence which sprang from an immediate and passionate sense of injustice.

In *Margaret* (1845) Sylvester Judd expressed a similar protest against the morality of capital punishment, though unlike Simms he preached a doctrine of universal love and brotherhood, looking forward to a perfectionist dream, to a New England apocalypse and utopia. After describing a bitter enmity between some New England townsfolk and Margaret's family, who lived on a wilderness pond, Judd embarked upon the subject of murder. A gross and drunken villager named Solomon Smith made indecent proposals to Margaret at a night husking bee. Margaret's brother, Chilion, who had been drinking and who already had a grudge against Smith, picked up a file and threw it, killing the villager. Persecuted by the cruel townsfolk, who delighted in the spectacle of executions, Chilion was tried and hanged for murder, though the killing had been neither premeditated nor deliberate. After a symbolic fire consumed the decadent town and church, a utopian village appeared, where criminals were unknown and where the gallows were replaced by a statue of Moses kneeling to Christ and surrendering to him the Book of the Hebrew Code.

Margaret is an involved and sentimental novel which nevertheless offers an interesting comment on the state of American society in 1845. Judd recognized the existing divisions, the fierce hostility, between neighboring groups which stimulated acts of retributive violence. Legal executions involved vengeance and group conflict as much

[25] *Ibid.*, p. 398.

as did illegal murder. Hanging was only murder by the majority. Possessing no impartial authority, no transcendent earthly power, society might be redeemed only by a spirit of love, by a recognition of man's universal brotherhood. If even the criminal belonged to the human family, the punishment of death could not be justified.

Public hangings not only gratified the mob's desire for blood and excitement, they also deprived sinners of the means of atonement. Simms's attitude toward the death penalty was clearly expressed in the advice given to Edward Clifford, the deluded and remorseful murderer in *Confession* (1841):

Life is a duty because it is an ordeal. You must preserve life, as a sacred trust, for this reason. Even if you were a felon— one wilfully resolving and coldly executing crime—you were yet bound to preserve life! Throw it away, and though you comply with the demand of social laws, you forfeit the only chance of making atonement to those which are far superior. . . . It was with this merciful purpose that God not only permitted Cain to live, but commanded that none should slay him.

Yet it is important to remember that this theory of reformation did not extend to villainous seducers.

Whenever the novelist approached the subject of a criminal trial, it was almost a rule to make the hero a defendant, to portray his hopeless struggle against crafty lawyers and inflamed public opinion, and to save him from conviction or execution by the appearance of an unexpected witness or by the accidental discovery of new information. It would be difficult to find a fictional murder trial in which an innocent man was acquitted or a guilty one convicted on the basis of the original evidence and testimony. This fact may be explained by the writer's desire to create suspense and dramatic effect; but such an explanation does not account for the running criticism of the judicial process, nor for the nearly universal assumption that justice triumphed only in spite of the courts. We may conclude, then, that many American writers from 1830 to 1860 accepted the belief of reformers that an innocent man might be convicted of murder and that the public anticipation of a hanging was evidence of depravity and not of Christian righteousness.

But literature was, as we have observed, a bridge between dominant values of tradition and the more temporary and changing values of special groups. Fictional plots and characters were often devices providing an opportunity for the examination of moral problems in concrete terms. If novelists sometimes explained the origins of human evil in accordance with theories of psychiatrists or reformers, they generally preserved the more traditional belief that evil, once created, must be destroyed. A man might be a villain because of faulty training, the environment of the city, or the corrupting effect of slavery, but as a villain he must die. When the struggle of competing brothers was transferred to the courtroom, the procedure of justice might be perverted by conspiracy, blinding the eyes of an ineffectual but well-meaning judge, but a higher justice was sure to triumph in the end; and death was the only positive symbol of an evil brother's defeat.

Unlike Simms, Cooper attacked the theory of reforming criminals as "mawkish philanthropy," but he was too skeptical to rely on human courts for absolute justice:

Bodies of men are proverbially heartless. They commit injustice without reflection, and vindicate their abuses without remorse. And yet it may be doubtful if either a nation, or an individual, ever tolerated, or was an accessary in, a wrong, that the act sooner or later did not recoil on the offending party, through that mysterious principle of right, which is implanted in the nature of things, bringing forth its own results as the seed produces its grain.[26]

In fiction, at least, the "mysterious principle of right" included the primitive law of retaliation—the belief that right could be vindicated only by the ultimate death of wrong. But if the source of justice lay in the individual's natural right of retaliation, a right which the courts could only imperfectly exercise, there remained the problem of how to kill an evil man without indulging in revenge and hatred. John Locke said that it should be done in accordance with the calm dictates of reason, and Timothy Dwight, representing traditional Protestant morality, ruled that criminals should be executed in the spirit of Christian benevolence. But it was evident that public executions, which as examples were intended symbolically to kill the evil impulses in spectators' hearts, actually aroused an aggressive passion, serving as a vicarious outlet for murderous desires. Hence writers of fiction attacked the bloodthirsty mobs who yearned for sensational spectacles, but searched, nevertheless, for means of justifying the penalty of death.

The murderer might have alienated his human rights and privileges, but his executioners, to absolve themselves from a similar guilt, were required to recognize his immutable status as a fellow man. Since this final sympathy was impossible in a public execution, many writers described the infliction of the death penalty as a primitive ritual, which, like lynching, was based on natural law. In Richard Hildreth's *The Slave* (1836) an overseer brutally killed the young wife of Thomas, a friend of the hero, Archy Moore. When Archy and Thomas captured the overseer in the wilderness, they decided to

[26] James Fenimore Cooper, *The Wing-and-Wing; or, Le Feu-Follet: A Tale* (New York, 1852), I, 71.

execute him for his crime, because southern justice was so corrupt that he could never be legally tried and convicted. Yet, when Thomas finally shot the overseer, Archy felt a revulsion and pity which evidenced moral sensibility.

In Cooper's *The Prairie* (1827) Ismael Bush knew that he must observe the law of God and Nature, but even this crude frontier patriarch did not enjoy the execution of his murderer brother-in-law. The hanging occurred in a bleak wasteland, far removed from shouting mobs and corrupt judges and governors. It was in such a spot, Cooper suggested, that justice was at once spontaneous and natural, and yet in harmony with the tribal laws of antiquity. When Abiram White had been placed on a rocky ledge, Ishmael tied a rope from his neck to a lonely willow tree. Thus the criminal was left to make peace with God and to execute himself by jumping from the ledge. Just as Deerslayer had embraced his first Indian victim, so Ishmael Bush forgave the murderer of his son and put a fragment of the Bible in his hand. Homicide was thus purified by a ritual which at once acknowledged the victim's essential humanity and made the executioner an agent of a higher power.

Along with the critics of capital punishment, American writers recognized the social and psychological origins of criminality, and they knew that the judicial process was not infallible and that executions gratified the worst passions of a depraved people. Yet they feared that without the certainty of a murderer's death, social order would collapse, leaving a land filled with blood. In our discussions of moral insanity, monomania, and revenge, we saw that there was a tendency to equate moral and physical alienation. Even though the murderer was influenced by external causes and did not consciously choose his own evil, he was nevertheless a renegade from the family, whose example endangered fundamental bonds of unity. Once the chain of revenge had begun, the aggressive impulses which were universal in man would destroy the fragile web of brotherhood, together with the restraints and self-limitations imposed by family obligations. Thus the execution of an alienated man gave proof of a united purpose and of an allegiance to necessary laws of restriction. But the supreme penalty could be justified only when people acknowledged that it was essentially a sacrifice to the gods of stability and virtue.

Long after our period of discussion, Herman Melville explored the deeper implications of individual and group homicide. Billy Budd's offense could be easily explained and understood, and, in a very real sense, he had not been responsible. Yet it was necessary that he should die, despite his lack of moral guilt. Otherwise, we assume, all human relationships would lapse into the moral ambiguity of *Pierre*. But if the arbitrary unity and virtue of society could be preserved only by the death of a scapegoat, Captain Vere, the vindicator of the right, knew that Billy's execution was a sacrifice to an abstract rule, whose purpose was control and discipline; and in this realization, he sensed the full significance of law.

Conclusion

TIS not only the mischief of diseases, and the villany of poysons, that make an end of us; we vainly accuse the fury of Gunnes, and the new invention of death: it is in the power of every hand to destroy us, and we are beholding unto every one we meet, he doth not kill us.

—Sir Thomas Browne

Want of a common Judge with Authority, puts all Men in a State of Nature: Force without Right, upon a Man's Person, makes a State of War, both where is, and is not, a common Judge.

—John Locke

CONCLUSION

THE relationship between men involves varying degrees of identification and sympathy, which may be defined as the projection to others of one's own desires, expectations, fears, and enjoyments. When sharp frustration or injury has stimulated an aggressive reaction in an individual, his mind converts the annoying person from an object of sympathy to an object of hatred. By severing the link of identification, the aggressor deprives his enemy of dignity and of benevolent human emotions. This is the process of alienation. At the same time, the aggressor's own consciousness of evil is projected to the alien, who becomes an embodiment or agent of all malicious force. Such a psychological process probably rationalizes most murders, as well as legal and illegal executions of a social outcast. In American fiction from 1798 to 1860 we have seen homicide explained in terms of moral alienation, which implied that the victim was guilty and deserving of punishment. Yet such human depravity was often pictured in fiction as the result of improper nurture in the family, of sexual corruption, or of city and frontier environments.

American writers of fiction generally rejected the theory of European conservatives that democracy leads inevitably to anarchy; however, they were conscious of the fact that American culture was characterized by excessive violence and by an absence or weakness of institutional forms which had traditionally promoted social unity and had stabilized the status, obligations, and expectations of individuals. In fiction such devices as the superman, the struggling brothers, and the husband who avenges his wife's dishonor reflected the uncertainty of a people who looked forward to unparalleled wealth and progress, but who lacked the justification and direction of absolute moral law. Those who believed that the only fundamental law emanated from the moral sense of individual men could find no voice of authority which would unite conflicting groups. If freedom assured a blissful and bountiful future, permitting each man to anticipate unlimited success, writers of fiction were occasionally sobered by the thought that a state of liberty was not so very different from a state of nature, that no common judge transmitted the supreme and unquestioned laws of God, and that every man and group might claim the authority and power to declare an act of war.

From about 1830 to 1860 American writers generally emphasized the importance of man's nonintellectual powers, including a sense which perceived virtue by the intensity of moral feeling. This romantic psychology was part of a larger reaction against the materialism and moral relativism of eighteenth-century thought. But when individual feeling was frankly recognized as the basis for normative judgment, morality might become obscured by the ambiguities of human passion. When ethical rules were conceived as the product of subjective feelings, and not as the immutable decree of God, revealed in Scripture or deduced by human reason, moral nurture replaced arbitrary command and obedience. For sensitive reformers, it was then evident that the moral sense of criminals had been either diseased or improperly nourished. Individual responsibility was undermined in another way when defenders of lynching found in the private moral feelings a justification for the sudden and "mystical" revenge of a mob. But if the various adaptations of the moral-sense theory led to ambiguity, most American writers implied that there was an inherent and passionate sense of justice in man which transcended both reason and human desire. Murderers might be the product of faulty nurture, but man intuitively sensed the divine command that only blood could atone for the shedding of blood.

BIBLIOGRAPHY

SINCE this study is not confined to American fiction, but ventures into such diverse fields as moral philosophy, theology, jurisprudence, criminology, and social history, the bibliography is highly selective. The following list is limited to works previously cited and to those books and articles which have influenced my interpretation of fictional attitudes toward homicide.

I. PRIMARY SOURCES

A. Nonfiction books, pamphlets, and articles

Aristides [pseud.]. *Strictures on the Case of Ephraim K. Avery, Originally Published in the "Republican Herald," Providence, R.I.* Providence, 1833.

[Ashmead, John W.] *Speech of John W. Ashmead, in the Case of the People vs. James Stephens, Indicted for Murder, in the Court of Oyer and Terminer, for the City and County of New York. Delivered March 25, 1859.* N.p., n.d.

Baldwin, Moses. *The Ungodly Condemned in Judgment: A Sermon Preached at Springfield, December 13th 1770. On Occasion of the Execution of William Shaw for Murder.* Boston, 1771.

Beasley, Frederic. *A Sermon on Duelling, Delivered in Christ-Church, Baltimore, April 28, 1811.* Baltimore, 1811.

Beccaria, Cesare. *An Essay on Crimes and Punishments. Translated from the Italian; with a Commentary Attributed to Mons. De Voltaire. . . .* London, 1767.

Beck, Theodric Romeyn. *Elements of Medical Jurisprudence.* Albany, 1823.

Beecher, Lyman. *The Remedy for Duelling: A Sermon Delivered before the Presbytery of Long-Island, at the Opening of Their Session, at Aquebogue, April 16, 1806.* . . . New York, 1809.

Bemis, George. *Report of the Case of John W. Webster . . . Indicted for the Murder of George Parkman . . . before the Supreme Judicial Court of Massachusetts; Including the Hearing on the Petition for a Writ of Error, the Prisoner's Confessional Statements . . . and an Appendix.* . . . Boston, 1850.

Bennet, John. *Letters to a Young Lady.* 7th ed. Philadelphia, 1818.

Bentham, Jeremy. *An Introduction to the Principles of Morals and Legislation.* London, 1879.

Blakey, Robert. *History of Moral Science.* 2nd ed. 2 vols. Edinburgh, 1836.

Bovee, Martin H. *Reasons for Abolishing Capital Punishment.* Chicago, 1876.

Bradford, William. *An Enquiry How Far the Punishment of Death Is Necessary in Pennsylvania.* . . . Philadelphia, 1793.

Brothers, Thomas. *The United States of North America as They Are; Not as They Are Generally Described: Being a Cure for Radicalism.* London, 1840.

Brown, David Paul. *Speech of David Paul Brown, in Defense of Alexander William Holmes . . . Indicted for Manslaughter upon the High Seas, April 21, 1842, before the Circuit Court of the United States, for the Eastern District of Pennsylvania.* Philadelphia, 1858.

Brown, Henry. *A Narrative of the Anti-Masonick Excitement in the Western Part of the State of New-York, during the Years 1826, '7, '8, and a part of 1829.* Batavia [N.Y.], 1829.

Bushnell, Horace. *Christian Nurture.* New York, 1860.

——. *Discourses on Christian Nurture.* Boston, 1847.

Butler, Joseph. *The Works of Joseph Butler, LL.D. Late Lord Bishop of Durham.* . . . 2 vols. Edinburgh, 1804.

Channing, William Ellery. *The Works of William E. Channing, D.D. With an Introduction.* Boston, 1899.

Chapin, Edwin H. *Duties of Young Women.* Boston, 1848.

Chapone, Hester. *Letters on the Improvement of the Mind, Addressed to a Lady.* Philadelphia, 1816.

Cheever, George Barrell. *Capital Punishment: The Argument of Rev. George B. Cheever, in Reply to J. L. O'Sullivan.* . . . New York, 1843.

Coleman, William. *Report of the Trial of Levi Weeks, on an Indictment for the Murder of Gulielma Sands,* . . . *Taken in Short Hand by the Clerk of the Court.* New York, 1800.

[*Commonwealth of Massachusetts.*] *House* [*Document*] *No. 32. Report Relating to Capital Punishment.* (February 1836.)

——. *House* [*Document*] *No. 149. Report of a Joint Special Committee on Capital Punishment.* (April 24, 1851.)

The Confession of Faith, Agreed Upon by the Assembly of Divines at Westminster. . . . Edinburgh, 1781.

The Confession of Jesse Strang, Who Was Convicted of the Murder of John Whipple. . . . Albany, 1827.

Constitution and Laws of the State of New Hampshire. . . . Dover [N.H.], 1805.

Dane, Nathan. *A General Abridgment and Digest of American Law, with Occasional Notes and Comments.* 8 vols. Boston, 1824.

Dickens, Charles. *American Notes.* London, 1842.

A Digest of the Laws of Texas: To Which is Subjoined an Appendix. . . . Comp. by Oliver C. Hartley, Philadelphia, 1850.

A Digest of the Laws of the State of Alabama: Containing All the Statutes of a Public and General Nature, in Force at the Close of the Session of the General Assembly, in January, 1833. Comp. by John G. Aikin, Philadelphia, 1833.

Down the River; or, Practical Lessons under the Code Duello. By an Amateur. New York, 1874.

Dunlop, John. *Anti-Duel; or, A Plan for the Abrogation of Duelling, Which Has Been Tried and Found Successful.* London, 1843.

Duyckinck, Evert A. and George L. *Cyclopaedia of American*

Literature; Embracing Personal and Critical Notices of Authors, and Selections from Their Writings. . . . 2 vols. New York, 1856.

Dwight, Timothy. *Theology Explained and Defended, in a Series of Sermons.* 12th ed. 4 vols. New York, 1846.

Dwight, William Theodore. *A Discourse on the Rightfulness and Expediency of Capital Punishments.* . . . Portland [Me.], 1843.

East, T. *The Memoirs of the Late Miss Emma Humphries, of Frome, England, with a Series of Letters to Young Ladies, on the Influence of Religion, in the Formation of Their Moral and Intellectual Character.* . . . Boston, 1819.

Emmons, Nathaniel. *The Works of Nathaniel Emmons.* . . . Vol. VI. Boston, 1842.

An Exercise in Declamation; in the Form of a Debate on Capital Punishment. At the Boston Latin School, Public Saturday, March 3, 1849. Boston, 1849.

Finney, Charles G. *Lectures on Systematic Theology.* Ed. by James H. Fairchild. Oberlin [O.], 1878.

The General Laws of Massachusetts, from the Adoption of the Constitution, to February, 1822. . . . *Revised and Published by Authority of the Legislature.* . . . 2 vols. Boston, 1823.

Graham, John. *Summing Up of John Graham, Esq., to the Jury, on the Part of the Defence, on the Trial of Daniel MacFarland.* . . . New York, 1870.

Greene, Samuel D. *The Broken Seal; or, Personal Reminiscences of the Morgan Abduction and Murder.* Boston, 1870.

Griesinger, Theodor. *Lebende Bilder aus Amerika.* Stuttgart, 1858.

Grund, Francis J. *The Americans in Their Moral, Social, and Political Relations.* 2 vols. London, 1837.

Hartley, David. *Observations on Man, His Frame, His Duty, and His Expectations. In Two Parts.* London, 1834.

Hermann Remson, the Great Louisiana Murderer. . . . *With His Strange and Unnatural Death, Sunk in the Quicksands of a Lonely Island.* . . . Philadelphia, 1855.

Hickok, Laurens P. *A System of Moral Science.* 3rd ed. New York, 1861.

Hill, Frederic. *Crime: Its Amount, Causes, and Remedies.* London, 1853.

Hobbes, Thomas. *Leviathan.* Ed. by A. D. Lindsay. New York, 1950.

Hopkins, Samuel. *The Works of Samuel Hopkins.* . . . 3 vols. Boston, 1854.

Howard, H. R., comp. *The History of Virgil A. Stewart, and His Adventure in Capturing and Exposing the Great "Western Land Pirate" and His Gang* . . . *also of the Trials, Confessions, and Execution of a Number of Murrell's Associates in the State of Mississippi during the Summer of 1835, and the Execution of Five Professional Gamblers by the Citizens of Vicksburg.* . . . New York, 1836.

——. *The Lives of Helen Jewett, and Richard P. Robinson, by the Editor of the New York "National Police Gazette."* . . . New York, n.d.

Hutcheson, Francis. *An Essay on the Nature and Conduct of the Passions and Affections. With Illustrations on the Moral Sense.* London, 1728.

——. *A System of Moral Philosophy, in Three Books.* . . . 2 vols. London, 1755.

Hutchinson, Aaron. *Iniquity Purged by Mercy and Truth: A Sermon Preached at Grafton, Oct. 23, 1768. Being the Sabbath after the Execution of Arthur, a Negro Man, at Worcester.* . . . Boston, 1769.

"Insanity—How Far a Legal Defence," *The American Review: A Whig Journal, Devoted to Politics and Literature,* XLV (Sept. 1848), 269–275.

Journal of the House of Representatives, of the State of Michigan, 1846. Detroit, 1846.

Journal of the Senate of the State of Michigan, 1846. Detroit, 1846.

Journals of the Senate and House [New Hampshire], 1842–1844. Concord [N.H.], 1842, 1843, 1844.

Kemble, Frances Anne. *Journal of a Residence on a Georgian Plantation in 1838–1839.* New York, 1863.

Kendall, E. A. *An Argument for Construing Largely the Right of an Appellee of Murder to Insist on Trial by Battle; and also for Abolishing Appeals.* . . . 3rd ed. London, 1818.

Laws of the State of Missouri; Revised and Digested by Authority of the General Assembly. 2 vols. St. Louis, 1825.

Laws of the State of New York, Revised and Passed at the Thirty-Sixth Session of the Legislators. Ed. by William P. Van Ness and John Woodworth. 2 vols. Albany, 1813.

Laws of the Territory of Michigan, Condensed, Arranged, and Passed by the Fifth Legislative Council. Detroit, 1833.

Lee, Samuel. *Capital Punishment. Speech of Rev. Samuel Lee . . . in the New-Hampshire Legislature, June Session, 1849.* N.p., n.d.

Leger, Theodore. *Animal Magnetism; or, Psycodunamy.* New York, 1846.

Life, Trial, Execution and Dying Confession of John Erpenstein, Convicted of Poisoning His Wife, and Executed in Newark, N.J., March 30, 1852. 2nd ed. Newark, 1852.

Livingston, Edward. *Argument of Edward Livingston, against Capital Punishment.* New York, 1847.

——. *A System of Penal Law, for the State of Louisiana.* . . . Philadelphia, 1833.

Locke, John. *An Essay Concerning Human Understanding.* 2 vols. London, 1726.

——. *An Essay Concerning the True, Original, Extent, and End of Civil-Government.* In *The Works of John Locke, Esq.,* 2nd ed., Vol. II. London, 1722.

Montagu, Basil, ed. *The Opinions of Different Authors upon the Punishment of Death.* . . . London, 1809.

"Moral Insanity," *Boston Medical and Surgical Journal,* XLIV (May 7, 1851), 285.

Moreau de Saint-Méry, Méderic L. E. *Voyage aux États-Unis de l'Amérique, 1793–1798.* Ed. by Stewart L. Mims. New Haven, 1913.

Niles' Weekly Register, 1825–1840.

Observations upon Duelling: With a Plan to Prevent the Fre-

quency of Single Combat. By an Irish Barrister. London, 1803.

O'Sullivan, John L. *Report in Favor of the Abolition of Death by Law, Made to the Legislature of the State of New York, April 14, 1841.* . . . 2nd ed. New York, 1841.

Paley, William. *Natural Theology.* New York, n.d.

——. *The Principles of Moral and Political Philosophy.* 7th ed. Philadelphia, 1788.

Parker, Theodore. *The Chief Sins of the People: A Sermon Delivered at the Melodeon, Boston, on Fast Day, April 10, 1851.* Boston, 1851.

——. *Discourse on the Transient and Permanent in Christianity; Preached at the Ordination of Mr. Charles C. Shackford.* . . . Boston, 1841.

——. *The Function and Place of Conscience in Relation to the Laws of Men: A Sermon for the Times; Preached on Sunday, September 22, 1850.* Boston, 1850.

——. *A Sermon of the Consequences of an Immoral Principle and False Idea of Life. Preached at the Music Hall, in Boston, on Sunday, November 26, 1854.* Boston, 1854.

——. *A Sermon of the Dangerous Classes in Society, Preached at the Melodeon, on Sunday, January 31.* Boston, 1847.

——. *A Sermon of the Moral Dangers Incident to Prosperity, Preached at the Music Hall, in Boston, on Sunday, November, 5, 1854.* Boston, 1855.

——. *A Sermon of the Public Function of Woman, Preached at the Music Hall, March 27, 1853.* Boston, 1853.

——. *A Sermon of War, Preached at the Melodeon, on Sunday, June 7, 1846.* Boston, 1846.

Parkman, George. *Management of Lunatics, with Illustrations of Insanity.* Boston, 1817.

Peirce, Cyrus. *Crime: Its Cause and Cure. An Essay.* Boston, 1854.

Philanthropos. *A Letter to Aaron Burr, Vice-President of the United States of America, on the Barbarous Origin, the Criminal Nature and the Baneful Effects of Duels; Occasioned by His Late Fatal Interview with the Deceased*

and Much Lamented General Alexander Hamilton. New
York, 1804.

"Phreno-Magnetism," *Boston Medical and Surgical Journal,*
XXIX (Nov. 1, 1843), 249–253.

*Piracy and Murder. Particulars of the Horrid and Atrocious
Murders, Committed by Four Spaniards on the Captain,
Passengers, and Crew of the Brig Crawford. . . . With an
Accurate Account of their Trials, Conviction, Sentence, and
Execution.* New York, 1827.

Prichard, James Cowles. *A Treatise on Insanity and Other Disorders Affecting the Mind.* Philadelphia, 1837.

*The Prisoners' Friend: A Monthly Magazine, Devoted to Crim-
inal Reform, Philosophy, Literature, Science and Art,* 1848–
1852.

Purrington, Tobias. *Report on Capital Punishment, Made to
the Maine Legislature in 1836. . . .* 3rd ed. Washington,
1852.

Rantoul, Robert. *Hon. Robert Rantoul, Jr.'s Letters on the
Death Penalty.* Boston, n.d.

Ray, Isaac. *A Treatise on the Medical Jurisprudence of Insanity.* Boston, 1838.

Reid, Thomas, *Essays on the Powers of the Human Mind.* 2
vols. Edinburgh, 1803.

*Remarks on Capital Punishments: To Which Are Added,
Letters of Morris N. B. Hull, &c.* Utica [N.Y.], 1821.

*Report of the Trial of Jason Fairbanks, on an Indictment for
the Murder of Miss Elizabeth Fales.* 2nd ed. Boston, 1801.

*Report of the Trial of William F. Comings, on an Indictment
for the Murder of his Wife, Mrs. Adeline T. Comings. At
the September Term of the Court of Common Pleas Holden
at Haverhill, in the County of Grafton, N.H. . . . Together
with His Life, Written by Himself.* Boston, 1844.

*The Revised Statutes of the State of Michigan, Passed and
Approved May 18, 1846.* Detroit, 1846.

*The Revised Statutes of the State of Missouri, Revised and
Digested by the Eighth General Assembly during the Years
One Thousand Eight Hundred and Thirty-Four, and One
Thousand Eight Hundred and Thirty-Five.* St. Louis, 1835.

The Revised Statutes of the State of New York, Passed during the Years One Thousand Eight Hundred and Twenty-Seven, and One Thousand Eight Hundred and Twenty-Eight. . . . 3 vols. Albany, 1829.

Romilly, Samuel. *Observations on the Criminal Law of England, as It Relates to Capital Punishments.* . . . London, 1810.

Rush, Benjamin. *Medical Inquiries and Observations, upon the Diseases of the Mind.* Philadelphia, 1812.

———. *An Oration Delivered before the American Philosophical Society, Held in Philadelphia on the 27th of February, 1786; Containing an Enquiry into the Influence of Physical Causes upon the Moral Faculty.* Philadelphia, 1786.

Sabine, Lorenzo. *Notes on Duelling, Alphabetically Arranged, with a Preliminary Historical Essay.* 2nd ed. Boston, 1856.

St. Clair, Henry. *The United States Criminal Calendar; or, An Awful Warning to the Youth of America.* . . . Boston, 1833.

Sampson, M. B. *Rationale of Crime, and Its Appropriate Treatment; Being a Treatise on Criminal Jurisprudence Considered in Relation to Cerebral Organization.* New York, 1846.

Sanford, H. S. *The Different Systems of Penal Codes in Europe; also, A Report on the Administrative Changes in France, since the Revolution of 1848.* Washington, 1854.

Sega, James. *An Essay on the Practice of Duelling, as It Exists in Modern Society. Occasioned by the Late Lamentable Occurrence near Philadelphia. Translated from Italian by the Author.* Philadelphia, 1830.

Selfridge, Thomas O. *A Correct Statement of the Whole Preliminary Controversy between Thomas O. Selfridge and Benjamin Austin; also, A Brief Account of the Catastrophe in State Street, Boston, on the 4th of August, 1806.* Charlestown [Mass.], 1807.

Seward, William H. *Argument of William H. Seward, in Defense of William Freeman, on His Trial for Murder, at Auburn, July 21st and 22nd, 1846. Reported by S. Blatchford.* 3rd ed. Auburn [N.Y.], 1846.

Sharp, Granville. *A Tract on Duelling: Wherein the Opinions of the Most Celebrated Writers on Crown Law Are Examined and Corrected.* . . . 2nd ed. London, 1790.

Sketch, of the Life of Miss Ellen Jewett, who was Murdered in the City of New York, on Saturday Evening, April 9, 1836. Boston, 1836.

Sketches of the Life and a Narrative of the Trial of James Hamilton, who was Tried, Convicted, and Hanged at Albany, the 6th of November, 1818, for the Murder of Major Benjamin Birdsall. . . . Albany, 1818.

Slicer, Henry. *A Discourse, in Which Is Considered the History, Character, Causes, and Consequences of Duels, with the Means of Prevention. Prepared to Be Delivered in the Capitol, by Henry Slicer, Chaplain to the Senate of the United States.* . . . Washington, 1838.

Spear, Charles. *Essays on the Punishment of Death.* 8th ed. Boston, 1844.

Sprague, William B. *Letters to Young Men, Founded on the History of Joseph.* 2nd ed. Albany, 1845.

State of New-York. [*Document*] *No. 109. In Assembly, March 14, 1851. Report of Select Committee on the Subject of Capital Punishment.* N.p., n.d.

The Statutes at Large of South Carolina; Edited, under Authority of the Legislature, by Thomas Cooper. 10 vols. Columbia [S.C.], 1837–1841.

Stewart, Dugald. *Elements of the Philosophy of the Human Mind.* 2 vols. in one. Boston, 1821.

——. *Outlines of Moral Philosophy. For the Use of Students in the University of Edinburgh.* Edinburgh, 1793.

Stout, Marion Ira. *"The Last Writing" of Marion Ira Stout; Containing His Confession, Revelations, and also His "So Called" Principles of Philosophy and Religion.* Rochester [N.Y.], 1858.

Sutherland, David. *A Sermon, Delivered at Haverhill, New Hampshire, August 12, 1806, at the Execution of Josiah Burnham, Who Was Executed for the Murder of Russell Freeman, Esq. and Capt. Joseph Starkweather, in the Haverhill Jail, on the 17th December, 1805.* Hanover [N.H.], 1806.

Tallack, William. *The Practical Results of the Total or Partial Abolition of Capital Punishment in Various Countries.* London, 1866.

Taylor, Timothy Alden. *The Bible View of the Death Penalty: also, A Summary of the Webster Case.* Worcester [Mass.], 1850.

Thacher, Thomas. *The Danger of Despising the Divine Counsel: Exhibited in a Discourse, Delivered at Dedham . . . September 13, 1801, the Lord's Day after the Execution of Jason Fairbanks.* Dedham [Mass.], 1802.

[Thompson, George.] *Life and Exploits of the Noted Criminal, Bristol Bill. By Greenhorn* [pseud.]. New York, n.d.

Tocqueville, Alexis de. *De la démocratie en Amérique.* 15th ed. 3 vols. Paris, 1868.

Townshend, Chauncy Hare. *Facts in Mesmerism, or Animal Magnetism. With Reasons for a Dispassionate Inquiry into It.* Boston, 1841.

Trial and Conviction of Dr. Stephen T. Beale; with the Letters of Chief Justice Lewis, and Judges Black and Woodward, on His Case. Philadelphia, 1855.

Trial and Execution of Bellingham, for the Murder of Mr. Perceval. N.p., 1812.

Trial of Alexander M'Leod, for the Murder of Amos Durfee; and as an Accomplice in the Burning of the Steamer Caroline . . . during the Canadian Rebellion in 1837–8. New York, 1841.

Trial of Amos Furnald for the Murder of Alfred Furnald, before the Superior Court of Judicature, Holden at Dover, within and for the County of Strafford, and State of New Hampshire. Reported by Richard Ela. Concord [N.H.], 1825.

Trial of Henry G. Green, for the Murder of His Wife. Troy [N.Y.], 1845.

Trial of Rev. Issachar Grosscup, for the Seduction of Roxana L. Wheeler . . . at the February Term of the Supreme Court, Held at Canandaigua, Ontario County. Canandaigua [N.Y.], 1848.

Trial of Robert M. Goodwin . . . on an Indictment of Manslaughter, for Killing James Stoughton, Esq. in Broadway, in the City of New-York, December 21, 1819. Reported by a Gentleman of the Bar. New York, 1820.

The Trial of William Corder, at the Assizes, Bury St. Edmunds, Suffolk, August 7th and 8th, 1828, for the Murder of Maria Marten, in the Red Barn, at Polstead. . . . 3rd ed. London, 1828.

The Truly Remarkable Life of the Beautiful Helen Jewett, Who Was so Mysteriously Murdered. Philadelphia, 1878.

"Unchastity," *New Englander,* XVII (May 1859), 469–488.

Upham, Thomas C. *Elements of Mental Philosophy, Embracing the Two Departments of the Intellect and the Sensibilities.* 3rd ed. 2 vols. Portland [Me.], 1839.

Warden, Robert B. *A Familiar Forensic View of Man and Law.* Columbus [O.], 1860.

Weems, Mason L. *God's Revenge against Adultery, Awfully Exemplified in the Following Cases . . . the Accomplished Dr. Theodore Wilson, (Delaware,) who for Seducing Mrs. Nancy Wiley, Had His Brains Blown out by Her Husband.* . . . 2nd ed. Philadelphia, 1816.

——. *God's Revenge against Murder; or, The Drown'd Wife, a Tragedy.* . . . 4th ed. Philadelphia, 1808.

West, Nathaniel. *An Address on Capital Punishment, Recently Delivered before the Westmoreland County Lyceum.* Pittsburgh, 1855.

Wharton, Francis. *Philosophy of Criminal Law.* Philadelphia, 1880.

——. *A Treatise on Mental Unsoundness, Embracing a General View of Psychological Law.* 4th ed. Philadelphia, 1882.

——. *A Treatise on the Criminal Law of the United States.* 3 vols. Philadelphia, 1874.

——. *A Treatise on the Law of Homicide in the United States: To Which is Appended a Series of Leading Cases.* 2nd ed. Philadelphia, 1875.

Williams, John M. *Extracts from a Charge Delivered to the Grand Jury at Northampton, at the March Term of the Court of Common Pleas, A.D. 1838.* Northampton [Mass.], 1838.

Wilson, John Lyde. *The Code of Honor; or, Rules for the Government of Principals and Seconds in Duelling.* Charleston [S.C.], 1838.

Wonderful Trial of Caroline Lohman, Alias Restell, with Speeches of Counsel, Charge of Court, and Verdict of Jury. 3rd ed. New York, 1847.

Woodward, S. B. "Moral Insanity," *Boston Medical and Surgical Journal,* XVIII (March 28, 1838), 124–126.

——. "Moral Insanity," *Boston Medical and Surgical Journal,* XXX (April 17, 1844), 228.

B. Works of fiction

(When a later edition has been used, the date of the first edition is given in brackets.)

Allston, Washington. *Monaldi: A Tale.* Boston, 1856 [1841].

[Arrington, Alfred W.] *The Rangers and Regulators of the Tanaha; or, Life among the Lawless: A Tale of the Republic of Texas.* By Charles Summerfield [pseud.]. New York, 1856.

Arthur, Timothy Shay. *Ten Nights in a Bar-Room, and What I Saw There.* Boston, 1855 [1854].

Awful Disclosures of Maria Monk, of the Hotel Dieu Convent of Montreal; or, The Secrets of the Black Nunnery Revealed. San Francisco, n.d. [1836].

Barker, Benjamin. *Blackbeard; or, The Pirate of the Roanoke: A Tale of the Atlantic.* Boston, 1847.

——. *Mary Morland; or, The Fortunes and Misfortunes of an Orphan.* Boston, 1845.

Bennett, Emerson. *The Bride of the Wilderness.* New York, 1854.

——. *Forest and Prairie; or, Life on the Frontier.* Philadelphia, 1860.

——. *Kate Clarendon; or, Necromancy in the Wilderness.* Philadelphia, 1854 [1848].

Bird, Robert Montgomery. *The Adventures of Robin Day.* New York, 1877 [1839].

——. *The Hawks of Hawk-Hollow.* Philadelphia, 1835.

———. *Nick of the Woods; or, The Jibbenainosay: A Tale of Kentucky.* Ed. by Cecil B. Williams. New York, 1939 [1837].

[Bourne, George.] *Lorette. The History of Louise, Daughter of a Canadian Nun, Exhibiting the Interior of Female Convents. . . .* New York, 1834 [1833].

Brackenridge, Hugh Henry. *Modern Chivalry.* Ed. by Claude M. Newlin. New York, 1937 [1792–1797].

Brown, Charles Brockden. *Arthur Mervyn; or, Memoirs of the Year 1793.* 2 vols. Philadelphia, 1887 [1799–1800].

———. *Edgar Huntly; or, Memoirs of a Sleep-Walker.* Ed. by David Lee Clark. New York, 1928 [1799].

———. *Ormond; or, The Secret Witness.* Ed. by Ernest Marchand. New York, 1937 [1799].

———. *Wieland; or, The Transformation, Together with Memoirs of Carwin the Biloquist.* Ed. by Fred Lewis Pattee. New York, 1926 [1798].

Caruthers, William Alexander. *The Knights of the Horseshoe: A Traditionary Tale of the Cocked Hat Gentry in the Old Dominion. . . .* New York, n.d. [1845].

Cobb, Sylvanus. *Fernando; or, The Moor of Castile: A Romance of Old Spain.* Boston, 1853.

———. *The Juggler of Nankin: The Grandee's Plot: A Story of the Celestial Empire.* New York, n.d. [18–?].

———. *The Maniac's Secret; or, The Privateer of Massachusetts Bay: A Story of the Revolution.* New York, n.d. [18–?].

———. *The Ocean Martyr; or, the Hunter Spy of Virginia. By Austin C. Burdick* [pseud.]. New York, n.d. [18–?].

Cooper, James Fenimore. *Afloat and Ashore: A Sea Tale.* New York, 1857 [1844].

———. *The Bravo: A Tale.* 2 vols. in one. New York, 1852 [1831].

———. *The Chainbearer; or, The Littlepage Manuscripts.* 2 vols. New York, 1852 [1845].

———. *The Crater; or, Vulcan's Peak: A Tale of the Pacific.* New York, 1861 [1847].

———. *The Deerslayer; or, The First War-Path.* New York, 1861 [1841].

———. *The Headsman; or, The Abbaye des Vignerons.* 2 vols. New York, 1852 [1833].

——. *The Heidenmauer; or, The Benedictines: A Legend of the Rhine.* New York, 1856 [1832].

——. *Jack Tier; or, The Florida Reef.* New York, 1896 [1848].

——. *The Last of the Mohicans: A Narrative of 1757.* Ed. by John B. Dunbar. Boston, 1898 [1826].

——. *Lionel Lincoln; or, The Leaguer of Boston.* 2 vols. New York, 1852 [1824–1825].

——. *Ned Myers; or, A Life before the Mast.* New York, 1852 [1843].

——. *The Oak Openings; or, The Bee-Hunter.* 2 vols. in one. New York, 1852 [1848].

——. *The Pathfinder; or, The Inland Sea.* New York, 1860 [1840].

——. *The Pilot: A Tale of the Sea.* New York, 1859 [1823].

——. *The Pioneers; or, The Sources of the Susquehanna.* New York, 1859 [1823].

——. *The Prairie: A Tale.* New York, 1859 [1827].

——. *The Red Rover.* New York, 1853 [1827–1828].

——. *The Sea Lions; or, The Lost Sealers.* New York, 1855 [1849].

——. *The Spy: A Tale of the Neutral Ground.* New York, 1859 [1821].

——. *The Two Admirals.* New York, 1853 [1842].

——. *The Water-Witch; or, the Skimmer of the Seas: A Tale.* 2 vols. in one. New York, 1852 [1831].

——. *The Ways of the Hour: A Tale.* New York, 1855 [1850].

——. *The Wept of Wish-ton-Wish: A Tale.* New York, 1857 [1829].

——. *The Wing-and-Wing; or, Le Feu-Follet: A Tale.* 2 vols. in one. New York, 1852 [1842].

——. *Wyandotté; or, The Hutted Knoll: A Tale.* New York, 1857 [1843].

Curtis, Newton Mallory. *The Black-Plumed Riflemen: A Tale of the Revolution.* New York, 1846.

——. *The Bride of the Northern Wilds: A Tale.* Albany, 1843.

——. *The Matricide's Daughter: A Tale of Life in the Great Metropolis.* N.p., n.d. [1850?].

——. *The Star of the Fallen: A Tale.* New York, n.d. [185–?].

——. *The Victim's Revenge: A Sequel to "The Matricide's Daughter" and "The Star of the Fallen."* New York, n.d. [185–?].

Dana, Richard Henry. *Poems and Prose Writings.* 2 vols. New York, 1849. [1833].

Durivage, Francis Alexander. *Edith Vernon; or, Crime and Retribution: A Tragic Story of New England.* Boston, 1845.

Fay, Theodore S. *The Countess.* 3 vols. London, 1840.

——. *Norman Leslie: A New York Story.* New York, 1869 [1835].

Field, Joseph M. *The Drama of Pokerville: The Bench and Bar of Jurytown, and Other Stories.* Philadelphia, 1847.

Flint, Timothy. *Francis Berrian; or, The Mexican Patriot.* London, 1841 [1826].

[Foster, Hannah Webster.] *The Coquette; or, The History of Eliza Wharton: A Novel Founded on Fact.* By a Lady of Massachusetts. Newburyport [Mass.], 1811 [1797].

Further Disclosures by Maria Monk, Concerning the Hotel Dieu Nunnery of Montreal; also, Her Visit to Nuns' Island. . . . New York, 1836.

Hall, James. *The Harpe's Head: A Legend of Kentucky.* Philadelphia, 1833.

——. *Legends of the West.* Cincinnati, 1857 [1832].

Hawthorne, Nathaniel. *The Complete Novels and Selected Tales of Nathaniel Hawthorne.* Ed. by Norman Holmes Pearson. New York, 1937.

——. *Mosses from an Old Manse.* Boston, 1882 [1846].

——. *Twice-Told Tales.* Boston, 1882 [1837].

[Hildreth, Richard.] *The Slave: or, Memoirs of Archy Moore.* 2 vols. Boston, 1836.

Hoffman, Charles Fenno. *Greyslaer: A Romance of the Mohawk.* 2 vols. New York, 1840.

Ingraham, Joseph Holt. *The Beautiful Cigar Girl; or, The Mysteries of Broadway.* New York, n.d. [1849].

——. *Frank Rivers; or, The Dangers of the Town. Founded upon Incidents in the Romantic Life and Tragic Death of Helen Jewett.* New York, n.d. [1843].

——. *The Midshipman; or, The Corvette and Brigantine: A Tale of Land and Sea.* Boston, 1845. [1844].

——. *The Quadroone; or, St. Michael's Day.* 2 vols. New York, 1841.

[Irving, Washington.] *A History of New York from the Beginning of the World to the End of the Dutch Dynasty . . . by Diedrich Knickerbocker* [pseud.]. In *The Works of Washington Irving.* Vol. IV. New York, 1897 [1809].

——. *The Sketch Book.* In *The Works of Washington Irving.* Vol. I. New York, 1897 [1819–1820].

——. *Tales of a Traveler.* In *The Works of Washington Irving.* Vol. II. New York, 1897 [1824].

Jackson, Daniel. *Alonzo and Melissa: or, The Unfeeling Father: An American Tale.* Philadelphia, 1830 [1811].

[Judd, Sylvester.] *Margaret: A Tale of the Real and the Ideal, Blight and Bloom. . . .* 2 vols. Boston, 1851 [1845].

[Judson, Edward Zane Carroll.] *The B'hoys of New York: A Sequel to the "Mysteries and Miseries of New York,"* by Ned Buntline [pseud.]. New York, n.d. [1850].

——. *The G'hals of New York: A Novel,* by Ned Buntline [pseud.]. New York, n.d. [1850].

——. *The Last of the Buccaneers: A Yarn of the Eighteenth Century,* by Ned Buntline [pseud.]. New York, 1856.

——. *The Mysteries and Miseries of New York: A Story of Real Life.* By Ned Buntline [pseud.]. New York, 1848.

——. *Ned Buntline's Life-Yarn.* New York, 1849.

——. *The Shell Hunter; or, An Ocean Love Chase.* New York, 1858.

Kennedy, John Pendleton. *Horse-Shoe Robinson: A Tale of the Tory Ascendency.* Philadelphia, 1852 [1835].

——. *Rob of the Bowl: A Legend of St. Inigoe's.* Philadelphia, 1860 [1838].

Lewis, Matthew Gregory. *The Monk.* Philadelphia, n.d. [1795].

Lippard, George. *The Empire City; or, New York by Night and Day. . . .* Philadelphia, 1864 [1850].

——. *New York: Its Upper Ten and Lower Million.* Cincinnati, 1853.

——. *The Quaker City; or, The Monks of Monk-Hall.* Philadelphia, 1845 [1844].

Lockwood, Ralph Ingersoll. *The Insurgents: An Historical Novel.* 2 vols. in one. Philadelphia, 1835.

Lytton, Edward Bulwer. *Paul Clifford.* In *The Novels of Lord Lytton.* Vol. XI. 2 vols. in one. New York, 1897 [1830].

——. *Pelham; or, Adventures of a Gentleman. To Which Is Added, Falkland.* In *The Novels of Lord Lytton.* Vol. IX. 2 vols. in one. New York, 1897 [1828].

——. *A Strange Story.* In *Bulwer's Works.* Vol. XIX. New York, n.d. [1862].

Melville, Herman. *Moby-Dick; or, The Whale.* New York, 1930 [1851].

——. *Omoo: A Narrative of Adventures in the South Seas.* New York, 1921 [1847].

——. *Pierre; or, The Ambiguities.* New York, 1852.

Neal, John. *The Down-Easters.* . . . 2 vols. New York, 1833.

——. *Errata; or, The Works of Will. Adams: A Tale by the Author of "Logan," "Seventy-six," and "Randolph."* 2 vols. New York, 1823.

——. *Logan: A Family History.* 2 vols. Philadelphia, 1822.

——. *Rachel Dyer: A North American Story.* Portland [Me.], 1828.

——. *Seventy-six.* 2 vols. Baltimore, 1823.

Paulding, James Kirke. *Koningsmarke; or, Old Times in the New World.* 2 vols. New York, 1836 [1823].

Poe, Edgar Allan. *The Works of Edgar Allan Poe.* Ed. by Edmund Clarence Stedman and George Edward Woodberry. 10 vols. Chicago, 1894.

Reynolds, George W. M. *The Mysteries of London.* 4 vols. London, 1845–1848.

[Rowson, Susanna Haswell.] *Charlotte: A Tale of Truth.* . . . Philadelphia, 1794.

Sedgwick, Catharine Maria. *Hope Leslie; or, Early Times in the Massachusetts.* 2 vols. New York, 1842 [1827].

——. *The Linwoods; or, "Sixty Years Since" in America.* 2 vols. New York, 1835.

Simms, William Gilmore. *Beauchampe; or, The Kentucky Tragedy*. New York, 1856 [1842].

——. *Border Beagles: A Tale of Mississippi*. New York, 1855 [1840].

——. *Charlemont; or, The Pride of the Village: A Tale of Kentucky*. New York, 1856.

——. *Confession; or, The Blind Heart*. Chicago, 1890 [1841].

——. *The Forayers; or, The Raid of the Dog-Days*. New York, 1882 [1855].

——. *Guy Rivers: A Tale of Georgia*. New York, 1855 [1834].

——. *Martin Faber: The Story of a Criminal*. New York, 1833.

——. *Mellichampe: A Legend of the Santee*. 2 vols. New York, 1836.

——. *The Partisan: A Romance of the Revolution*. New York, 1854 [1835].

——. *Richard Hurdis: A Tale of Alabama*. New York, 1882 [1838].

——. *The Wigwam and the Cabin; or, Tales of the South*. Philadelphia, 1853 [1845].

——. *The Wigwam and the Cabin, Second Series*. Philadelphia, 1853 [1845].

——. *Woodcraft; or, Hawks about the Dovecoat: A Story of the South at the Close of the Revolution*. New York, 1882 [1854].

——. *The Yemassee: A Romance of Carolina*. New York, n.d. [1835].

Stowe, Harriet Beecher. *Dred: A Tale of the Great Dismal Swamp*. 2 vols. Boston, 1856.

——. *Uncle Tom's Cabin; or, Life among the Lowly*. 2 vols. Boston, 1852.

Sue, Eugène. *The Mysteries of Paris: A Novel*. Trans. by Charles H. Town. New York, 1843 [1842].

Thompson, Daniel Pierce. *The Green Mountain Boys: A Historical Tale of the Early Settlement of Vermont*. New York, 1927 [1839].

[Thompson, George.] *Dashington; or, The Mysteries of a Private Mad-House*. By Greenhorn [pseud.]. New York, n.d. [185–?].

Webber, Charles Wilkins. *Tales of the Southern Border*. Philadelphia, 1855 [1853].

II. SECONDARY SOURCES

A. Articles

Cassity, John Holland. "Personality Study of 200 Murderers," *Journal of Criminal Psychopathology*, II (Jan. 1941), 296–304.

Curti, Merle. "The Great Mr. Locke. America's Philosopher, 1783–1861," *Huntington Library Bulletin*, XI (April 1937), 107–151.

Hinsie, L. E. "A Contribution to the Psychopathology of Murder—Study of a Case," *Journal of Criminal Psychopathology*, II (July 1940), 1–20.

Karpman, Ben. "Criteria for Knowing Right from Wrong," *Journal of Criminal Psychopathology*, II (Jan. 1941), 376–386.

Maughs, Sydney. "A Concept of Psychopathy and Psychopathic Personality: Its Evolution and Historical Development," *Journal of Criminal Psychopathology*, II (Jan. 1941), 329–356.

Mills, Charles K. "Benjamin Rush and American Psychiatry," reprinted from the *Medico-Legal Journal* (Dec. 1886).

Orians, G. Harrison. "The Romance Ferment after Waverley," *American Literature*, III (Jan. 1932), 408–431.

Post, Albert. "Michigan Abolishes Capital Punishment," *Michigan History Magazine*, XXIX (January–March 1945), 44–50.

Reinhardt, John E. "The Evolution of William Ellery Channing's Sociopolitical Ideas," *American Literature*, XXVI (May 1954), 154–165.

Riegel, Robert E. "The American Father of Birth Control," *New England Quarterly*, VI (Sept. 1933), 470–490.

Schlesinger, Arthur M. "Political Mobs and the American Revolution, 1765–1776," *American Philosophical Society Proceedings*, IC (Aug. 30, 1955), 244–250.

Wertham, Frederic. "The Matricidal Impulse," *Journal of Criminal Psychopathology*, II (April 1941), 455–464.

Winters, Warrington, "Unusual Mental Phenomena in the Life and Works of Charles Dickens," *Summaries of Ph.D. Theses, University of Minnesota*, V (1951), 147–151.

Wright, Lyle H. "A Statistical Survey of American Fiction, 1774–1850," *Huntington Library Quarterly*, II (April 1939), 313–321.

B. Books

Alexander, Franz, and William Healy. *Roots of Crime. Psychoanalytic Studies*. New York, 1935.

Allen, Hervey. *Israfel: The Life and Times of Edgar Allan Poe*. 2 vols. New York, 1926.

Babbitt, Irving. *Rousseau and Romanticism*. New York, 1955.

Baldwin, James M. *History of Psychology: A Sketch and an Interpretation*. 2 vols. New York, 1913.

Barnes, Harry Elmer, and Negley K. Teeters. *New Horizons in Criminology*. 2nd ed. New York, 1951.

——. *Society in Transition*. New York, 1939.

——. *The Story of Punishment: A Record of Man's Inhumanity to Man*. Boston, 1930.

Bayard, Thomas Francis. *"Unwritten Law." An Address Delivered before the Phi Beta Kappa Society of Harvard University . . . June 28, 1877*. Boston, 1877.

Bernard, L. L., and Jessie Bernard. *Origins of American Sociology: The Social Science Movement in the United States*. New York, 1943.

Bjerre, Andreas. *The Psychology of Murder: A Study in Criminal Psychology*. Trans. by E. Classen. London, 1927.

Bleyer, Willard Grosvenor. *Main Currents in the History of American Journalism*. Boston, 1927.

Boas, George, ed. *Romanticism in America*. Baltimore, 1940.

Bonaparte, Marie. *The Life and Works of Edgar Allan Poe: A Psycho-Analytic Interpretation*. London, 1949.

Bonar, James. *Moral Sense*. London, 1930.

Brooks, Van Wyck. *The World of Washington Irving*. New York, 1944.

Brown, Herbert Ross. *The Sentimental Novel in America, 1789–1860*. Durham [N.C.], 1940.

Bryce, James. *Studies in History and Jurisprudence.* New York, 1901.

Bye, Raymond T. *Capital Punishment in the United States.* Philadelphia, 1919.

Cahn, Edmond N. *The Sense of Injustice: An Anthropocentric View of Law.* New York, 1949.

Calhoun, Arthur W. *A Social History of the American Family from Colonial Times to the Present.* 3 vols. in one. New York, 1945.

Cardozo, Benjamin N. *Law and Literature.* New York, 1931.

Cash, W. J. *The Mind of the South.* Garden City [N.Y.], 1954.

Cattell, James M. *Psychology in America.* New York, 1929.

Catton, Joseph. *Behind the Scenes of Murder.* New York, 1940.

Clark, David Lee. *Charles Brockden Brown: Pioneer Voice of America.* Durham [N.C.], 1952.

Cockburn, John. *The History of Duels.* 2 vols. Edinburgh, 1888.

Coleman, J. Winston. *The Beauchamp-Sharp Tragedy.* Frankfort (Kentucky), 1950.

——. *Famous Kentucky Duels: The Story of the Code of Honor in the Bluegrass State.* Frankfort, 1953.

Collins, Varnum Lansing. *President Witherspoon.* 2 vols. Princeton [N.J.], 1925.

Cowie, Alexander. *The Rise of the American Novel.* New York, 1948.

Cutler, James Elbert. *Lynch-Law: An Investigation into the History of Lynching in the United States.* New York, 1905.

Damon, S. Foster. *Thomas Holley Chivers, Friend of Poe.* New York, 1930.

Davis, Curtis Carroll. *Chronicler of the Cavaliers: A Life of the Virginia Novelist Dr. William A. Caruthers.* Richmond [Va.], 1953.

Dearden, Harold. *The Mind of the Murderer.* New York, n.d.

Deegan, Dorothy Yost. *The Stereotype of the Single Woman in American Novels: A Social Study with Implications for the Education of Women.* New York, 1951.

Deutsch, Albert. *The Mentally Ill in America: A History of Their Care and Treatment from Colonial Times.* New York, 1937.

DeVoto, Bernard. *Mark Twain's America.* Boston, 1932.

Dillon, John F. *The Laws and Jurisprudence of England and America: Being a Series of Lectures Delivered Before Yale University.* Boston, 1894.

Dollard, John, Neal E. Miller, *et al. Frustration and Aggression.* New Haven [Conn.], 1939.

Dunlap, George Arthur. *The City in the American Novel, 1789–1900.* Philadelphia, 1934.

Douthwaite, L. C. *Mass Murder.* New York, 1929.

Ellis, Havelock. *Studies in the Psychology of Sex.* 6 vols. Philadelphia, 1924.

Fay, Jay W. *American Psychology before William James.* New Brunswick [N.J.], 1939.

Fish, Carl Russell. *The Rise of the Common Man, 1830–1850.* [A History of American Life, Vol. VI.] New York, 1927.

Fluegel, John Carl. *A Hundred Years of Psychology, 1833–1933.* London, 1951.

——. *Man, Morals and Society: A Psycho-analytic Study.* New York, 1947.

Foster, Hugh Frank. *A Genetic History of the New England Theology.* Chicago, 1907.

Foust, Clement E. *The Life and Dramatic Works of Robert Montgomery Bird.* New York, 1919.

Frazer, Sir James George. *The Golden Bough.* One vol. ed. New York, 1948.

Freud, Sigmund. *Civilization and Its Discontents.* Trans. by Joan Riviere. London, 1930.

——. *Collected Papers,* Vol. V. Ed. by James Strachey. London, 1950.

——. *The Future of an Illusion.* Trans. by W. D. Robson-Scott. London, 1928.

——. *A General Introduction to Psychoanalysis.* Trans. by Joan Riviere. Garden City [N.Y.], 1943.

——. *Group Psychology and the Analysis of the Ego.* Trans. by James Strachey. New York, n.d.

——. *Psychopathology of Everyday Life.* London, 1917.

——. *Totem and Taboo: Resemblances between the Psychic*

Lives of Savages and Neurotics. Trans. by A. A. Brill. New York, 1918.

Fromm, Erich. *Escape from Freedom.* New York, 1941.

——. *The Forgotten Language: An Introduction to the Understanding of Dreams, Fairy Tales and Myths.* New York, 1951.

Gamble, Thomas. *Savannah Duels and Duellists, 1733–1877.* Savannah, 1923.

Garnett, A. Campbell. *The Mind in Action: A Study of Motives and Values.* London, 1931.

Gehman, Richard. *A Murder in Paradise.* New York, 1954.

Goodwin, John C. *Insanity and the Criminal.* New York, 1924.

Grossman, James. *James Fenimore Cooper.* (The American Men of Letters Series.) New York, 1949.

Guttmacher, Manfred S., and Henry Weihoffen. *Psychiatry and the Law.* New York, 1952.

Haroutunian, J. *Piety versus Moralism: The Passing of the New England Theology.* New York, 1932.

Harrison, M. Clifford. *Social Types in Southern Fiction.* Ann Arbor, 1921.

Hoag, Ernest Bryant, and Edward Huntington Williams. *Crime, Abnormal Minds, and the Law.* Indianapolis, 1923.

Hurst, James Willard. *The Growth of American Law: The Law Makers.* Boston, 1950.

Jones, Howard Mumford. *The Pursuit of Happiness.* Cambridge [Mass.], 1953.

Kane, Harnett C. *Gentlemen, Swords and Pistols.* New York, 1951.

Kardiner, Abram, *et al. The Psychological Frontiers of Society.* New York, 1947.

Lawrence, D. H. *Studies in Classic American Literature.* Garden City [N.Y.], 1951.

Lee, James Melvin. *History of American Journalism.* Boston, 1917.

Lichtenstein, Perry M. *A Doctor Studies Crime.* New York, 1934.

Lounsbury, Thomas R. *James Fenimore Cooper.* (American Men of Letters Series.) Boston, 1882.

Lovejoy, Arthur O. *Essays in the History of Ideas*. Baltimore, 1948.

McCarthy, Charles. "The Anti-Masonic Party," *Annual Report of the American Historical Association for the Year 1902* (Washington, 1903), I, 367–559.

MacLean, Kenneth. *John Locke and English Literature of the Eighteenth Century*. New Haven, 1936.

Martin, John Bartlow. *Why Did They Kill?* New York, 1953.

Matthiessen, F. O. *American Renaissance*. New York, 1941.

Miller, Justin. *Handbook of Criminal Law*. St. Paul [Minn.], 1934.

Monaghan, Jay. *The Great Rascal: The Life and Adventures of Ned Buntline*. Boston, 1951.

Murphy, Gardner, *et al. Experimental Social Psychology*. New York, 1937.

Parrington, Vernon Louis. *Main Currents in American Thought*. One vol. ed. New York, 1930.

Pearson, Edmund. *Dime Novels; or, Following an old Trail in Popular Literature*. Boston, 1929.

——. *Instigation of the Devil*. New York, 1930.

——. *More Studies in Murder*. New York, 1936.

——. *Murder at Smutty Nose and Other Murders*. New York, 1926.

——. *Studies in Murder*. New York, 1924.

Pillsburgy, W. B. *The History of Psychology*. New York, 1929.

Raphael, David Daiches. *The Moral Sense*. London, 1947.

Reik, Theodor. *The Unknown Murderer*. Trans. by Katherine Jones. London, 1936.

Richardson, Edgar P. *Washington Allston: A Study of the Romantic Artist in America*. Chicago, 1948.

Riesman, David, *et al. The Lonely Crowd: A Study of the Changing American Character*. New Haven, 1950.

Riley, I. Woodbridge. *American Philosophy: The Early Schools*. New York, 1907.

Roback, Abraham A. *History of American Psychology*. New York, 1952.

Roughead, William. *Malice Domestic*. Edinburgh, 1928.

Sanger, William W. *The History of Prostitution: Its Extent, Causes, and Effects throughout the World.* New York, 1897.

Sellin, Thorsten, ed. *Murder and the Penalty of Death.* (The Annals of the American Academy of Political and Social Sciences, vol. 284.) Philadelphia, 1952.

Simpson, Helen, *et al. The Anatomy of Murder.* New York, 1937.

Smith, Henry Nash. *Virgin Land: The American West as Symbol and Myth.* Cambridge [Mass.], 1950.

Spiller, Robert E., *et al. Literary History of the United States.* 3 vols. New York, 1948.

Stauffer, Vernon. *New England and the Bavarian Illuminati.* New York, 1918.

Stephen, Sir James Fitzjames. *A General View of the Criminal Law of England.* 2nd ed. London, 1890.

Stevens, William Oliver. *Pistols at Ten Paces: The Story of the Code of Honor in America.* Boston, 1940.

Truman, Ben C. *The Field of Honor: Being a Complete and Comprehensive History of Duelling in all Countries. . . .* New York, 1884.

Two Centuries' Growth of American Law, 1701–1901. By Members of the Faculty of the Yale Law School. New York, 1901.

Van Doren, Carl. *The American Novel, 1789–1939.* Rev. ed. New York, 1940.

Watson, David Kemper. *Growth of the Criminal Law of the United States.* (House of Representatives Doc. no. 362, 57th Cong., 1st sess.) Washington, n.d.

Wertham, Frederic. *Dark Legend: A Study in Murder.* New York, 1941.

——. *The Show of Violence.* New York, 1948.

White, Walter. *Rope and Faggot: A Biography of Judge Lynch.* New York, 1929.

Wiley, Lulu Rumsey. *The Sources and Influence of the Novels of Charles Brockden Brown.* New York, 1950.

Winters, Yvor. *Maule's Curse: Seven Studies in the History of American Obscurantism.* Norfolk [Conn.], 1938.

Zilboorg, Gregory, and George W. Henry. *A History of Medical Psychology.* New York, 1941.

INDEX

341